Practical Web Development with Haskell

Master the Essential Skills to Build Fast and Scalable Web Applications

Ecky Putrady

APress®

Practical Web Development with Haskell

Ecky Putrady
Singapore, Singapore, Singapore

ISBN-13 (pbk): 978-1-4842-3738-0   ISBN-13 (electronic): 978-1-4842-3739-7
https://doi.org/10.1007/978-1-4842-3739-7

Library of Congress Control Number: 2018962969

Managing Director, Apress Media LLC: Welmoed Spahr
Acquisitions Editor: Jade Scard
Development Editor: James Markham
Coordinating Editor: Nancy Chen

Cover designed by eStudioCalamar

Cover image designed by Freepik (www.freepik.com)

Distributed to the book trade worldwide by Springer Science+Business Media New York, 233 Spring Street, 6th Floor, New York, NY 10013. Phone 1-800-SPRINGER, fax (201) 348-4505, e-mail orders-ny@springer-sbm.com, or visit www.springeronline.com. Apress Media, LLC is a California LLC and the sole member (owner) is Springer Science + Business Media Finance Inc (SSBM Finance Inc). SSBM Finance Inc is a **Delaware** corporation.

For information on translations, please e-mail rights@apress.com, or visit www.apress.com/rights-permissions.

Apress titles may be purchased in bulk for academic, corporate, or promotional use. eBook versions and licenses are also available for most titles. For more information, reference our Print and eBook Bulk Sales web page at www.apress.com/bulk-sales.

Any source code or other supplementary material referenced by the author in this book is available to readers on GitHub via the book's product page, located at www.apress.com/9781484237380. For more detailed information, please visit www.apress.com/source-code.

Printed on acid-free paper

Table of Contents

About the Author

 **Ecky Putrady** is a software engineer with extensive experience in developing web applications. Specializing in Java, Ecky discovered Haskell four years ago and was amazed by the potential the language could bring. Although resources were scarce, he learned the language by reading multiple blog posts and participating in active discussions in the Haskell community. That arduous process is what motivated him to write this book, and he hopes that new future practitioners of Haskell will become productive quickly.

About the Technical Reviewers

Taylor Fausak is the lead developer at ITProTV. He has nearly a decade of web development experience and supports the Haskell community by publishing the Haskell Weekly newsletter. Find him online at `https://taylor.fausak.me`.

Samuli Thomasson is a self-taught programmer since 2008 and has been hacking in Haskell since 2012. He has worked at Nokia and currently at Relex Solutions as an Integration Specialist. He is interested in the application of mathematics in practical software development.

Acknowledgments

I would like to express my appreciation and thanks to the amazing people who have helped me in writing this book.

Thank you to Yolanda, who encouraged me to step beyond my comfort zone by writing this book and has provided me with continuous support in the process.

Thank you to my parents for their words of encouragement and support.

Thank you to Keke for various tips and support. The book would not be completed without her insights.

Thank you to the awesome editorial team of Apress: Nancy Chen and Jim Markham. It has been a positive working experience for me. Without them, the book would not be completed.

Thank you to the technical reviewers: Taylor Fausak and Samuli Thomasson. Their insights have helped improve the technical quality of this book and me as a practicing Haskell developer.

Thank you to the awesome people of the Haskell community that I can't name one by one. The community has been very friendly and helpful for me when learning Haskell for the first time.

Finally, thanks to you, dear reader, to have chosen this book as your resource to learn Haskell.

Introduction

Why Haskell

I was instantly hooked into Haskell when I stumbled upon this piece of code:

```
quicksort :: (Ord a) => [a] -> [a]
quicksort [] = []
quicksort (x:xs) =
  let smallerSorted = quicksort [a | a <- xs, a <= x]
      biggerSorted = quicksort [a | a <- xs, a > x]
  in  smallerSorted ++ [x] ++ biggerSorted
```

It is indeed not the most efficient implementation of a quicksort algorithm, but it is so terse while fully capturing the main idea of quicksort. I find it to be elegant.

Haskell is infamously known as a difficult programming language to learn. It is true, but only if you are accustomed to OOP or an imperative way of thinking. If you are already familiar with Java, you can spend a weekend learning C# and be productive with it. It's because they are quite similar enough. The same thing cannot be said for Haskell. Haskell is significantly different from those programming languages. You need to think differently. And this way of thinking takes time to learn. In my experience, learning Haskell is like learning Java or C# for the first time when you have no prior knowledge of programming.

So why would one want to invest time to build applications in Haskell? What makes it worth the initial learning curve?

Haskell is a statically typed programming language. Statically typed languages are languages in which the types are checked at compile time. It prevents you from doing stupid things, like passing in a string to a function that expects an integer. It is always better to catch these problems up front rather than three days later in production when a specific input is sent to the system. You might have lost the context already and you are supposed to enjoy your weekend!

Most statically-typed programming languages are correlated with verbosity. It is a sound statement. Since you are required to annotate the types, you are indeed writing more code. For example, in Java, you would write something like this:

```java
public String hello(String name) {
  return "Hello, " + name + "!";
}
```

See the `String` there? It's a type that you need to tell the compiler so that it can check your code for correctness.

Fortunately, Haskell has type inference. Type inference allows you to omit the types almost entirely. The compiler will still be able to tell you if your code is not correct. The same example can be rewritten in Haskell as:

```haskell
hello name = "Hello, " ++ name ++ "!"
```

In this example, the compiler knows that `name` must be a string because the operations being applied to it are string operations.

The preceding example also shows how Haskell code could be so terse. Besides the syntax, there are many other features in Haskell that help you write concise code, such as higher order function and partial function applications. These features, for example, allow you to replace loops with a one-liner. It's powerful for processing and transforming data.

Learning Haskell did change the way I think about programming. In OOP, I used to think in terms of long-lived "organisms" called "objects" interacting with each other. I used to think about how to structure my objects into the correct hierarchy. That's how OOP is taught. Remember the "Cat extends Animal" in OOP 101?

After learning Haskell, I think in terms of data transformation. What I usually do in my work so far can be boiled down to just transforming one kind of data into another kind of data. It's straightforward. I notice that I now write less code to achieve the same amount of functionalities with fewer defects.

Nowadays, you might have noticed that mainstream programming languages include more and more functional programming constructs. Java 8, for example, introduces "Optional" (from Haskell's "Maybe"), and most importantly, lambda function. Recently created programming languages like Swift, Kotlin, or Scala also favor immutability, a concept from functional programming. It's more apparent now where the industry is heading.

So, again, why would one want to invest time to build applications in Haskell? The short answer is, Haskell lets you write applications faster and more correctly.

What This Book Is About

As I have said earlier, Haskell is infamously difficult to learn. Part of it is because there are not many resources on the subject yet, especially if you want to apply Haskell to your day-to-day job. If you investigate mainstream programming languages, there are a lot of resources that teach you how to use them.

This book is about being practical with Haskell. I learned that there are a lot of resources about Haskell aimed at beginners of the language. They teach you how to read and write Haskell code. However, there is almost no resource once you are familiar with Haskell and want to tackle bigger projects. I was struggling with these:

1. How would I structure my Haskell code to build bigger applications?

2. What are the best practices?

3. What are the development tools to make me more productive?

4. What are the good libraries to use?

It took me quite some time to figure all those out. The available resources are not complete and are scattered across blog posts and forum threads. This book aims to provide complete and structured information on such topics.

In this book, we will be focusing on web development. If you are a web developer aspiring to build systems with Haskell, then you will greatly benefit from this book. If you are not a web developer, you may find the approach of building bigger Haskell applications that you see in this book will also be applicable to your domain.

Intended Audience

The intended audience of this book is people who have basic knowledge of web development. You should know how HTTP works. For example, HTTP request, HTTP response, headers, cookies, etc. You also need to know a little bit about HTML, CSS, and Javascript.

You also need to have basic knowledge of Haskell. You should be familiar with the syntax and basic typeclasses like Applicative, Functor, and Monad. You should also know about Monad Transformer or mtl, like MonadReader. If you are unable to understand what the following code snippet does, then you might have a slight difficulty following along.

```
hello :: (MonadReader String m, MonadIO m) => m ()
hello = do
  name <- ask
  liftIO $ putStrLn $ "Hello, " <> name <> "!"

newtype AppT a = AppT
  { unAppT :: ReaderT String IO a
  } deriving (Applicative, Functor, Monad, MonadReader String, MonadIO)

main :: IO ()
main = flip runReaderT "World" $ unAppT hello
```

Project Overview

Since this book is all about being practical, then what's more practical than building a project? In this book, we will build a working user authentication feature. That feature might sound simple, but it's actually complex. Let's see the requirements:

1. Registration Page

   a. User should be able to register with email and password

   b. Upon registration, an email verification link is sent to the user's email

2. Login Page

   a. User should be able to login with email and password

   b. User should not be able to login with invalid email and password combination

   c. User should not be able to log in if the email has not been verified

3. Email Verification Page

   a. User should be informed if the verification link is incorrect

   b. User's email should be verified by visiting this page

4. User Page

   a. User should be redirected to Login Page if the user is not authenticated

   b. User should be able to see the user's email if the user is authenticated

5. Input validation

   a. Email is case insensitive and should be unique across the whole system

   b. Email should be in the correct format

   c. Password should have length of more than 5, and contain number, uppercase letter, and lowercase letter

6. Misc

   a. All of the preceding should be accessible in HTML format

   b. All of the preceding should be accessible RESTful API format

Let's analyze the requirements and break them down into manageable pieces. One thing to note is that we will handle this like we do in a real production system; we will be relying a lot on many external systems such as databases and queues. So, don't be overwhelmed as it's as practical as the real-world challenges.

We need to store user information, such as email and password, so we obviously need data storage. A common choice for this type of application is an SQL-based storage, for example, PostgreSQL. In this book, we will use exactly that.

Email is sent after a user is registered into the system. Sending email is usually a time-consuming process. We typically don't want to make the user wait, as it impacts the user experience. A standard solution to this problem is to send the email in the background, so it doesn't block the user from proceeding. A naive solution is to spawn a thread to send the email. This approach has a problem: we can't recover the email sending job if the application crashes or restarted for deployment. A better alternative method, which is also a standard solution, is to publish the email sending job to a queueing system, such as RabbitMQ. Our application listens to the queueing system and acts on the received job. Another advantage of such an approach is the job can be distributed to multiple workers. In this book, we will learn the latter approach.

When the user is logged in, we want to give the user a token so that we can authenticate the user without him/her sending credentials all the time. Since we will be building a web application, the common solution is to pass the token as a cookie. Most browsers send the cookie back to the server for subsequent interactions. In the server side, we need to store the token somewhere to identify the user from that token. A common solution is to store it in an in-memory storage system. Example systems are Redis and Memcached. In this book, we will use Redis.

This seemingly simple feature requires knowledge of many concepts of web development as well as how to implement them in Haskell. The business logic in this feature is not complicated, but we need to interface with many external systems like databases and queues.

This system architecture is common in today's web-based systems. After completing this book, you are expected to be able to use the knowledge to build such systems.

Book Structure

The book is structured chronologically, akin to how you would build an application like the one previously mentioned.

We will start our journey in Chapter 1, in which we will be setting up a productive Haskell development environment.

In Chapter 2, we will learn some libraries that help us do the basic, bread-and-butter tasks that we often encounter when building web applications.

In Chapter 3, we will build the main business logic of our project. We will learn how to structure the code such that the business logic is decoupled from external systems.

In Chapter 4, we will learn about logging—an important component that allows us to troubleshoot issues in production.

Chapters 5 and 6 explore how to interact with external systems, specifically databases and queues.

Chapters 7, 8, and 9 are all about web programming. Chapter 7 is about writing a RESTful web server. In Chapter 8, we will be building a web server that has the same functionality offered in Chapter 7, but via HTML pages instead of RESTful API. Finally, Chapter 9 explains about working with an HTTP client to interact with an external web server.

In Chapter 10, we will be working on configuration management. Configuration management is important, as usually we ship our application to multiple environments and the configuration for each environment might be different.

Chapter 11 explores automated testing. Testing is an integral part of the development process that ensures the quality of our application. The Haskell type system helps eliminate a certain class of bugs, but not all. So, having automated testing is still important in Haskell codebase.

Finally, we will learn about deployment of Haskell application in Chapter 12. We will be using Docker to deploy our Haskell application. In addition to that, we will also explore some tools that help ensure our code is of high quality.

CHAPTER 1

Getting Started

In this chapter, we will set up a Haskell development environment from scratch. The setup includes the compiler, the IDE, and any other tools to the point you are at the most productive level for developing Haskell applications. We will also briefly discuss hpack and cabal, tools for building Haskell applications.

Stack

The easiest way to get started developing Haskell is by using stack. stack is a command line application that does a bunch of things, like scaffolding a project, downloading and setting up dependencies (including the compiler), run test, build application, and many more.

You can install stack by using either one of the following commands:

```
$ brew install haskell-stack # for homebrew users
$ curl -sSL https://get.haskellstack.org/ | sh
$ wget -qO- https://get.haskellstack.org/ | sh
```

After stack is installed, we can create a new project by typing this command:

```
$ stack new hauth
```

In this case, hauth is the name of our project. You may supply other names if you wish to create a project with a different name. This stack command will create a new folder with the same name as the project. We will look into that in more detail shortly.

Now that the project is created, we need to download and set up the project dependencies. Go into the project folder and run stack setup.

```
$ cd hauth
$ stack setup
```

© Ecky Putrady 2018
E. Putrady, *Practical Web Development with Haskell*, https://doi.org/10.1007/978-1-4842-3739-7_1

`stack setup` downloads the necessary dependencies of your project. One of the dependencies is GHC, The Glasgow Haskell Compiler. Do note that GHC is only installed when you don't have it on your system yet. Get a coffee or stretch, as the setup process might take some time.

Next, we want to try to build the project.

```
$ stack build
```

This command downloads the necessary external packages from Stackage,[1] a package repository for Haskell; then you build your application. The build result is then stored in `.stack-work/install/<your os>/lts-<version>/<ghc version>/bin/`.

In practice, you usually want to pass in `--pedantic` as the argument of the command. This argument makes the build process check for common bad practices when writing Haskell code and will fail the build if those bad practices are found in your code. It's a must-have if you want to deploy your application to production.

You may run the application with either one of the following commands:

```
$ stack exec hauth-exe
$ .stack-work/install/<your os>/lts-<version>/<ghc version>/bin/hauth-exe
```

For running the tests, the command is `stack test`. Since we have not yet implemented any test, it will just print "Test suite not yet implemented" text to the console. You will usually use a test library that does assertions and outputs nicely formatted test results.

Last but not least, you may run the REPL (Read-Eval-Print-Loop) using `stack repl`. REPL is an essential tool for developing Haskell applications. REPL allows you to test and prototype new code quickly.

Haskell IDE

It's certainly possible to develop Haskell applications with any plain text editor. However, it's not the most efficient way to write Haskell code. In this section, we will set up our text editor to be more productive when developing Haskell applications.

---

[1]`www.stackage.org/`

Popular text editor options are emacs, vim, Atom, and Visual Studio Code. In this book, we will use Visual Studio Code. Visual Studio Code is more user-friendly than emacs and vim. Visual Studio Code is also free and cross-platform.

First, let's install Visual Studio Code by visiting the official site[2] and follow the installation instruction there. The installation should be very straightforward.

Next, we install the necessary Visual Studio Code plugin for Haskell. The one that we want to install is **Haskero**. We install from within the Visual Studio Code itself. Go to the "Extensions" tab, search for "Haskero," and press "Install," as shown in Figure 1-1.

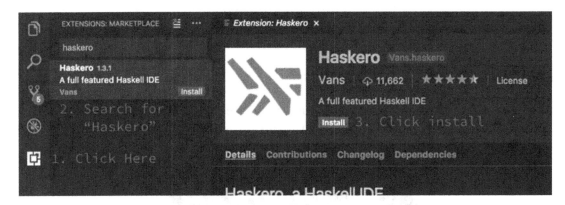

Figure 1-1. *Haskero installation*

Haskero has a dependency on **Intero**. Intero is the backend for the IDE-like functionalities. Haskero is the binding for Visual Studio Code. We install Intero by typing this command at the root of our project:

```
$ stack build intero
```

Once Intero is installed, we may restart the Visual Studio Code and you'll see that Haskero should function correctly. For example, you may see type signature when you hover over a function, as shown in Figure 1-2.

---

[2]https://code.visualstudio.com

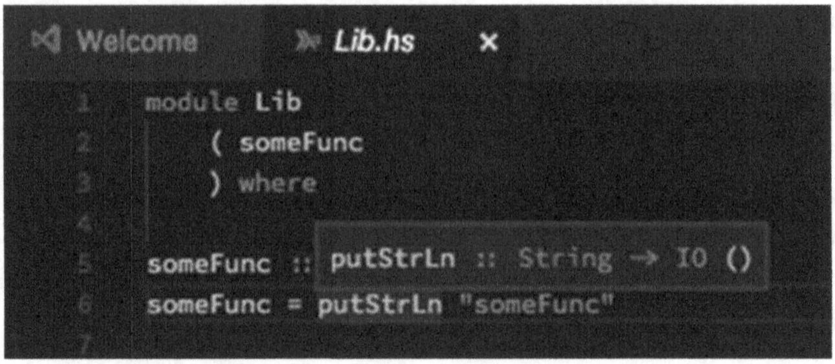

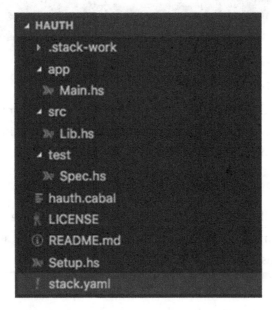

Figure 1-2. *Haskero in action*

Default Project Structure

After creating a new project with stack, you should see the same generated files as shown in Figure 1-3. In this section we will explore those files in more detail.

Figure 1-3. *Default project structure*

Both the src and app folders contain Haskell code. The src folder is meant to contain library code. If there's a part of your project that can be reused in another context, then put it here. The app folder is meant to contain executable code. The code here depends on code in the src folder.

In practice, however, if you create a web application, it doesn't matter where you put the code. I usually put most of my code in the src folder, and the code in the app folder only calls a one-liner function to kick off the application.

test folder, as the name suggests, contains test code.

hauth.cabal is the build file. This file is read by cabal, the build tool for Haskell. stack wraps cabal and provides a nicer command line interface to do common development tasks. In practice, however, you rarely need to deal with cabal directly. You'll most likely work with stack exclusively. We'll look into the detail of cabal files shortly.

Setup.hs is used by cabal for the build process. Most of the time, you don't need to touch this file.

stack.yaml is where you define the configuration for stack. There are many configuration parameters in this file, but most of the time you'll only deal with extra-deps. extra-deps contains a list of Haskell packages that are not available in Stackage.

The Build Configuration

In this section, we will look in more detail into hauth.cabal, a cabal file. As I have briefly mentioned before, the cabal file is the build file. It contains configuration for building your project. For example, it defines other packages that your project depends on.

Let's open the hauth.cabal file to see what it looks like. On the first few lines, you will see name, version, license, etc., which are self-explanatory. Following those lines is the library block.

```
library
  hs-source-dirs:    src
  exposed-modules:   Lib
  build-depends:     base >= 4.7 && < 5
  default-language:  Haskell2010
```

This section defines the library files in your project. `hs-source-dirs` defines which folder in our project the source codes exists. In our case, it's in the `src` folder. `exposed-modules` are the modules that are available to users who import the package; in this case the value is `Lib`. Let's see the first few lines of the `src/Lib.hs` file:

```
module Lib
    ( someFunc
    ) where
```

This file defines a module named `Lib`, which is the one being included in `exposed-modules` field.

If we create a new module, let's say `Hello`, and we want to expose it, then we need to add it in the `exposed-modules`, like so:

```
exposed-modules:    Lib, Hello
```

Not shown here is a field called `other-modules`. This works like `exposed-modules`, but the modules won't be exposed to the users of your library. It means that the users of this package will not be able to import those modules. The use-case of `other-modules` is when you have modules that are internal to your package.

The `build-depends` field defines external libraries that we depend on. The one that has been defined now is `base >= 4.7 && < 5`. This means that we depend on the `base` library with any version equal to or greater than 4.7 but less than version 5.

The next following blocks are `executable` and `test-suite`, which have the same fields as the `library` block. Those fields have the same functionalities as we have explored previously.

As you have seen earlier, if we add a new module, we need to add it in either `other-modules` or `exposed-modules`. This is slightly cumbersome when you have a lot of modules since you need to add it manually. Also, if you happen to need to use the same library in both `library` and `executable`, then you also need to list it twice in both blocks. This is also slightly cumbersome.

To remedy this issue, there is a tool that is supported out-of-the-box by `stack`: `hpack`.[3] Both the `hpack` file and `cabal` file have the same purpose of defining the build configuration. The advantage of using `hpack` is that it is less verbose by fixing issues that I've mentioned before. For example, you don't need to list each module in either

---

[3]https://github.com/sol/hpack

exposed-modules or other-modules. Another advantage is in the file format. hpack uses YAML[4] as the file format. The YAML format is quite popular, and chances are you and other people are already familiar with it.

In this book, we will use hpack for its simplicity and efficiency. First, let's generate our hpack file from our cabal file.

```
$ stack install hpack-convert # install the converter tool
$ ~/.local/bin/hpack-convert # convert
```

hpack-convert finds the cabal file in the current directory and converts that to package.yaml. If you read the package.yaml file, the format should be very similar to the cabal file.

hpack (the application) actually does nothing more than converting the hpack file to a cabal file. This cabal file is still the one being used to build the application. However, stack supports hpack so transparently it's as if you don't need the cabal file at all. When you run stack build, stack will run hpack (the application) to convert the hpack file to a cabal file before finally building the application.

Let's see this in action. Change some values in the field to see how the cabal file is generated after the change. Set the values of the following fields with your details, for example:

```
author: Ecky Putrady
maintainer: eckyp@example.com
copyright: 2017 Ecky Putrady
```

Then build the application using stack build. Notice that now, the cabal file contents are updated with values that we have set.

```
author:      Ecky Putrady
maintainer:  eckyp@example.com
copyright:   2017 Ecky Putrady
```

When we run stack build, stack automatically looks for package.yaml. If the file is found, stack automatically generates the cabal file. This cabal file is then used for building the application. If you are using git, it's a good idea to list the cabal file in .gitignore, since our "source of truth" for the build configuration is now package.yaml.

---

[4]http://yaml.org

Summary

In this chapter, we have learned to set up various tools for working with Haskell efficiently.

We have learned about `stack`, a command-line tool for managing Haskell projects. We learned some `stack` commands that we will use most often:

1. *stack new*: for creating a new project

2. *stack setup*: for setting up Haskell development environment

3. *stack build*: for building the application

4. *stack exec*: for executing the binary that have been created by `stack build`

5. *stack test*: for running tests

We have set up Visual Studio Code, our text editor of choice for writing Haskell. We have also installed `Haskero`, a Visual Studio Code plugin that enables IDE-like functionality for Haskell.

We have learned about `cabal`, the build tool and dependency manager for Haskell. We have also learned to work with `cabal` files. Since there are some downsides to `cabal`, we use another tool, `hpack`, to manage the build configuration. By using `hpack`, we write the build configuration in YAML format and it will then be translated to a `cabal` file.

CHAPTER 2

Practical Haskell

As web developers, we face so many challenges daily to complete our tasks. For example, we might need to find an element matching a predicate in a collection, parse this JSON to compute some other values, replace the text in this paragraph to something else, and many more. Each of those challenges is not particularly hard, but it's not very easy either. Most importantly, it's not very related to your problem domain. It's just not practical and efficient to rewrite such code over and over again. In this chapter, we will learn to be practical. We will learn about essential libraries that help you with common, day-to-day tasks as a web developer.

We will be using REPL, a lot as it helps us experiment with code faster. This is also for giving you a real-world example on how REPL is helpful for code exploration and prototyping. Whenever you see a > in a code block example, it means we are in a REPL. You can get into REPL by typing `stack repl` in the command line.

ClassyPrelude

Prelude is the base library that comes with GHC. It provides standard functionalities that you would want when working with Haskell. However, the default prelude has some downsides. One of them is the exposure of partial function. Partial function is a function that throws an error on specific inputs. One such example is `head`. It throws an error when you give it an empty list.

```
> head []
*** Exception: Prelude.head: empty list
```

Partial function is dangerous because it is unpredictable. It's best to avoid working with or creating such a function as much as possible.

© Ecky Putrady 2018
E. Putrady, *Practical Web Development with Haskell*, https://doi.org/10.1007/978-1-4842-3739-7_2

Another downside of the default prelude is that it doesn't include libraries that you will almost always use when building Haskell applications. Some examples of the libraries are text and containers. It means you will always need to list them in your dependency and import them in almost each of your Haskell files.

Due to those problems, there are multiple prelude alternatives created by the Haskell community, for example, Protolude and ClassyPrelude. In this book, we will be using ClassyPrelude. I find it to be the most enjoyable to work with compared with other alternatives. To enable ClassyPrelude, add the following lines at the root of our package.yml:

```
dependencies:
- base
- classy-prelude

default-extensions:
- NoImplicitPrelude
- OverloadedStrings
```

We put them in the root because we will use ClassyPrelude and base in our library, executable, and test files.

The default-extensions block contains a list of language extension. For this case, we put in NoImplicitPrelude, which instructs the compiler not to import the default prelude implicitly. We will learn about the OverloadedStrings language extension shortly.

If you run stack build, you'll notice that there will be an error similar to the following:

```
/Users/ecky/Projects/hauth/src/Lib.hs:5:13:  error:
    Not in scope: type constructor or class 'IO
```

It says that the type IO is not found. This type was exported in the default prelude and implicitly imported. Now that we don't import the prelude implicitly, the IO type is not available anymore, and that makes the compilation fail.

To fix this, simply import ClassyPrelude into those files. Specifically, you need to import it into src/Lib.hs, app/Main.hs, and test/Spec.hs. Now you may run stack build again, and the compilation should be successful.

ClassyPrelude documentation might be hard to digest. There are two places to look for its capabilities: the ClassyPrelude[1] itself and MonoTraversable.[2] ClassyPrelude is built on top of MonoTraversable. Many functionalities exposed by ClassyPrelude are provided by MonoTraversable. In the following sections, we will explore some functionalities provided by both libraries.

String, Text, and ByteString

Haskell has five string-like types: String, Text, LText, ByteString, and LByteString. Each of them has different use cases. Let's look into them in more detail.

String is a list of characters ([Char]). The good thing about String being a list of characters is that most list operations can be reused for String. However, String is not really efficient for text processing. This type is generally frowned upon by the community, and it's best to avoid using this type for public APIs.

Text is an array of Unicode characters. It's more efficient than String because the characters are stored in a contiguous block of array. The Haskell community has generally converged to use this type instead of String for representing text.

LText is the lazy variant of Text. You can think of it as [Text]. LText is useful in certain situations where you have a very big text you want to process. If you use Text, then the whole text will need to reside in memory. That might be problematic if the whole text doesn't fit in memory. In this case, LText helps because it stores only chunks of the text in memory at a given time.

ByteString is an array of bytes. If you are familiar with Java, ByteString is equal to byte[]. We mostly use it for serializing data to be sent over a network or saved into a file.

Similar to Text, ByteString also has a lazy variant called LByteString that has the same use cases as the LText counterpart.

With all these different string types, you are likely to encounter cases where you need to convert from one type to another. ClassyPrelude provides some functions to do just that, as you can see in Table 2.1.

---

[1]www.stackage.org/package/classy-prelude
[2]www.stackage.org/package/mono-traversable

Table 2-1. *Functions to Convert Between* String, LText, Text, LByteString, *or* ByteString

From	To	Function
String	Text	fromString
String	LText	fromString
String	ByteString	fromString
String	LByteString	fromString
Text	LText	fromStrict
Text	ByteString	encodeUtf8
Text	LByteString	(fromStrict . encodeUtf8)
Text	String	unpack
LText	Text	toStrict
LText	ByteString	(toStrict . encodeUtf8)
LText	LByteString	encodeUtf8
LText	String	unpack
ByteString	LByteString	fromStrict
ByteString	Text	decodeUtf8
ByteString	LText	(fromStrict . decodeUtf8)
ByteString	String	(unpack . decodeUtf8)
LByteString	ByteString	toStrict
LByteString	Text	(toStrict . decodeUtf8)
LByteString	LText	decodeUtf8
LByteString	String	(unpack . decodeUtf8)

When you type any string in Haskell, like "Hello," the type will automatically be String. As mentioned a few paragraphs back, String is generally avoided. We want to make it a Text most of the time. By looking at Table 2-1, we can easily convert String to Text by using fromString. However, this means we need to litter our code base with fromString anywhere. That would not look great! This is where the OverloadedStrings language extension comes to the rescue. It allows you to write a normal string like "Hello" and it will be converted to any of those five string-like types based on the context. To be precise, OverloadedStrings allows you to build any type that is an instance of IsString typeclass. The five string-like types just happen to be an instance of that typeclass.

Data Structures and Operations

ClassyPrelude includes many data structures and tons of operations that work with the data structure. The documentation for them is available in MonoTraversable. However, as we are being practical, we don't need to be familiar with all of them to get by. We can get things done by knowing only a few of them. Most of the time, the data structures that we will work with are List, Map, and Set.

Lists are created by using the [] or (:) notation. I'm pretty sure you are familiar with that already.

```
> [1,2,3]
[1,2,3]
> 1 : 2 : 3 : []
[1,2,3]
> 1 : [2,3]
[1,2,3]
```

Now let's take a look at Map.

```
> mapFromList [(1,'a'), (2,'b'), (2,'c')] :: Map Int Char
fromList [(1,'a'),(2,'c')]
> let m1 = mapFromList [("hello", "world"), ("foo", "bar"), ("foo", "hey")]
:: Map Text Text
> m1
fromList [("hello","world"),("foo","hey")]

> mapToList m1
[("hello", "world"), ("foo", "hey")]
```

Maps are initialized using the `mapFromList` function by providing a list of key-value tuples as its argument. The `:: Map Int Char` is required because `mapFromList` is polymorphic. It's ambiguous for the compiler, as there are multiple types that fulfill the constraints. To fix that, we need to give the compiler a hint on the exact type we are instantiating.

In case there are multiple entries of the same keys, the last one being listed will be kept in the map. The entries before that are omitted.

Map is meant to be printed as `fromList ...`, so don't be surprised if the representation of it is not what you usually see in other programming languages.

If you need to convert `Map` back to `List`, the function to use is `mapToList`.

Let's explore Set next.

```
> let s1 = setFromList [2,3,2,4,1] :: Set Int
> s1
fromList [1,2,3,4]

> setToList s1
[1,2,3,4]
```

Sets are created by using `setFromList`. As you can see, it is quite similar to `Map`. If you need to convert `Set` back to `List`, the function to use is `setToList`.

As I have said earlier, there are tons of operations to do useful stuff with `List`, `Map`, and `Set`. You will notice that some functions can work with multiple container types, as shown with "Y" in Table 2-2. For all the functions in Table 2-2, the ones that can work on `List` will also work on string-like types.

Table 2-2. *Some Functions Provided in ClassyPrelude and on Which Container Types They Can Work*

Function	List	Set	Map
headMay	Y	Y	Y
lastMay	Y	Y	Y
zip	Y	-	-
map	Y	-	Y
filter	Y	-	-
foldr	Y	Y	Y
sortOn	Y	-	-
groupAllOn	Y	-	-
intercalate	Y	-	-
take	Y	-	-
drop	Y	-	-
null	Y	Y	Y
length	Y	Y	Y
elem	Y	Y	Y
(<>)	Y	Y	Y
(\\)	-	Y	Y
member	-	Y	Y
intersect	-	Y	Y
keys	-	Y	Y
unionWithKey	-	-	Y
mapWithKey	-	-	Y

I really suggest you take some time to read the documentation to get the full idea of the capabilities. Alternatively, you can play around with autocompletion in REPL to explore the variants of the listed functions. For example, `drop` has another variant:

```
> drop -- press TAB here
drop      dropWhile
```

Date and Time

The canonical library for dealing with date and time in Haskell is the `time`[3] library. People coming from other programming languages must find the library unintuitive. Reading the documentation would not help much as well, since there is almost no example of what to use on what occasion. This is why we have a dedicated section for it. Here, we will only look at the important bits and cover the common use cases so you can get productive quickly.

For enabling a `time` package in our project, let's add it to our `package.yaml` file:

```
dependencies:
- time
```

The first thing to do to work with this library effectively is to understand the types. The following types are the ones that you are most likely to work with:

1. *UTCTime*: This type is used to reference an event in absolute time. It contains date and time information, up to picoseconds precision.

2. *NominalDiffTime*: This type is used to represent the duration between two `UTCTime`s. Internally it contains a fixed point number representing the difference in picoseconds. Do note that the value might be negative.

3. *TimeZone*: The representation is minutes offset from UTC.

4. *ZonedTime*: This type contains date and time information, like `UTCTime`, but with the addition of `TimeZone`. We use this to refer to an event in a specific time zone.

There are multiple ways to construct `UTCTime`. The first approach is to get the current `UTCTime`. The function to use in this case is `getCurrentTime`. `getCurrentTime` is an impure action, as represented by the `IO` in the type.

```
> import Data.Time
> :t getCurrentTime
getCurrentTime :: IO UTCTime
> getCurrentTime
2017-11-14 23:50:49.576744 UTC
```

---

[3]`www.stackage.org/package/time`

The second approach is to supply seconds since epoch. The function to use is posixSecondsToUTCTime. There is also the utcTimeToPOSIXSeconds function to convert in reverse direction.

```
> import Data.Time.Clock.POSIX
> let t1 = posixSecondsToUTCTime 60.500
> t1
1970-01-01 00:01:00.5 UTC
> utcTimeToPOSIXSeconds t1
60.5s
```

Another option is to parse date time from text.

```
> let dateTimeFormat = iso8601DateFormat (Just "%H:%M:%S%Q%z")
> let parseISO = parseTimeM True defaultTimeLocale dateTimeFormat
> parseISO "2019-01-08T12:45:30.550+0800" :: Maybe UTCTime
Just 2019-01-08 04:45:30.55 UTC
> parseISO "2019-01-08T12:45:30.550+0800" :: Maybe ZonedTime
Just 2019-01-08 12:45:30.55 +0800
```

Since parseTimeM is polymorphic, we need to define the return value that we want. In the preceding example, we converted a string to both UTCTime and ZonedDateTime. Notice that when we define UTCTime, the time is automatically converted to UTC.

The second to last parameter of parseTimeM function is the date and time format. For a complete listing of the format syntax, please refer to the official documentation.[4]

There is also the formatTime function that accepts a format and various time types, including UTCTime, and returns a string of that time adhering to the given format.

The format syntax is the same one as we have seen previously.

For converting between UTCTime and ZonedTime, we use zonedTimeToUTC and utcToZonedTime.

```
> zt <- getZonedTime
> zt
2017-11-15 08:24:28.191892 +08
> zonedTimeToUTC zt
2017-11-15 00:24:28.191892 UTC
```

---

[4]www.stackage.org/haddock/lts-9.13/time-1.6.0.1/Data-Time-Format.html

```
> ut <- getCurrentTime
> ut
2017-11-15 00:28:39.924547 UTC
> let sgt = minutesToTimeZone (8 * 60) -- +0800
> utcToZonedTime sgt ut
2017-11-15 08:28:39.924547 +0800
```

UTCTime supports comparison.

```
> t0 <- getCurrentTime
> t1 <- getCurrentTime
> t0 < t1
True
> t0 >= t1
False
```

Unlike UTCTime, ZonedTime doesn't support comparison. However, you may convert ZonedTime to UTCTime first, with the functions we have seen earlier, before doing the comparison.

Another common use case is to get the duration between times. The function to use is diffUTCTime. It accepts two UTCTime and returns NominalDiffTime. NominalDiffTime is not an absolute number. It might be a negative number, depending on the UTCTimes input.

```
> :t diffUTCTime
diffUTCTime :: UTCTime -> UTCTime -> NominalDiffTime
> diffUTCTime t0 t1 -- assuming we already have t0 & t1 from before
-5.983774s
> diffUTCTime t1 t0
5.983774s
```

NominalDiffTime supports numeric operation like addition and subtraction. Although not commonly used, multiplication and division are also supported.

```
> let diff = realToFrac 60 :: NominalDiffTime
> diff + diff
3600s
> diff - diff
0s
```

As you have seen, to build a `NominalDiffTime` from a number, the function to use is `realToFrac`. You might be baffled with the `realToFrac`. How is this unintuitive name used to build `NominalDiffTime`? `realToFrac` converts any type that is an instance of `Real` to any type that is an instance of `Fractional`. `NominalDiffTime` is an instance of `Fractional` class, while the number we supplied is an instance of `Real` class.

For accessing and modifying specific component of the time-related types, the `time` package doesn't give us any convenient function. Fortunately, there is another library to do just that: `time-lens`.[5] Let's add it to our `package.yaml` file.

```
dependencies:
- time-lens
```

The main functions are `getL`, `modL`, and `setL`. They are used for getting, modifying, and setting, respectively. The first parameter for these functions is the date and time component you want to tweak. The available components are `timeZone`, `seconds`, `minutes`, `hours`, `day`, `month`, and `year`.

```
> zt <- getZonedTime
> zt
2017-11-16 05:39:21.457841 +08
> (getL timeZone zt, getL seconds zt, getL minutes zt, getL hours zt)
(+08,21.457841000000,39,5)
> (getL day zt, getL month zt, getL year zt) (16,11,2017)
> modL day (+20) zt
2017-12-06 05:39:21.457841 +08
> setL year 1000 zt
1000-11-16 05:39:21.457841 +08
```

If you want to modify multiple components at once, I find the cleaner way to do it is to compose the modifier functions using (`.`).

```
> setL month 12 . modL day (subtract 1) $ zt
2017-12-15 05:39:21.457841 +08
```

That's it. The functions and types along with the preceding example usage should be enough for working with date and time in Haskell.

---

[5]`www.stackage.org/package/time-lens`

Regular Expression

Regular expression (Regex) is another tool that we often use on day-to-day basis. We use regular expression for text manipulation, capturing input based on a pattern, and input validation.

There are many packages for doing regular expression, but the one that I find to be complete and easiest to use is pcre-heavy.[6] Let's learn to work with this package by updating our package.yaml file.

```
dependencies:
- pcre-heavy
```

If you encounter any issue while compiling, you may need to have the pcre and pkg-config package installed in your system. In MacOS, this is quite simple if you use homebrew. Just issue brew install pcre pkg-config and you are golden.

In addition to the package dependency mentioned, we also need to use the QuasiQuotes language extension.

This extension basically allows you to process something during compile time. We will see the usage of it shortly. Let's add that extension in our package.yaml.

```
default-extensions:
- QuasiQuotes
```

Now that we have listed the required package and language extension, we can start playing around with the library.

```
> import Text.Regex.PCRE.Heavy -- 1
> let regex1 = [re|^(hell.), (.+)!$|] -- 2
> let regex2 = [re|(hel|] -- 3
Exception when trying to run compile-time code:
        Text.Regex.PCRE.Light: Error in regex: missing )
> asText "Mamamia" =~ regex1 - 4
False
> asText "hello, world!" =~ regex1 -- 5
True
> asByteString "hello, world!" =~ regex1
True
```

---

[6]www.stackage.org/package/pcre-heavy

```
> scan regex1 "hello, world!" :: [(Text, [Text])] -- 6
[("hello, world!",["hello","world"])]
> scan regex1 "hello, world!" :: [(String, [String])]
[("hello, world!",["hello","world"])]

> gsub [re|\d+|] "x" "1 and 2 and 3" :: Text -- 7
"x and x and x"
> sub [re|\d+|] "x" "1 and 2 and 3" :: Text -- 8
"x and 2 and 3"
```

Example (1) shows how to import the package. To create a regular expression, we use the [re| ...|], a functionality from QuasiQuotes language extension, as shown in (2). The nice thing about using QuasiQuotes is that your regular expression is validated at compile time. If you create an invalid regular expression, an error will be thrown at compile time. Example (3) shows such a scenario. Notice that the error message is "Error in regex: missing)." Useful, isn't it?

To check whether a string matches a regular expression, we use the =~ function as shown in examples (4) and (5). It returns a Bool (True or False). =~ accepts any string-like argument. The compiler might get confused about exactly which string we want. asText is a function from ClassyPrelude that coerces a plain string like "hello, world" to Text. This way, the compiler can infer that the actual type that we want is Text. ClassyPrelude comes with other type-coercing functions as well. Please do check its documentation to learn more.

scan is a function to do regular expression capture. The usage is shown in example (6). scan returns a list of tuples. The first part of the tuple is the whole matching segment. The second part of the tuple is a list of captured groups. The tuple is polymorphic, meaning it might be ambiguous for the compiler to guess which string-like type we meant. The :: [(Text, [Text])] is there to give a hint to the compiler on which type to return.

gsub and sub are used for text replacement. The difference is that gsub replaces all matching instances, while sub only replaces the first matching instance. The usage of both functions is shown in example (7) and (8).

We are now ready to be productive with regular expressions.

JSON

Although there are many other alternative for data exchange format, JSON is the lingua-franca of the web. Communication between microservices? Most likely JSON. RESTful API response? Most likely JSON. It's crucial to be able to work with JSON in today's software development. In this section we will learn about aeson,[7] the most popular library for working with JSON.

aeson represents JSON in Haskell with a type called Value.

```
data Value
  = Object Object
  | Array Array
  | String Text
  | Number Scientific
  | Bool Bool
  | Null
type Object = HashMap Text Value
type Array = Vector Value
```

You might see some unfamiliar types. I'll quickly explain them to avoid confusion. Vector is a data structure from the vector library. Vector is similar to List. The difference is that List is basically a linked list, while Vector is an array. Vector fits the use case where you want to have a fast index access. Scientific is a type from the scientific package that represents an arbitrary-precision number. In practice, you'll use it just like any other number.

It's easy to build Value by hand. Let's say we want to build a JSON like the following:

```
{
    "id": 123,
    "name": "Ecky",
    "hobbies": ["Running", "Programming"],
    "country": null
}
```

---

[7]www.stackage.org/package/aeson

Then we build it like the following:

```
> import Data.Aeson
> :{
| object [ "id" .= 123
|        , "name" .= "Ecky"
|        , "hobbies" .= [ "Running", "Programming" ]
|        , "country" .= Null
|        ]
| :}
Object (fromList [("country",Null),("name",String "Ecky"),("id",Number 123.0),
("hobbies",Array [String "Running",String "Programming"])])
```

Writing a Value instance by hand might be a hassle in certain situations. Your domain types usually are not aeson's Value. Wouldn't it be nice if we can convert basic data types directly? Fortunately, we can. toJSON is the function we use to convert Haskell types to Value. toJSON accepts a value that is an instance of ToJSON typeclass. aeson has already implemented a ToJSON instance for basic data types so we can use it without writing our own implementation.

```
> toJSON "asdf" String "asdf"
> toJSON 1990
Number 1990.0
> let m1 = mapFromList [("hello", "world"), ("dunk", "dunk")] :: Map Text Text
> toJSON m1
Object (fromList [("hello",String "world"),("dunk",String "dunk")])
```

In contrast, fromJSON converts Value to any Haskell types that implement a FromJSON instance. Like ToJSON, aeson also has implemented instances for basic data types. fromJSON returns Result a to signal whether the conversion is a success or a failure.

```
> let j1 = toJSON m1
> fromJSON j1 :: Result (Map Text Text)
Success (fromList [("dunk","dunk"),("hello","world")])
> fromJSON j1 :: Result Text
Error "expected Text, encountered Object"
```

Value represents JSON within Haskell, but we usually want to work with a string that is a JSON. Fret not, as this is easy to do with aeson. encode is the function to convert any ToJSON instance to LByteString. Once we have LByteString, we can convert it to another string-like type using a function that we have seen in a previous section.

```
> encode m1 -- m1 from previous code block
"{\"dunk\":\"dunk\",\"hello\":\"world\"}"
> encode j1 -- j1 from previous code block "{\"hello\":\"world\",\"dunk\":\
"dunk\"}"
```

As you can see, Value (j1) itself is an instance of ToJSON. So, if we happen to build Value manually and want to convert it to LByteString, then we can use encode.

Astute readers might wonder if types like tuple, Maybe, or Either have ToJSON instance. Unsurprisingly, they do. So how are they encoded? Let's just try them out.

```
> encode (Just "Hello")
"\"Hello\""
> encode (Nothing :: Maybe Text) -- Nothing is ambiguous "null"
> encode (1, "two", 3.3)
"[1,\"two\",3.3]"
> encode (Left "Hello" :: Either Text Text)
"{\"Left\":\"Hello\"}"
> encode (Right "World" :: Either Text Text)
"{\"Right\":\"World\"}"
```

Now that we have seen how to convert a Haskell type to a JSON string, we might also want to convert in the other direction. The function to look for is eitherDecode. This function converts LByteString to any FromJSON instance. It returns Either String Value to a signal parsing failure if any. aeson comes with FromJSON implementation of many basic types. In the following example, we will see how the same json string can be decoded to Value and to Map Text Text.

```
> let json = encode j1 -- j1 from previous code block
> json
"{\"hello\":\"world\",\"dunk\":\"dunk\"}"
> eitherDecode json :: Either String Value
Right (Object (fromList [("hello",String "world"),("dunk",String "dunk")]))
> eitherDecode json :: Either String (Map Text Text)
```

```
Right (fromList [("dunk","dunk"),("hello","world")])
> eitherDecode json :: Either String Text
Left "Error in $: expected Text, encountered Object"
```

But wait, we usually have our own types, right? As we have seen, we are able to encode and decode any basic types to a JSON string. Now how do we convert from a JSON string to our own data structure? It's simple; we just need to implement a ToJSON and FromJSON instance for our data structure.

Let's say we have the following type:

```
data User = User
  { userId :: Int, userName :: Text, userHobbies :: [Text]
  } deriving (Show)
```

We then implement the ToJSON and FromJSON instance for that type:

```
instance ToJSON User where
  toJSON (User uId name hobbies) = object [ "id" .= uId , "name" .= name,
    "hobbies" .= hobbies ]
```

```
instance FromJSON User where
  parseJSON = withObject "User" $ \v ->
    User <$> v .: "id"
         <*> v .: "name"
         <*> v .: "hobbies"
```

Now we should be able to encode and decode the type to a JSON string. Let's try that out in REPL.

```
> let encoded = encode $ User 1 "Ecky" ["Running", "Programming"]
> encoded
"{\"name\":\"Ecky\",\"id\":1,\"hobbies\":[\"Running\",\"Programming\"]}"

> eitherDecode encoded :: Either String User
Right (User {userId = 1, userName = "Ecky", userHobbies =
["Running","Programming"]})
```

Sweet, we are now able to convert our data structure directly to JSON and vice versa.

The functions for parsing JSON that we've seen in the previous code block might look like they need more explanation. But actually, once you have seen the documentation,[8] you will surely know what to use.

Let's take a brief detour to talk about field names. In Haskell, field name is the same as function. If you have two records with the same field name in a module, the compiler will refuse to compile. Let me show you an example:

```
data User = User { age :: Int }
data Country = Country { age :: Int }
```

The preceding code won't compile because of the name clash for age. A common solution to fix that is to simply prefix the field name with the type's name. In this case, the field names will be "userAge" and "countryAge."

Now back again to JSON. Writing FromJSON and ToJSON instances by hand is easy, but boring. Fortunately, aeson provides a way to generate those instances using a language extension called TemplateHaskell. Let's try that out, shall we?

```
default-extensions:
- TemplateHaskell
```

Now replace the ToJSON and FromJSON instances with this one-liner:

```
$(deriveJSON defaultOptions "User)
```

Let's see what JSON is produced now in REPL.

```
> encode $ User 1 "Ecky" ["Running", "Programming"] "{\"userId\":1,
\"userName\":\"Ecky\",\"userHobbies\":[\"Running\",\"Programming\"]}"
```

Cool! It looks similar, but the field names are a little bit off. We want the user part to be omitted. If we look into defaultOptions docs,[9] it actually has the capability to modify the field name using fieldLabelModifier. Let's try that out. Change the previous code to the following:

```
import Language.Haskell.TH.Syntax (nameBase)
import Data.Aeson.TH

$(let structName = nameBase "User
```

---

[8]www.stackage.org/haddock/lts-9.13/aeson-1.1.2.0/Data-Aeson.html
[9]www.stackage.org/haddock/lts-9.13/aeson-1.1.2.0/Data-Aeson-TH.html

```
    lowercaseFirst (x:xs) = toLower [x] <> xs
    lowercaseFirst xs = xs
    options = defaultOptions
                { fieldLabelModifier = lowercaseFirst . drop (length
                                structName)
                }
 in  deriveJSON options ''User)
```

Also, we need to import the `template-haskell`[10] package to our `package.yaml` for the preceding code to compile.

```
dependencies:
- template-haskell
```

The preceding code begs more explanation. `fieldLabelModifier` has `String ->` `String` as it's type signature. This function accepts a field name as an input and outputs another `String` that will be used as the field name in JSON. In our case, this function will receive `"userId,"` `"username,"` and `"userHobbies."` `lowercaseFirst` is a simple function to convert the first letter of any `String` to lowercase. `''User` is a functionality provided by `Template Haskell` language extension to get the full qualified name of any Haskell type. Then, we apply the `nameBase` function provided by `template-haskell` to get only the type name. In this particular case `''User` yields `"Lib.User."` When we apply nameBase to it, we get just `"User."` In `fieldLabelModifier`, we basically drop the first few letters and convert the first letter to lowercase. This converts `"userHobbies"` to `"hobbies."`

Let's see how our preceding code affect the JSON string produced.

```
> encode $ User 1 "Ecky" ["Running", "Programming"] "{\"id\":1,\"name\":
\"Ecky\",\"hobbies\":[\"Running\",\"Programming\"]}"
```

Our custom data structure is now converted to JSON correctly as we wanted. `deriveJSON` also generates a `FromJSON` instance, which means we can convert the JSON string back to our Haskell type.

```
> let json = encode $ User 1 "Ecky" ["Running", "Programming"]
> eitherDecode json :: Either String User
Right (User {userId = 1, userName = "Ecky", userHobbies =
                    ["Running","Programming"]})
```

---

[10]www.stackage.org/package/template-haskell

As you can see, the preceding logic produces a `camelCase` field name for the JSON. Some people might prefer to use `snake_case` for field names. Fortunately, aeson provides a utility function to do that.

```
camelTo2 :: Char -> String -> String
```

Here's a usage example:

```
camelTo2 '_' 'CamelAPICase' == "camel_api_case"
camelTo2 '-' 'userHobbies' == "user-hobbies"
```

Should you want the produced JSON to have `snake_case` as the field name, then you may use `camelTo2` as an alternative to `lowercaseFirst`.

Not all Haskell types are naively convertible to JSON. Let's see how `deriveJSON` works with such Haskell types. Let's say we have the following types that we want to convert to JSON:

```
data Test
  = TestNullary
  | TestUnary Int
  | TestProduct Int Text Double
  | TestRecord { recA :: Bool, recB :: Int }
$(deriveJSON defaultOptions "Test")
```

Next, let's play around with REPL and see how it's encoded.

```
> encode $ TestNullary
"{\"tag\":\"TestNullary\"}"
> encode $ TestUnary 10
"{\"tag\":\"TestUnary\",\"contents\":10}"

> encode $ TestProduct 10 "Hello" 3.14 "{\"tag\":\"TestProduct\",\"contents
\":[10,\"Hello\",3.14]}"

> encode $ TestRecord True 10
"{\"tag\":\"TestRecord\",\"recA\":true,\"recB\":10}"
```

As you can see, the sum type constructor will be encoded using the `"tag"` field. The content of product type will be encoded as a JSON array in a field named `"contents"`. For record types, unsurprisingly, the field names become the field names of the produced JSON.

That's all we need to productively work with JSON in Haskell.

Exception Handling

It's inevitable that things can go wrong at runtime. For example, we try to write a file but there's not enough disk space. Or maybe we open an HTTP connection but are unable to reach the server. In general, any IO operation may fail at runtime. For these cases, Haskell represents the exceptional cases as Exception. Haskell Exceptions are unchecked, meaning there's nothing in the type signature that signals that an exception will be thrown. So we need to be careful when reading the documentation of the packages we are using, as it usually mentions that some exceptions might be thrown.

Based on how the exception is thrown, we have three types of exceptions: impure exception, synchronous exception, and asynchronous exception.

Impure exception is a kind of exception that is thrown inside a pure context. An example would be:

```
isBelow10 :: Int -> Bool
isBelow10 n = if n < 10 then True else error "above 10!"
```

Haskell is a lazy programming language. Values are not evaluated until it's truly necessary. The implication of this is that the program might crash at an unpredictable location when evaluating values that happen to be an exception. Let's see an example:

```
isBelow10 :: Int -> Either Text ()
isBelow10 n = if n < 10 then Right () else Left (error "above 10!")

let result = isBelow10 20
run :: IO ()
run =
  case result of
    Left e -> do
      putStrLn "something went wrong!"
      putStrLn e
    Right _ ->
      putStrLn "All good!"
```

If you execute the run function from the preceding snippet you'll find the following output:

```
something went wrong!
*** Exception: above 10!
```

That may look counterintuitive at first, especially if you come from strict programming languages background. You might expect that the program should crash on the first call of isBelow10, specifically the isBelow10 20. However, what we find is that "something went wrong" is still being printed. The reason for this behavior is that the error is not evaluated until it's really used. It is finally being used on the putStrLn e call. Since e is not evaluated until that point, "something went wrong!" is still being printed. Being aware of this behavior helps when you need to debug your program. In general, it's more ideal if you never use an impure exception at all.

The second kind of exception is synchronous exception. This exception is generated by the current thread. We generally want to catch this kind of exceptions and recover from it. We will see later how to do that.

The third kind of exception is asynchronous exception. This exception is generated by different thread or by the runtime system. For example, the race function (that you have access to once you have imported ClassyPrelude) will run two actions on separate threads and kill the longer running one with asynchronous exception once the shorter running one finishes. Unlike a synchronous exception, you usually don't want to recover from an asynchronous exception.

The package that allows us to work with exceptions is safe-exceptions.[11] The modules in this package are re-exported in ClassyPrelude. So, if you have imported ClassyPrelude into your module, you immediately have access to it.

Any type that you wish to throw and catch as exceptions needs to be an instance of the Exception typeclass. For example:

```
data ServerException
  = ServerOnFireException
  | ServerNotPluggedInException
  deriving (Show)
instance Exception ServerException
```

To throw a synchronous exception, the function to use is throw, defined as follows:

```
throw :: (MonadThrow m, Exception e) => e -> m a
```

To catch a synchronous exception, the function to use is catch, defined as follows:

```
catch :: (MonadCatch m, Exception e) => m a -> (e -> m a) -> m a
```

---

[11]www.stackage.org/lts-10.3/package/safe-exceptions-0.1.6.0

An example use of throw and catch is as follows:

```
throw ServerOnFireException `catch` (\e -> putStrLn $ show (e :: ServerException))
```

We need to explicitly tell the catch handler to handle ServerException, otherwise it won't compile because it's ambiguous for the compiler.

In addition to catch, there are other ways to handle synchronous exception.

```
handle :: (MonadCatch m, Exception e) => (e -> m a) -> m a -> m a
try :: (MonadCatch m, Exception e) => m a -> m (Either e a)
```

handle is basically the same as catch. The difference is that the arguments' order is flipped. try, on the other hand, is a bit different. It returns an Either where the Left contains the exception (if m a generates an exception) and the Right contains the result of running m a provided m a doesn't generate any exception.

Now that we have a basic understanding of how to manage exceptions in Haskell, let's see a more complicated example:

```
data ServerException
  = ServerOnFireException
  | ServerNotPluggedInException
  deriving (Show)

instance Exception ServerException

data MyException
  = ThisException
  | ThatException
  deriving (Show)

instance Exception MyException

run :: IO () -> IO ()
run action =
  action
    `catch` (\e -> putStrLn $ "ServerException: " <> tshow (e :: ServerException))
    `catch` (\e -> putStrLn $ "MyException: " <> tshow (e :: MyException))
    `catchAny` (\e -> putStrLn $ tshow e)
```

Here, we define two exception types: ServerException and MyException. We also define a run function that runs the action and has multiple catch blocks. The last catch block is catchAny. catchAny has the following type signature:

```
catchAny :: MonadCatch m => m a -> (SomeException -> m a) -> m a
```

Basically, catchAny is just a catch where e is specialized to SomeException. SomeException is a catch-all type for exception. So it means that any exception will be caught in the catchAny block.

Now, let's load the preceding code into REPL and try to execute the following commands:

```
> run (throw ServerOnFireException)
ServerException: ServerOnFireException

> run (throw ThisException)
MyException: ThisException

> run (throwString "unexpected exception")
Control.Exception.Safe.throwString called with:

unexpected exception
```

On the first call to the run function, we throw ServerOnFireException. This exception is then caught in the first catch block.

On the second call to the run function, we throw ThisException type. Notice that it's caught in the second catch block. Since the first block's exception type doesn't match the thrown exception type, the block is not executed and is skipped.

Finally, on the third call to run function, we throw a StringException (from the throwString function). We don't define any specific catch block for StringException, but we define a catchAny block. Since catchAny catches any type of exception, then StringException is cast as SomeException and handled there.

Summary

In this chapter, we have seen how to use various libraries for doing day-to-day tasks in Haskell. The libraries that we have covered are:

1. *classy-prelude*: for working with common data structures

2. *aeson*: for working with JSON

3. *time and time-lens*: for working with date and time

4. *pcre-heavy*: for working with regular expression

5. *safe-exception*: for working with exceptions

CHAPTER 3

Domain Modeling

In this chapter, we will start writing pieces of code that are truly related to our project. At the end of this chapter, we will have a working authentication feature backed by an in-memory database.

Port and Adapter Architecture

Before writing any code, it's worthwhile to think through the architecture first. It helps to give us a big picture of how the application will be laid out. It guides us to structure the interaction between components so that we can make sense of the application as a whole.

The architecture pattern that we want to follow is **Port and Adapter Architecture**. This architecture was first introduced by Alistair Cockburn in a blog post back in 2005.[1] Since then, variations of this architecture pattern have emerged, such as Onion Architecture[2] and Clean Architecture.[3] They have slight differences in the details, but the essence is still the same.

The main intent of Port and Adapter Architecture is to allow an application to be driven by users, programs, or automated test and to be developed in isolation from its eventual runtime external dependencies such as databases and queues. This pattern strictly separates what's internal from what's external to the application. The internal part contains the main business or **domain logic** and should never depend on the external part. The external and internal parts interact with each other through the use of **Port** and **Adapter**. Figure 3-1 illustrates this architecture.

---

[1]https://web.archive.org/web/20180822100852/

[2]http://jeffreypalermo.com/blog/the-onion-architecture-part-1/

[3]https://blog.8thlight.com/uncle-bob/2012/08/13/the-clean-architecture.html

© Ecky Putrady 2018

E. Putrady, *Practical Web Development with Haskell*, https://doi.org/10.1007/978-1-4842-3739-7_3

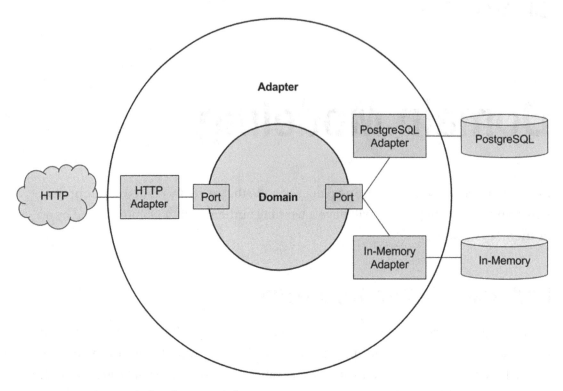

Figure 3-1. *Port and Adapter architecture*

Port is a "contract" on how external entities may interact with the application. In Java, for example, Ports are most likely to be represented using an interface. In Haskell, it could be a typeclass.

In addition to Port, there is the notion of Adapter. Adapter is a component that bridges between the Port and external entities. It translates the protocol that a Port understands to protocol that external entities understand. For example, if the external entity is an SQL database, then the adapter's job is to translate the Port's protocol into SQL.

This architecture is very useful to keep your application maintainable. Over time, the codebase would become more complex. Without guidance on where to put which code, the codebase will become messy.

Another advantage is having clear separation between the domain logic and the delivery mechanism. The Web, for example, is a delivery mechanism. Command line interface is another delivery mechanism. If you keep them separated from domain logic, it's easier to deliver your application through other mechanisms. The same argument also applies to databases and queues. If in the future you want to switch those to different technologies, you can just write another adapter without touching any of the domain logic.

So how does this architecture apply to our program? Our application is about authentication. So, for the domain part, we have authentication domain logic. It contains functionalities such as user registration and user login. As discussed in Chapter 1, the application interacts with multiple databases and uses HTTP as the delivery mechanism. So, here is the list of external entities that we will need to interact with:

1. InMemory database

2. PostgreSQL

3. Redis

4. RabbitMQ

5. Email

6. HTTP with RESTful API

7. HTTP with HTML

We will structure our source code to strictly follow the architecture. At the root level, we have two folders: Domain and Adapter. Domain logic code should be put inside Domain folder. Inside the Adapter folder, we have folders representing each external entity, such as InMemory and PostgreSQL. Code for which the main focus is to bridge external entities and the domain should be put here. In summary, our folders should be like the following:

```
Domain/
Adapter/
  InMemory/
  PostgreSQL/
  Redis/
  RabbitMQ/
  Email/
  HTTP/
    Web/
    API/
```

Auth Data Structure

We will begin our implementation by getting the data structure right. In this section, we will start by defining our data structure and implement the necessary validations logic.

Types Definition

A common practice for developing Haskell applications is by starting with type definitions. The Haskell type system is rich. We have sum types, product types, constraints, etc. In general we want to model everything as precisely as possible. We want to make illegal values or states irrepresentable in the type system. This way, some classes of bugs that may possible in other programming language will not even compile in Haskell. We will see an example of this shortly. Once we have types defined, programming Haskell feels very much like filling in the blanks.

In order to define types, we need to look into some of the requirements:

1. User should be able to register with email and password

2. Email is case insensitive and should be unique across the whole system

3. Email should be in the correct format

4. Password should have length of more than five and contain number, uppercase letter, and lowercase letter

We know that registration accepts email and password, so Auth is naturally a record with such data.

```
data Auth = Auth
  { authEmail :: Text
  , authPassword :: Text
  } deriving (Show, Eq)
```

Requirements points 2 to 4 state the validations that need to take place on registration. However, I see two kinds of validation there. The kind that depends on the application state and the kind that is independent of application state. "Email should be unique across the whole system" is the former kind. In order to validate this, we need to query the system state and see if the same email has already registered. The other validations, like "Email should be in correct format" are the latter kind.

The reason I made this distinction is because each kind has a different preferable way to implement. For the independent kind, it is better to make such a value irrepresentable in our types in the first place. The Auth record that we defined earlier is too loose. We can create an Auth with an invalid email format. Ideally, the compiler should refuse to create an Auth record if the email format is invalid. We will see how to do that shortly.

For the dependent kind, there is no choice other than to handle the error at runtime. In our case, the error is represented as RegistrationError. For now, the error that we have is only because of duplicate email.

```
data RegistrationError
  = RegistrationErrorEmailTaken
  deriving (Show, Eq)
```

As we have seen, the Auth record is not good enough since it still allows invalid email to be passed in. Let's make the Auth record stricter.

```
newtype Email = Email { emailRaw :: Text } deriving (Show, Eq)

rawEmail :: Email -> Text
rawEmail = emailRaw

mkEmail :: Text -> Either [Text] Email
mkEmail = undefined

newtype Password = Password { passwordRaw :: Text } deriving (Show, Eq)

rawPassword :: Password -> Text
rawPassword = passwordRaw

mkPassword :: Text -> Either [Text] Password
mkPassword = undefined

data Auth = Auth
  { authEmail :: Email
  , authPassword :: Password
  } deriving (Show, Eq)
```

We create a newtype for Email. We also create a function called mkEmail. This function accepts Text and returns an Either of [Text] or Email. The [Text] contains error messages. For email, the error message might be only one, such as "invalid format." For password, however, there might be multiple errors, such as "length should be more than 5" and "should contain number."

As an alternative to Text for representing error, we could define our own sum types for those errors. For example:

```
data EmailValidationErr = EmailValidationErrInvalidEmail

mkEmail :: Text -> Either [EmailValidationErr] Email
mkEmail = undefined

data PasswordValidationErr = PasswordValidationErrLength Int
  | PasswordValidationErrMustContainUpperCase
  | PasswordValidationErrMustContainLowerCase
  | PasswordValidationErrMustContainNumber

mkPassword :: Text -> Either [PasswordValidationErr] Password
mkPassword = undefined
```

Using sum types to define an error is useful if we want to act based on the type of the error. For validation-related errors, we usually just want to display the error as-is to the user without doing anything specific based on the error type. That's why we will stick with Text as the error type.

The main idea of creating newtypes for Email is that we won't export the constructor of Email and only allow Email construction through the use of the mkEmail function. This way, it is guaranteed at compile time that any Email that is used in the domain is always valid. We use the same approach for Password as well. This pattern is known as **smart constructor**.

Validation Implementation

We need some helper functions to implement the mkEmail and mkPassword functions. From the requirements, we know that we need to check the following:

1. Whether the text has some specified length

2. Whether the text matches he specified regex

Those functions are general enough and can be used for other purposes. So let's create them in the Domain.Validation module.

```
module Domain.Validation where

import ClassyPrelude
import Text.Regex.PCRE.Heavy
```

We import Text.Regex.PCRE.Heavy because we will need to validate based on regular expression.

We also define Validation type. Validation is a synonym for function that receives any input and returns a Maybe of any error message e. It returns Nothing if the input is valid and otherwise if not valid.

```
type Validation e a = a -> Maybe e
```

Next, we define the validate function. This function receives three inputs:

1. (a -> b): a constructor function, which will be called if validation passes

2. [Validation a]: a list of validation functions

3. a: the value we want to validate

It outputs an Either of error messages or b, a successful value.

```
validate :: (a -> b) -> [Validation e a] -> a -> Either [e] b
validate constructor validations val =
  case concatMap (\f -> maybeToList $ f val) validations of
    []    -> Right $ constructor val
    errs  -> Left errs
```

The concatMap here applies each validation to val and then concatenate the results. Then we check whether the result is an empty list or not. If it is an empty list, meaning there is no error message, we know that the value passes all validations. If that's the case, then we just apply the constructor function to the value and return it as Right. On the other hand, if there are error messages being returned, we know that the value does not pass validations, so we return Left with the error messages. The usage of this might be clearer once you see how it's being employed.

41

Next, we create some validation functions. From our requirement, we know that we need to check for length and regular expression. Let's first create a length checking validation.

```
rangeBetween :: (Ord a) => a -> a -> e -> Validation e a
rangeBetween minRange maxRange msg val =
  if val >= minRange && val <= maxRange then Nothing else Just msg

lengthBetween :: (MonoFoldable a) => Int -> Int -> e -> Validation e a
lengthBetween minLen maxLen msg val =
  rangeBetween minLen maxLen msg (length val)
```

We define two functions: rangeBetween and lengthBetween. rangeBetween checks whether the input value is within a specified range. An example would be "is this number between 5 and 10?". However, instead of just a number, our function works for all types that can be compared, thanks to the Ord constraint. lengthBetween internally uses rangeBetween. It makes sense, because length is just a number and we can check whether a number is within the specified range using rangeBetween. MonoFoldable constraint is there because we use the length function from ClassyPrelude. This basically means that this function works for all types that have length, for example Set, List, or Map. Both functions accept an error message as the third argument. This error message will be used when the validation doesn't pass.

The next function that we want to define is the regular expression check. The function is simple enough: just check whether the value matches a given regex.

```
regexMatches :: Regex -> e -> Validation e Text
regexMatches regex msg val =
  if val =~ regex then Nothing else Just msg
```

Let's try the code we just wrote in REPL.

```
> :l Domain.Validation

> lengthBetween 1 5 "err" "12345"
Nothing
> lengthBetween 1 5 "err" "123456"
Just "err"
```

```
> regexMatches [re|^hello|] "err" "hello world"
Nothing
> regexMatches [re|^hello|] "err" "failed world"
Just "err"

> let mustContainA = regexMatches [re|A|] "Must contain 'A'"
> let mustContainB = regexMatches [re|B|] "Must contain 'B'"
> validate id [ mustContainA, mustContainB ] "abc"
Left ["Must contain 'A'","Must contain 'B'"]
> validate id [ mustContainA, mustContainB ] "ABc"
Right "ABc"
```

Great, the code work as expected.

mkEmail and mkPassword Implementation

Now that we have handy validation functions, let's go back to Domain.Auth and finish up the mkEmail and mkPassword functions.

First, we import the validation module that we have just created along with the regular expression library.

```
import Domain.Validation
import Text.Regex.PCRE.Heavy
```

Next, we implement the mkEmail function. For email, we simply use regular expression check. Don't put too much effort on understanding the regular expression for email as it's not our main goal here. We pass Email as the first argument of validate function. Remember that Email is a constructor for Email newtype.

```
mkEmail :: Text -> Either [Text] Email
mkEmail = validate Email
    [ regexMatches
      [re|^[A-ZO-9a-z._%+-]+@[A-Za-zO-9.-]+\.[A-Za-z]{2,64}$|]
      "Not a valid email"
    ]
```

Password is a bit more complicated, as we have many checks to do. Per the requirements, we would need to check the length and whether the password contains number, uppercase letter, and lowercase letter. Actually, the requirement doesn't say anything about the maximum password length. However, I think having a maximum length check would not hurt.

```
mkPassword :: Text -> Either [Text] Password
mkPassword = validate Password
      [ lengthBetween 5 50 "Should between 5 and 50"
      , regexMatches [re|\d|] "Should contain number"
      , regexMatches [re|[A-Z]|] "Should contain uppercase letter"
      , regexMatches [re|[a-z]|] "Should contain lowercase letter"
      ]
```

Let's try that again in REPL.

```
> :l Domain.Auth

> mkEmail "test"
Left ["Not a valid email"]

> mkEmail "test@example.com"
Right (Email {emailRaw = "test@example.com"})

> mkPassword "ABC"
Left ["Should between 5 and 50","Should contain number","Should contain
lowercase letter"]

> mkPassword "1234ABCdef"
Right (Password {passwordRaw = "1234ABCdef"})
```

Congratulations, you have just learned how to create safer domain types with validations!

Registration

In the previous section, we defined and put necessary validations to our essential data structure. In this section, we will continue building on top of that to finish the registration scenario.

Types Definition

Registration would require us to store the authentication. This storage could be PostgreSQL or in-memory database. In addition to that, we also need to send an email verification link. As we have explored previously in the architecture section, we will need some Ports to interact with this storage and notification system. We will use Haskell typeclass to represent the Port.

```haskell
type VerificationCode = Text

class Monad m => AuthRepo m where
  addAuth :: Auth -> m (Either RegistrationError VerificationCode)

class Monad m => EmailVerificationNotif m where
  notifyEmailVerification :: Email -> VerificationCode -> m ()
```

AuthRepo contains functions for interaction with the authentication repository. For now, we only need to add an authentication into the repository. EmailVerificationNotif represents the notification system where email will be dispatched to the user. All of these typeclasses are constrained by Monad typeclass, since inherently these operations have side effects.

Finally, the type signature for the registration function would be as follow:

```haskell
register :: (AuthRepo m, EmailVerificationNotif m)
         => Auth -> m (Either RegistrationError ())
register auth = undefined
```

Implementation

Now let's implement the register function.

```haskell
import Control.Monad.Except

register :: (AuthRepo m, EmailVerificationNotif m)
         => Auth -> m (Either RegistrationError ())
register auth = runExceptT $ do
  vCode <- ExceptT $ addAuth auth
  let email = authEmail auth
  lift $ notifyEmailVerification email vCode
```

What we do in this function is to add the Auth to the repository using the addAuth function provided by AuthRepo typeclass. addAuth returns a VerificationCode. We then use it along with email to notify the user for email verification.

We also need to import Control.Monad.Except for ExceptT and runExceptT. By using ExceptT, we can short-circuit the logic if addAuth auth returns a Left. The lines following that line will not be evaluated. runExceptT converts an ExceptT into Either. You will need to put mtl in package.yml to use ExceptT.

```
dependencies:
- mtl # NEW
```

In order to run this code, we now need to implement an instance of AuthRepo and EmailVerificationNotif typeclass. Let's write a temporary code for an implementation over IO. What this implementation does is to just print something to the screen. Please note that this code is temporary and we will remove it once we have implemented a proper storage implementation.

```
instance AuthRepo IO where
  addAuth (Auth email pass) = do
    putStrLn $ "adding auth: " <> rawEmail email
    return $ Right "fake verification code"

instance EmailVerificationNotif IO where
  notifyEmailVerification email vcode =
    putStrLn $ "Notify " <> rawEmail email <> " - " <> vcode
```

Now let's get into REPL and see our implementation in action:

```
> :l Domain.Auth

> let Right email = mkEmail "test@example.com"
> let Right password = mkPassword "1234ABCdef"
> let auth = Auth email password
> register Auth
adding auth: test@example.com
Notify test@example.com - fake verification code
Right ()
```

As you can see, our implementation works as expected. Later we will use a proper storage implementation instead of just printing a message to the screen.

Email Verification

In this section, we will look into the next feature that we will be building: Email verification. We will follow the previous approach by starting with the type definition and finally implementing the necessary functions.

Types Definition

The requirements regarding email verification are as follow:

1. Email verification page

    1. User should be informed if the verification link is incorrect

    2. User's email should be verified by visiting this page

Although the requirement is web focused, we can imagine that a web route handler calls a function in our domain with some verification code as the input and our function will return an error if the verificaton code is incorrect.

Verifying email requires interaction with an authentication repository. For this, we introduce a new function in the AuthRepo typeclass, setEmailAsVerified.

```
class Monad m => AuthRepo m where
  setEmailAsVerified :: VerificationCode -> m (Either
  EmailVerificationError ())
```

We have a type for email verification error: EmailVerificationError. For now, the error is only because of invalid code, in which we represent it as EmailVerificationErrorInvalidCode.

```
data EmailVerificationError = EmailVerificationErrorInvalidCode
  deriving (Show, Eq)
```

The function that we will use to verify email is verifyEmail, which accepts a VerificationCode and returns an Either of EmailVerificationError and ().

```
verifyEmail :: AuthRepo m
            => VerificationCode -> m (Either EmailVerificationError ())
            verifyEmail = undefined
```

47

Implementation

Let's move onward to `verifyEmail` implementation.

```
verifyEmail :: AuthRepo m
            => VerificationCode -> m (Either EmailVerificationError ())
            verifyEmail = setEmailAsVerified
```

This feels like a waste of effort, since we basically just create a synonym for a function in AuthRepo. However, I would argue keeping things like this is good in the long run because it maintains consistency. This also prepares us should we want to extend the functionality in email verification. For example, we might want to log certain things or notify other systems if the email has been verified.

We won't be running our code, since there's nothing much to show.

Login and Resolving Session

In this section, we will work on the login functionality. The requirement says the following for login:

1. Login Page

    1. User should be able to log in with email and password

    2. User should not be able to log in with invalid email and password combination

    3. User should not be able to log in if the email has not been verified

In addition to the requirement listed, we will also have a session mechanism. This is a very common practice in web applications. The basic idea is that we want to give the user a temporary "ticket" after logging in to our system. The user can use this ticket for further actions that require authentication.

Types Definition

Let's start by defining the types. Login functionality essentially receives an `Auth` and returns a `SessionId`. We know that this functionality needs to query the repository of registered `Auth` and to write the mapping of `SessionId` to `UserId` in another repository. Login may also fail due to invalid authentication or if the email has not verified. So, we can define them as follows:

```haskell
type UserId = Int

type SessionId = Text

data LoginError = LoginErrorInvalidAuth
  | LoginErrorEmailNotVerified
  deriving (Show, Eq)

class Monad m => AuthRepo m where
  findUserByAuth :: Auth -> m (Maybe (UserId, Bool))

class Monad m => SessionRepo m where
  newSession :: UserId -> m SessionId

login :: (AuthRepo m, SessionRepo m)
      => Auth -> m (Either LoginError SessionId)
login = undefined
```

We define `UserId` as an alias for `Int`. We choose to do so over defining a newtype because unlike `Email` and `Password`, there's no specific constraint required on `UserId`. There is, however, an advantage if we define a newtype for it like so:

```haskell
newtype UserId = UserId Int
```

It ensures that we won't mix `Int` that is meant to represent `UserId` to other `Int` that represents something else, for example, `OrderId`. In my experience, I rarely do that kind of mistake and making it a newtype makes it a bit cumbersome to use. So I rarely wrap these in a newtype. It might be different in your experience. You can always use this approach if it suits your need better.

Moving on, we introduce a new function in `AuthRepo`, `findUserByAuth`. This function returns a `Maybe (UserId, Bool)`. The `Bool` part is used to represent whether the email has been verified or not. We will need it to fulfill a requirement where we want to reject logins with unverified email.

In addition to the authentication repository, login also needs to interact with the session repository. When the user logs in, we need to create a new session for that user. The function to do that is `newSession`.

There are two possible errors that may happen when the user tries to log in: when the email and password combination is incorrect, and when the email is not yet verified. We represent those errors as `LoginErrorInvalidAuth` and `LoginErrorEmailNotVerified`, respectively.

In addition to the `login` function, we also need to resolve `SessionId` back to `UserId`. For this use case, we have the `resolveSessionId` function. The return value of this function is a `Maybe UserId` instead of just `UserId` because the session might be invalid or expire, in which case no `UserId` can be resolved from that `SessionId`. This function obviously needs to query the repository of sessions, so we add a new function in `SessionRepo` called `findUserIdBySessionId`.

```
class Monad m => SessionRepo m where
  findUserIdBySessionId :: SessionId -> m (Maybe UserId)

resolveSessionId :: SessionRepo m => SessionId -> m (Maybe UserId)
resolveSessionId = findUserBySessionId
```

`resolveSessionId` is now just a synonym for `findUserBySessionId`. This seems like unnecessary boilerplate. However, let's keep it for now for consistency and possible future functionality additions.

Implementation

We only have one hole to fill in, the `login` function. We implement it as follows:

```
login :: (AuthRepo m, SessionRepo m)
      => Auth -> m (Either LoginError SessionId)
login auth = runExceptT $ do
  result <- lift $ findUserByAuth auth
```

```
case result of
  Nothing -> throwError LoginErrorInvalidAuth
  Just (_, False) -> throwError LoginErrorEmailNotVerified
  Just (uId, _) -> lift $ newSession uId
```

We first use the findUserByAuth function to find a user id from Auth. The result is then pattern matched; in the case of Nothing, we signal an invalid authentication error. In the case of Just (_, False), we signal an email not verified error. Otherwise, we just create a new session using the newSession function.

User Page

The last requirement that we want to implement is the following:

1. User Page

   1. User should be redirected to the Login Page if the user is not authenticated

   2. User should be able to see the user's email if the user is authenticated

We can ignore the first requirement, as it's web application centric. For now, our concern is that there should be a domain function to get Email from UserId. Obviously, this requires interaction with the authentication repository. So, let's introduce another function.

```
class Monad m => AuthRepo m where
  findEmailFromUserId :: UserId -> m (Maybe Email)

  getUser :: AuthRepo m => UserId -> m (Maybe Email)
  getUser = findEmailFromUserId
```

We return a Maybe Email because we can't guarantee that the given UserId always exists in our system.

Similar to the preceding, we also have a seemingly unnecessary function that just wraps a function in AuthRepo. Bear with it for now as we shall see how this is useful in Chapter 11 (Testing).

Exposing Safe Functions

Not all functions and types that we have defined are meant to be used by the user of this module. For example, we don't want the user of this module to use the constructor of `Email` and `Password` directly, so that they cannot create `Email` and `Password` with invalid values. To achieve that, we simply don't export those constructors. Our module will then have the following export:

```
module Domain.Auth (
  -- * Types
  Auth(..),
  Email,
  mkEmail,
  rawEmail,
  Password,
  mkPassword,
  rawPassword,
  UserId,
  VerificationCode,
  SessionId,
  RegistrationError(..),
  EmailVerificationError(..),
  LoginError(..),

  -- * Ports
  AuthRepo(..),
  EmailVerificationNotif(..),
  SessionRepo(..),

  -- * Use cases
  register,
  verifyEmail,
  login,
  resolveSessionId,
  getUser
)
```

In-Memory Database

Up until this point, we have finished the implementation of the main domain logic. However, it's still unusable because the logic requires a repository to store the data. In this chapter, we will create one implementation of such a data repository. For simplicity, we will store all of the data in-memory. It's not usable for production, but it's great for getting started. In later chapters, we will learn how to use other databases for storing the data.

We start by learning thea concept of Software Transactional Memory in Haskell. This concept is necessary to learn, knowing that our in-memory database will be read and written concurrently. Without understanding this concept, our implementation might fail in a concurrent scenario. We will then continue to implement each function in the typeclasses that we've defined in previous sections.

Software Transactional Memory

In an imperative programming language, like Java, having a mutable state is easy and the norm. Just declare a variable and change it as necessary. However, extra care needs to be taken in a concurrent scenario. Consider a registration process. The process would be: read the list of authentications, insert a new authentication, and store this whole list back—very straightforward. Now consider what happens if there are multiple registration processes that happen concurrently. The following scenario could happen:

1. *Process A*: Get the list of authentications; it's an empty list.

2. *Process B*: Get the list of authentications; it's an empty list.

3. *Process A*: Append the list with authentication A; it's currently a list with one element: A.

4. *Process B*: Append the list with authentication B; it's currently a list with one element: B.

5. *Process A*: Store the list of authentications.

6. *Process B*: Store the list of authentications.

In the preceding scenario, authentication A will be lost. It's because process B overwrites what process A has done. For mitigating this issue, we need to use a locking mechanism. It's not a very straightforward process; if you are not careful, you may hit deadlock.

In Haskell, there is a library to mitigate the aforementioned issue. The library is called stm.[4] It's re-exported in ClassyPrelude. Since we use ClassyPrelude, we can use it without importing any other packages.

stm has a data type called TVar. Think of it as a box containing a value that can be mutated atomically. TVar can be created with the newTVarIO function. Let's try it out in REPL.

```
> :t newTVarIO :: a -> IO (TVar a)
> tvar <- newTVarIO 10
```

In the preceding snippet, we create a new TVar with a value of 10. For reading and writing, the functions to use are readTVar and writeTVar, respectively. Both of these functions return an STM monad. We can then use atomically to convert STM into IO.

```
> :t readTVar
readTVar :: TVar a -> STM a
> :t writeTVar
writeTVar :: TVar a -> a -> STM ()
> :t atomically
atomically :: MonadIO m => STM a -> m a
> let add5 = readTVar tvar >>= \val -> writeTVar tvar (val + 5)
> :t add5
add5 :: STM()

> atomically $ readTVar tvar
10
> atomically add5
> atomically $ readTVar tvar
15
```

In the preceding example, we defined a new function add5, which adds 5 to tvar. Then, we executed that using the atomically function and we observed that the value in tvar is mutated from 10 to 15.

---

[4]https://www.stackage.org/package/stm

STM operation can be nested, for example:

```
> atomically $ add5 >> add5
> atomically $ readTVar tvar
25
```

One common case is when we want to just read the value contained in TVar in IO monad without doing any write back. As we have seen so far, the way to do it is quite verbose, `atomically $ readTVar tvar`. Fortunately, there is an alias for that: `readTVarIO`.

```
> readTVarIO tvar
25
```

The increment works correctly in a single-threaded scenario. How about a concurrent scenario? Will it also work? Let's find out.

```
> tvar <- newTVarIO 0
> let add1 = readTVar tvar >>= \val -> writeTVar tvar (val + 1)
> let add1Actions = replicate 100 add1 :: [STM ()]
> mapConcurrently atomically add1Actions
> readTVarIO tvar
100
```

In the preceding example, we initialized a TVar with a starting value of 0. We then defined a function to increment the value inside tvar by one. The mapConcurrently function is used to apply the actions concurrently. In this case, the actions are 100 add1s. As we have seen, the increment also works correctly in a concurrent scenario.

That concludes our crash course on Haskell's STM. In short, if you want a safe mutable variable in Haskell, you almost always want to use STM. You can be productive in using STM by just remembering a few functions: newTVarIO, readTVar, writeTVar, and atomically.

Repositories Implementation

Now that we've learned about STM, let's use it for our repositories implementation. We will write our code in a new module `Adapter.InMemory.Auth`.

```
module Adapter.InMemory.Auth where

import ClassyPrelude
import qualified Domain.Auth as D
```

Besides the usual `ClassyPrelude`, we need to import `Domain.Auth`. We also make it a qualified import to avoid name collision.

Since we want to store the data in memory, we need to define a data structure to hold all these data. Here's one I came up with:

```
data State = State
  { stateAuths :: [(D.UserId, D.Auth)]
  , stateUnverifiedEmails :: Map D.VerificationCode D.Email
  , stateVerifiedEmails :: Set D.Email
  , stateUserIdCounter :: Int
  , stateNotifications :: Map D.Email D.VerificationCode
  , stateSessions :: Map D.SessionId D.UserId
  } deriving (Show, Eq)
```

If you try to compile this, you would get an error saying `Email` needs to be an instance of `Ord` typeclass. This error comes up because we have `Set D.Email`. `Set` requires the element to be an instance of `Ord` typeclass. No need to worry, because we can have GHC generate such an instance. Simply add `Ord` in the `deriving` clause of `Email` newtype.

```
newtype Email = Email { rawEmail :: Text } deriving (Show, Eq, Ord)
```

`stateAuths` is a list of `UserId` and `Auth` pairs that is used for storing user authentications. We will use `stateUserIdCounter` for generating a unique `UserId`. `stateAuths` is defined as a list of tuple instead of a `Map`, because our algorithm needs to traverse to the values as we will see later. `Map` is great if we want a random access based on a key.

`stateUnverifiedEmails` is a `Map` of `VerificationCode` and `Email`. We use `VerificationCode` as a key, since our use case is to look up an `Email` by `VerificationCode`. We also have `stateVerifiedEmails` that is a `Set` of `Email`. We use this `Set` to check whether an email is verified or not.

stateSessions is a mapping of SessionId and UserId. We use this structure to look up UserId from SessionId.

Last but not least is stateNotification. This represents notification that is sent to an Email. Having this state around would be handy for automated testing.

We also define initialState. This is used when we start the application.

```
initialState :: State
initialState = State
  { stateAuths = []
  , stateUnverifiedEmails = mempty
  , stateVerifiedEmails = mempty
  , stateUserIdCounter = 0
  , stateNotifications = mempty
  , stateSessions = mempty
  }
```

Since we want to implement each function in repositories, let's copy over all those functions here with slight modifications.

```
import Data.Has

type InMemory r m = (Has (TVar State) r, MonadReader r m, MonadIO m)

addAuth :: InMemory r m
        => Auth -> m (Either RegistrationError VerificationCode)
addAuth = undefined

setEmailAsVerified :: InMemory r m
                   => VerificationCode -> m (Either EmailVerificationError ())
setEmailAsVerified = undefined

findUserByAuth :: InMemory r m
               => Auth -> m (Maybe (UserId, Bool))
findUserByAuth = undefined

findEmailFromUserId :: InMemory r m
                    => UserId -> m (Maybe Email)
findEmailFromUserId = undefined
```

```
notifyEmailVerification :: InMemory r m
                        => Email -> VerificationCode -> m ()
notifyEmailVerification = undefined

newSession :: InMemory r m
           => UserId -> m SessionId
newSession = undefined

findUserIdBySessionId :: InMemory r m
                      => SessionId -> m (Maybe UserId)
findUserIdBySessionId = undefined
```

The modification that we did is just adding a new constraint, InMemory r m, in the beginning of each function. InMemory r m basically says: "The following computation works for any m that is an instance of MonadIO and MonadReader r, where r is any structure that has TVar State."

We need MonadIO because we need to do IO, such as changing the content of the TVar and generating a random string.

We need the Has (TVar State) r, MonadReader r m constraint because in each function we need access to the state. In this case, we choose to thread the state through MonadReader. Otherwise, we need to pass in the state as a function argument, such as:

```
setEmailAsVerified :: TVar State
                   -> VerificationCode -> IO (Either EmailVerification
                   Error ())
```

The implication of such function design is that whoever calls the function needs to explicitly pass the state. Once you need to call such functions deep in the call chain, those functions get unwieldly pretty fast.

Has a r comes from the data-has[5] package. If you try to compile the preceding code, you may encounter a compile error. That's because we have not added that package to our project yet. Let's edit our package.yaml to be the following:

```
dependencies:
- data-has # New!
```

---

[5]www.stackage.org/package/data-has

In addition to `data-has`, we also need to enable two new language extensions. Let's add those to our `package.yaml`:

```
default-extensions:
- ConstraintKinds
- FlexibleContexts
```

`ConstraintKinds` language extension allows you to write something like this:

```
type InMemory r m = (Has (TVar State) r, MonadReader r m, MonadIO m)
```

Without this language extension, you have to write the full constraints in each function type signature, such as:

```
addAuth :: (Has (TVar State) r, MonadReader r m, MonadIO m)
        => Auth -> m (Either RegistrationError VerificationCode)
```

It's slightly unpleasant because it's too long. Imagine writing that if you have so many functions requiring the same constraint.

SessionRepo Implementation

`findUserBySessionId` is a simple one. We just get the current state and then look for `SessionID` in `stateSessions` structure.

```
findUserIdBySessionId :: InMemory r m
                      => D.SessionId -> m (Maybe D.UserId)
findUserIdBySessionId sId = do
  tvar <- asks getter
  liftIO $ lookup sId . stateSessions <$> readTVarIO tvar
```

`getter` is a function that comes from `data-has`. It has the type signature of `Has a t => t -> a`. From the type signature, we can infer that this function simply gets an `a` from `t`, provided `t` has `a`, as implied by `Has a t` constraint.

`newSession` is another simple one. First, we need to generate a unique and random `SessionID`. We implement it by generating a random sixteen alphanumeric letters using `stringRandomIO` from the `Text.StringRandom` module. Sixteen is picked arbitrarily, as I think it would generate a unique enough string for our use case. Since it's just random letters, there is no guarantee that it will be unique. So, we will reduce the collision probability even further by prefixing it with `UserId`, since we know `UserID` is unique. Once we have this `SessionId`, we just need to insert it in `stateSessions`.

```haskell
import Text.StringRandom

newSession :: InMemory r m
           => D.UserId -> m D.SessionId
newSession uId = do
  tvar <- asks getter
  sId <- liftIO $ ((tshow uId) <>) <$> stringRandomIO "[A-Za-z0-9]{16}"
  atomically $ do
    state <- readTVar tvar
    let sessions = stateSessions state
        newSessions = insertMap sId uId sessions
        newState = state { stateSessions = newSessions }
    writeTVar tvar newState
    return sId
```

For this to compile, we need to list `string-random` as our dependency in the package.yaml file.

```yaml
dependencies:
- string-random # NEW!
```

`string-random` might not be available in Stackage. If that's the case, then we need to add it in stack.yaml.

```yaml
extra-deps:
- string-random-0.1.0.0
```

EmailVerificationNotif Implementation

`EmailVerificationNotif` typeclass has only one function: `notifyEmailVerification`. It's also a simple one, as we just need to insert the given `VerificationCode` to `stateNotifications`.

```
notifyEmailVerification :: InMemory r m
                       => D.Email -> D.VerificationCode -> m ()
notifyEmailVerification email vCode = do
  tvar <- asks getter
  atomically $ do
    state <- readTVar tvar
    let notifications = stateNotifications state
        newNotifications = insertMap email vCode notifications
        newState = state { stateNotifications = newNotifications }
    writeTVar tvar newState
```

The next function that we will implement is actually only useful for testing purposes. Since we fake email notification by storing it in a memory, there is no way to get the verification code unless we provide a function to get it. This function does just that. It simply looks up the stateNotifications by that Email.

```
getNotificationsForEmail :: InMemory r m
                       => D.Email -> m (Maybe D.VerificationCode)
getNotificationsForEmail email = do
  tvar <- asks getter
  state <- liftIO $ readTVarIO tvar
  return $ lookup email $ stateNotifications state
```

AuthRepo Implementation

Let's move on to the four functions in AuthRepo. The first one that we want to implement is findEmailFromUserId. What we need to do here is to read stateAuths and find one entry that matches the given UserId and get the Email out of that entry.

```
findEmailFromUserId :: InMemory r m
                   => D.UserId -> m (Maybe D.Email)
findEmailFromUserId uId = do
  tvar <- asks getter
  state <- liftIO $ readTVarIO tvar
  let mayAuth = map snd . find ((uId ==) . fst) $ stateAuths state
  return $ D.authEmail <$> mayAuth
```

findUserByAuth is slightly more complicated. We first need to look up UserId from the given Auth. If such Auth is not found, then return Nothing. If it's found, then we need to check whether the Email is verified or not by checking with stateVerifiedEmails. The result of this check is then put into the return value.

```
findUserByAuth :: InMemory r m
                => D.Auth -> m (Maybe (D.UserId, Bool))
findUserByAuth auth = do
  tvar <- asks getter
  state <- liftIO $ readTVarIO tvar
  let mayUserId = map fst . find ((auth ==) . snd) $ stateAuths state
  case mayUserId of
    Nothing -> return Nothing
    Just uId -> do
      let verifieds = stateVerifiedEmails state
          email = D.authEmail auth
          isVerified = elem email verifieds
      return $ Just (uId, isVerified)
```

For setEmailAsVerified, the basic idea is to look up an Email in stateUnverifiedEmails from the given VerificationCode and move it into stateVerifiedEmails. Since VerificationCode might not map to any Email, we may throw EmailVerificationErrorInvalidCode.

```
setEmailAsVerified :: InMemory r m
                   => D.VerificationCode
                   -> m (Either D.EmailVerificationError ())
setEmailAsVerified vCode = do
  tvar <- asks getter
  atomically . runExceptT $ do
    state <- lift $ readTVar tvar
    let unverifieds = stateUnverifiedEmails state
        verifieds = stateVerifiedEmails state
        mayEmail = lookup vCode unverifieds
    case mayEmail of
      Nothing -> throwError D.EmailVerificationErrorInvalidCode
      Just email -> do
```

```
    let newUnverifieds = deleteMap vCode unverifieds
        newVerifieds = insertSet email verifieds
        newState = state
          { stateUnverifiedEmails = newUnverifieds
          , stateVerifiedEmails = newVerifieds
          }
    lift $ writeTVar tvar newState
```

addAuth is the most complex one so far. First, we generate a random VerificationCode using the similar mechanism as generating SessionId. Then, we check whether the email is a duplicate by traversing stateAuths. If it is a duplicate, we return a RegistrationErrorEmailTaken error. Otherwise, we continue to insert the user's Auth into stateAuths. UserId is generated using a counter. We simply increment the counter by one when generating a new UserId. Since we also want users to verify their email, we store the Email along with VerificationCode in stateUnverifiedEmails.

```
addAuth :: InMemory r m
        => D.Auth -> m (Either D.RegistrationError D.VerificationCode)
addAuth auth = do
  tvar <- asks getter

  -- gen verification code
  vCode <- liftIO $ stringRandomIO "[A-Za-z0-9]{16}"

  atomically . runExceptT $ do
    state <- lift $ readTVar tvar
    -- check whether the given email is duplicate
    let auths = stateAuths state
        email = D.authEmail auth
        isDuplicate = any (email ==) . map (D.authEmail . snd) $ auths
    when isDuplicate $ throwError D.RegistrationErrorEmailTaken
    -- update the state
    let newUserId = stateUserIdCounter state + 1
        newAuths = (newUserId, auth) : auths
        unverifieds = stateUnverifiedEmails state
        newUnverifieds = insertMap vCode email unverifieds
```

```
        newState = state
          { stateAuths = newAuths
          , stateUserIdCounter = newUserId
          , stateUnverifiedEmails = newUnverifieds
          }
    lift $ writeTVar tvar newState
    return vCode
```

Verification in REPL

As usual, whenever we write a new code, the quickest way to get feedback whether our code is correct is to just try it out in REPL.

```
> :l Adapter.InMemory.Auth
> let email = D.mkEmail "ecky@test.com"
> let passw = D.mkPassword "1234ABCDefgh"
> let auth = either undefined id $ D.Auth <$> email <*> passw

> s <- newTVarIO initialState

> addAuth s auth
Right "aBNhtG653Bga9kas"
> findUserByAuth s auth
Just (1,False)
> findEmailFromUserId s 1
Just (Email {rawEmail = "ecky@test.com"})
> newSession s 1
"1gkCTScCqWePhMg66"
> findUserIdBySessionId s "1gkCTScCqWePhMg66"
Just 1
```

Great; so far it looks correct.

Tying Everything Together

Let's take a step back and recap what we have done so far. We have defined types that are required to fulfill our project requirements. We also have implemented the main domain logic, like registering and logging in a user. We have created a few typeclasses to manage side-effecting parts of our application. Last but not least, we have implemented an in-memory implementation for the side-effecting part.

What's missing is to be able to tie the in-memory implementation with our domain logic. This section will guide you on how to do that. Let's start by opening the `Lib` module and import both the domain and in-memory implementation.

```
import qualified Adapter.InMemory.Auth as M
import Domain.Auth
```

Next, we define the application state. For now, the application state is just the same as the in-memory state. In the future, our application state might contain a connection to databases or queues. We also create a monad transformer stack for our application, `App`. Since our application only needs to read from the "environment," which is the `State`, and also do IO, then `ReaderT State IO a` should be sufficient. The function `run` is a helper to unwind the `App` stack into an IO.

```
type State = TVar M.State
newtype App a = App
  { unApp :: ReaderT State IO a
  } deriving (Applicative, Functor, Monad, MonadReader State, MonadIO)

run :: State -> App a -> IO a
run state = flip runReaderT state . unApp
```

In order for the preceding code to work, we need to enable another language extension: `GeneralizedNewtypeDeriving`. Let's add that to our `package.yaml`.

```
default-extensions:
- GeneralizedNewtypeDeriving # NEW!
```

Next, we create instances of `AuthRepo`, `EmailVerificationNotif`, and `SessionRepo` for `App`. These instances are the glue between in-memory implementation and domain logic. In general, we just delegate the calls to in-memory implementations.

```
instance AuthRepo App where
  addAuth = M.addAuth
  setEmailAsVerified = M.setEmailAsVerified
  findUserByAuth = M.findUserByAuth
  findEmailFromUserId = M.findEmailFromUserId

instance EmailVerificationNotif App where
  notifyEmailVerification = M.notifyEmailVerification

instance SessionRepo App where
  newSession = M.newSession
  findUserIdBySessionId = M.findUserIdBySessionId
```

And with that, we are done. But let's write a simple program using it to see it in action.

```
someFunc :: IO ()
someFunc = do
  state <- newTVarIO M.initialState
  run state action

action :: App ()
action = do
  let email = either undefined id $ mkEmail "ecky@test.com"
      passw = either undefined id $ mkPassword "1234ABCDefgh"
      auth = Auth email passw
  register auth
  Just vCode <- M.getNotificationsForEmail email
  verifyEmail vCode
  Right session <- login auth
  Just uId <- resolveSessionId session
  Just registeredEmail <- getUser uId
  print (session, uId, registeredEmail)
```

This simple program shows how the code is meant to be used. First, we initialize the state. Then use the run function using the initialized state. The program registers a user using the given Auth. Since we know it's using the in-memory implementation, we get the verification code using the getNotificationsForEmail helper function. Once we get the verification code, we verify the email using it. After that, we log in, resolve the session, and get the user email. Finally, we print what we have.

If we run it in REPL, here's what we get:

```
> someFunc
("1zAfj9UFJFD7J4edE",1,Email {rawEmail = "ecky@test.com"})
```

Summary

In this chapter, we have built an authentication feature with in-memory database.

We started by exploring **Port and Adapter** architecture. This architecture should help to keep our code base maintainable, and strictly separate what are the domain and the external of the application.

After that, we started defining the types for our application. We want to make our types as precise as possible to the requirements, that is, illegal states should not compile. One example of this is that we strictly use the **smart constructor** approach to define Email and Password type. We then separate the side-effecting part of our application using typeclass.

We briefly learned about STM and used it for out in-memory database implementation. We learned the problem STM solves, which is concurrent read and write, and how easily the STM interface solves the problem.

Finally, we tie everything together by creating our own monad transformer stack and defining typeclass instances for repositories that we defined in our domain.

CHAPTER 4

Logging

If you put any system in production, logging is an essential part that you want to get right. Without logging, it would be very hard to troubleshoot production issues that may appear. In this chapter, we will learn about how to do logging in Haskell.

When `putStrLn` Is Not Enough

The easiest way to get started with logging is to just use `putStrLn` that comes with `ClassyPrelude`. After all, logging basically is just printing something while the application is running, right? Well, not quite true. There are various requirements for logging in production scenarios. For starters, you may want to attach extra information along with each log, such as on which line the log is created or arbitrary information such as user ID. It is cumbersome and error prone to manually add such information on each call to `putStrLn`. Another thing to consider is about performance. We need to design our `putStrLn` call so that it doesn't flush the text on every call. It would slow down the application. It's best to buffer the texts for quite some time before finally flushing.

Considering the preceding points, we learned that `putStrLn` is only half of the solution for logging. In the following sections we'll learn to use a package that helps with the logging scenario.

© Ecky Putrady 2018
E. Putrady, *Practical Web Development with Haskell*, https://doi.org/10.1007/978-1-4842-3739-7_4

Katip

If you look into available packages for logging, you will find plenty of them. Some of the most popular ones are `logging-effect`,[1] `monad-logger`,[2] and `katip`.[3] In this book, we will learn about Katip. I find that Katip is the most flexible to use, while providing sensible defaults.

Before writing any log, it's best to spend some time to learn important concepts in Katip so that you can use it effectively beyond the examples presented in this book.

Log Structure

The first concept to understand is `Item  a`. It's a data structure that Katip uses to represent the actual log item. We will explore some of the following fields.

```haskell
data Item a = Item
  { _itemApp        :: Namespace
  , _itemNamespace  :: Namespace
  , _itemEnv        :: Environment
  , _itemHost       :: HostName
  , _itemProcess    :: ProcessID
  , _itemSeverity   :: Severity
  , _itemThread     :: ThreadIdText
  , _itemPayload    :: a
  , _itemMessage    :: LogStr
  , _itemTime       :: UTCTime
  , _itemLoc        :: Maybe Loc
}
```

`_itemApp` represents the name of the application. `_itemNamespace` represents the "area" of the application. `Namespace` is basically just a wrapper around `[Text]` and intended to represent a hierarchy from general to specific. Let's say your application consists of two big components: web server and worker. You can put `["webserver"]` and `["worker"]` as `_itemNamespace` respectively to inform where the log originates from.

---

[1]`www.stackage.org/package/logging-effect`
[2]`www.stackage.org/package/monad-logger`
[3]`www.stackage.org/package/katip`

`Environment` is basically a wrapper for `Text`. `_itemEnv` is meant to represent the environment name where the log originates from. For example, "Prod" or "Staging."

`HostName` is a synonym for `String`. `_itemHost` records the hostname of the node where the log is produced. It would be helpful if your application runs on multiple nodes. Once the logs are collected in a single place (e.g., via the ELK[4] stack), it will be easy to identify which node actually produced this log.

`_itemMessage` contains the message for the log. `LogStr` is a wrapper for `Text` that provides a more efficient text concatenation.

`_itemLoc` contains the information of exact location, such as filename and line number where the log is produced.

`_itemPayload` is a generic type. In general, you can put anything here as long as it can be serialized to JSON and have a `ToObject` instance. Practically, though, you are most likely just to use the one that has already been provided by Katip: `SimpleLogPayload`. We will see later on how to use it.

`_itemSeverity` informs the severity of this particular log message. Katip defines eight level of severity, as we can see in the following:

```
data Severity
  = DebugS
  | InfoS
  | NoticeS
  | WarningS
  | ErrorS
  | CriticalS
  | AlertS
  | EmergencyS
```

There is no clear guideline on how to choose the right severity. However, I consistently use the following guidelines:

1. `DebugS` for logs that are meaningful only for the developer and operation team, for example, logging which database the application connects to.

2. `InfoS` for logs that are business- or domain-specific events, such as "user registered" or "user published a new post."

---

[4]www.elastic.co/elk-stack

3. Warnings for oddities that are recovered automatically. Too many of these might indicate that there is something wrong in the system. For example, if you are issuing an HTTP request but the server is unavailable and you provide a fallback, then it is a good candidate for logging at this level.

4. Errors for events that need to be actionable by someone. For example, if customer's payment failed to be captured, usually a manual process needs to be carried out to resolve the issue.

Scribe

Scribe is a component that does the actual writing of the log to the external system. It receives an Item that we have seen above, formats it as required, and writes it to the external system. Since the formatting and where the log is sent are up to Scribe implementation to decide, the implementation may choose to log the format as syslog and write it to a file on disk or maybe format it as JSON and send it to ElasticSearch.

Katip provides a default Scribe implementation:

```
mkHandleScribe
  :: ColorStrategy -> Handle -> Severity -> Verbosity -> IO Scribe

data ColorStrategy = ColorLog Bool
  | ColorIfTerminal
```

Handle could be stdout, stderr, or a file. The function formats the logs to be something like this:

```
[2016-05-11  21:01:15][MyApp][Info][myhost.example.com][1724][Thre
adId 1154][main:Helpers.Logging Helpers/Logging.hs:32:7] Started
```

It accepts Severity as a parameter. It means that it will not write a log that has severity below the given parameter. For example, if you set the Severity to Errors but the log's severity is Infos, then that log will not be written.

Verbosity has four levels and is defined as follow:

```
data Verbosity = V0 | V1 | V2 | V3
```

It is meant to control how verbose the log will be printed. V3 is the most verbose, while V0 is the least verbose. The log format that we have seen previously is printed using V2 as the input parameter.

Of course, you can create your own Scribe implementation. Scribe is defined as follows:

```
data Scribe = Scribe
  { liPush            :: LogItem a => Item a -> IO ()
  , scribeFinalizer :: IO ()
  }
```

liPush is the function that is supposed to transform and push a log item into the external system. scribeFinalizer is a function that will be called when the scribe is no longer used. If it's not relevant, you can just put return () for this function implementation.

KatipContext

KatipContext is a typeclass that provides functionality to do contextual logging. By "contextual," I mean the logging will get the various informations from the environment and attach it to the log. The following snippet shows how KatipContext is being used:

```
logSomething :: (KatipContext m) => m ()
logSomething = do
  $(logTM) InfoS "Log in no namespace"
  katipAddNamespace "ns1" $
    $(logTM) InfoS "Log in ns1"
  katipAddNamespace "ns2" $ do
    $(logTM) WarningS "Log in ns2"
    katipAddNamespace "ns3" $
      katipAddContext (sl "userId" $ asText "12") $ do
        $(logTM) InfoS "Log in ns2.ns3 with userId context"
        katipAddContext (sl "country" $ asText "Singapore") $
          $(logTM) InfoS "Log in ns2.ns3 with userId and country context"
```

The main function for logging is logTM. You might be wondering why it needs to be wrapped with strange $(..) notation. It's because logTM is meant to be evaluated at compile time using the TemplateHaskell language extension. This function only receives two inputs: the severity and the log message. However, under the hood, this function also populates the various fields for Item structure that we have seen earlier, such as _itemLoc and _itemNamespace. This information is available from LogEnv, a data structure that can be obtained in KatipContext. We will see the details of LogEnv later.

katipAddNamespace and katipAddContext both temporarily alter the LogEnv structure. Since we do logging inside the altered LogEnv, the resulting Item object will be different. In the preceding example, logTM actions that are being called under katipAddNamespace "ns2" will produce an Item that has "ns2" in its namespace.

katipAddContext accepts SimpleLogPayload as the first argument. Actually, it accepts something more general than that, but in most cases SimpleLogPayload should be what you want. This first argument will be present in the resulting Item's payload field.

You can think of SimpleLogPayload as a map in which the key is Text and the value is Value from aeson. SimpleLogPayload can be created by using the sl function. Here's the sl function:

```
sl :: ToJSON a => Text -> a -> SimpleLogPayload
```

It says that it takes Text, which is the key, and value of anything that is an instance of ToJSON. SimpleLogPayload is an instance of Monoid, which means you can combine multiple SimpleLogPayloads into one, as in:

```
combined :: SimpleLogPayload
combined = (sl "userId" "12") <> (sl "country" "Singapore")
```

In the case of combination with the same key, the latter value will overwrite the former values.

LogEnv

LogEnv is defined as follow:

```
data LogEnv = LogEnv
  { _logEnvHost    :: HostName
  , _logEnvPid     :: ProcessID
  , _logEnvApp     :: Namespace
  , _logEnvEnv     :: Environment
  , _logEnvTimer   :: IO UTCTime
  , _logEnvScribes :: M.Map Text ScribeHandle
  }
```

You have seen most of the preceding fields in Item. However, _logEnvTimer and _logEnvScribes need a bit more explanation. _logEnvTimer is an IO action that is used to get the current time. _logEnvScribes is a collection of Scribes that are registered in this environment. You may have multiple Scribes registered. Each Item will be processed by each Scribe. For example, you might have two Scribes, the one that writes to stdout and the one that writes to ElasticSearch. In that case, Item will be written to stdout and also shipped to ElasticSearch.

There are a few helpful operations that Katip has provided us to work with LogEnv. initLogEnv is a function that creates LogEnv with a sensible default.

```
initLogEnv :: Namespace -> Environment -> IO LogEnv
```

It's important to note that initLogEnv uses the AutoUpdate[5] package for _logEnvTimer. By using AutoUpdate, basically _logEnvTimer won't give a super precise timing. It's because the current time information is cached for a few milliseconds. This helps with performance when a lot of logging is happening at the same time. In case you want a precise logging time, you can just replace it with getCurrentTime like the code snippet below:

```
preciseLogEnv = do
  le <- initLogEnv mempty "repl"
  return $ le { _logEnvTimer = getCurrentTime }
```

registerScribe, as the name suggests, is a function to modify the given LogEnv to add a new Scribe.

```
registerScribe :: Text -> Scribe -> ScribeSettings -> LogEnv -> IO LogEnv
```

The first parameter represents the name of the Scribe. ScribeSettings is basically a configuration on how much we should buffer the logs before we flush them to the external system. This is mostly for performance reasons. For simplicity, we can just use the ScribeSettings provided by Katip, defaultScribeSettings. These settings set the buffer size to 4096.

```
closeScribes :: LogEnv -> IO LogEnv
```

---

[5]www.stackage.org/package/auto-update

`closeScribes` basically flushes the remaining log in the buffer of each `Scribe` so that they are written to the external system. This will also execute the `scribeFinalizer` function that exists in the `Scribe`. Ideally, this function should be called upon application termination to make sure that all is being written to the external system.

Working with Katip

Phew, we have explored the important concepts of Katip. Now let's see how to tie all of the concepts together so that we have a better idea of how to work with it.

First, we need to import Katip and enable the `TemplateHaskell` language extension in our `package.yaml` file.

```
dependencies:
- katip # new

default-extensions:
- TemplateHaskell
```

Let's write some temporary code in the `Lib` module for simplicity to experiment with Katip.

```
import Katip

runKatip :: IO ()
runKatip = withKatip $ \le ->
  runKatipContextT le () mempty logSomething

withKatip :: (LogEnv -> IO a) -> IO a
withKatip app =
  bracket createLogEnv closeScribes app
  where
    createLogEnv = do
      logEnv <- initLogEnv "HAuth" "dev"
      stdoutScribe <- mkHandleScribe ColorIfTerminal stdout InfoS V2
      registerScribe "stdout" stdoutScribe defaultScribeSettings logEnv
```

```
logSomething :: (KatipContext m) => m ()
logSomething = do
  $(logTM) InfoS "Log in no namespace"
  katipAddNamespace "ns1" $
    $(logTM) InfoS "Log in ns1"
  katipAddNamespace "ns2" $ do
    $(logTM) WarningS "Log in ns2"
    katipAddNamespace "ns3" $
      katipAddContext (sl "userId" $ asText "12") $ do
        $(logTM) InfoS "Log in ns2.ns3 with userId context"
        katipAddContext (sl "country" $ asText "Singapore") $
          $(logTM) InfoS "Log in ns2.ns3 with userId and country context"
```

Try to run runKatip in REPL to see the results. You should see that the logs containing various information are printed in the terminal similar to the following:

```
[2018-05-09 13:08:58][HAuth][Info][machine][56579][ThreadId 281]
[main:Lib Lib.hs:116:5] Log in no namespace
[2018-05-09 13:08:58][HAuth.ns1][Info][machine][56579][ThreadId 2
81][main:Lib Lib.hs:118:7] Log in ns1
[2018-05-09 13:08:58][HAuth.ns2][Warning][machine][56579][ThreadI
d 281][main:Lib Lib.hs:120:7] Log in ns2
[2018-05-09 13:08:58][HAuth.ns2.ns3][Info][machine][56579][Thread
Id 281][userId:12][main:Lib Lib.hs:123:11] Log in ns2.ns3 with us
erId context
[2018-05-09 13:08:58][HAuth.ns2.ns3][Info][machine][56579][Thread
Id 281][country:Singapore][userId:12][main:Lib Lib.hs:125:13] Log
 in ns2.ns3 with userId and country context
```

Let's look a bit closer at the preceding code snippet to understand what it does. withKatip is a function where we initialize and close LogEnv. It accepts another function (LogEnv -> IO a), which basically means any IO action that has direct dependency to LogEnv.

```
bracket :: MonadMask m => m a -> (a -> m b) -> (a -> m c) -> m c
```

`bracket` is a function that comes from `ClassyPrelude`. It's meant to be used for safe resource allocation and deallocation. The resource could be anything, like a database connection or file handle. In our case, the resource is `LogEnv`. It is "safe" because it handles error that may arise. If an error is thrown, then the resource is deallocated before rethrowing the error.

`bracket` accepts three parameters:

1. `m a`: the function that allocates the resource a

2. `(a -> m b)`: the function that deallocates or frees the resource a

3. `(a -> m c)`: the function that uses the resources after it's allocated and before it's deallocated

We deallocate `LogEnv` using the `closeScribes` function that we have previously seen, to make sure that the logs in the buffer are flushed.

`createLogEnv` is a helper function that we define to initialize the `LogEnv`. We use `initLogEnv` that we have seen previously, to create `LogEnv` with sensible defaults. We then create a `Scribe` that writes to `stdout`. The `Scribe` is then registered to the `LogEnv` that we have just created.

The `runKatip` function internally calls `withKatip` to get the reference to `LogEnv`. This `LogEnv` is then passed on to `runKatipContextT`. The second and third arguments of `runKatipContextT` are the initial payload and initial namespace, respectively. We use `()` for empty payload and `mempty` for empty namespace. `runKatipContextT` essentially unwraps `KatipContextT m a` to `m a`. It's analog to `ReaderT` and `runReaderT`. As you might have noticed, `KatipContextT` is an instance of `KatipContext` typeclass.

Integrating Log in Our Project

Now back to our project; what are the things that we want to log? We want to log events that are "state changing" and meaningful for the business. For our case it should be:

1. User registration

2. User login

3. Email verification

In addition to that, we also want to put the user ID in each log when applicable. It would be helpful for troubleshooting issues. We can just filter the log with a specific user id and see what activities the user did in our system.

Now that we have decided what the important logs are, let's consider what needs to be changed. We need to change the following type signatures in the Domain.Auth module:

```
 class (Monad m) => AuthRepo m where
-  addAuth :: Auth -> m (Either RegistrationError VerificationCode)
+  addAuth :: Auth -> m (Either RegistrationError (UserId,
                            VerificationCode))
-  setEmailAsVerified :: VerificationCode -> m (Either EmailVerificationError ())
+  setEmailAsVerified :: VerificationCode
+                          -> m (Either EmailVerificationError (UserId, Email))
```

As we have explored previously, we want to add user ID in the log context. So, we modified some of our repo's functions to return UserId along with the usual values.

Next, we modify the register function to the following:

```
+ withUserIdContext :: (KatipContext m) => UserId -> m a -> m a
+ withUserIdContext uId = katipAddContext (sl "userId" uId)

- register :: (AuthRepo m, EmailVerificationNotif m)
+ register :: (KatipContext m, AuthRepo m, EmailVerificationNotif m)
           => Auth -> m (Either RegistrationError ())
  register auth = runExceptT $ do
-  vCode <- ExceptT $ addAuth auth
+  (uId, vCode) <- ExceptT $ addAuth auth
   let email = authEmail auth
   lift $ notifyEmailVerification email vCode
+  withUserIdContext uId $
+    $(logTM) InfoS $ ls (rawEmail email) <> " is registered successfully"
```

We introduced the withUserIdContext helper function as shorthand for appending UserId to the log context.

The register function now has another constraint: KatipContext m. This allows logging-related functions from Katip to be used here. The last two lines of the function are where we do the logging. We use the withUserIdContext helper function that we have defined in the preceding code to embed UserId to the log context. Then print an

Info-level log informing that this particular email and user are successfully registered. You might be confused about ls. logTM expects to receive LogStr as the last parameter. ls basically converts string-like types to LogStr.

We also need to modify the verifyEmail function as in the following. This should be straightforward to understand, as it is very similar to the preceding change.

```
- verifyEmail :: (AuthRepo m)
+ verifyEmail :: (KatipContext m, AuthRepo m)
              => VerificationCode -> m (Either EmailVerificationError ())
- verifyEmail = setEmailAsVerified
+ verifyEmail vCode = runExceptT $ do
+   (uId, email) <- ExceptT $ setEmailAsVerified vCode
+   withUserIdContext uId $
+     $(logTM) InfoS $ ls (rawEmail email) <> " is verified successfully"
+   return ()
```

The login function also needs to change. Again, it is very similar like before.

```
- login :: (AuthRepo m, SessionRepo m)
+ login :: (KatipContext m, AuthRepo m, SessionRepo m)
        => Auth -> m (Either LoginError SessionId)
  login auth = runExceptT $ do
    result <- lift $ findUserByAuth auth
    case result of
      Nothing -> throwError LoginErrorInvalidAuth
      Just (_, False) -> throwError LoginErrorEmailNotVerified
-     Just (uId, _) -> lift $ newSession uId
+     Just (uId, _) -> withUserIdContext uId . lift $ do
+       sId <- newSession uId
+       $(logTM) InfoS $ ls (rawEmail $ authEmail auth) <> " logged in
+       successfully"
+       return sId
```

Since we changed the type signatures of AuthRepo, we also need to adjust the repo implementation as well. Let's open the Adapter.InMemory.Auth module. The first function that we need to change is addAuth. The only change we need to do is to also return the UserId at the end of the function.

```
  addAuth :: InMemory r m
-         => D.Auth -> m (Either D.RegistrationError D.VerificationCode)
+         => D.Auth -> m (Either D.RegistrationError (D.UserId,
                                 D.VerificationCode))
  addAuth auth = do
  -- code does not change, except below:
-   return vCode
+   return (newUserId, vCode)
```

Another function that we need to modify is setEmailAsVerified.

```
+ orThrow :: MonadError e m => Maybe a -> e -> m a
+ orThrow Nothing e   = throwError e
+ orThrow (Just a) _  = return a

  setEmailAsVerified :: InMemory r m
                     => D.VerificationCode
-                    -> m (Either D.EmailVerificationError ())
+                    -> m (Either D.EmailVerificationError (D.UserId,
                             D.Email))
  setEmailAsVerified vCode = do
    tvar <- asks getter
    atomically . runExceptT $ do
      state <- lift $ readTVar tvar
      let unverifieds = stateUnverifiedEmails state
-         verifieds = stateVerifiedEmails state
          mayEmail = lookup vCode unverifieds
-     case mayEmail of
-       Nothing -> throwError D.EmailVerificationErrorInvalidCode
-       Just email -> do
-         let newUnverifieds = deleteMap vCode unverifieds
-             newVerifieds = insertSet email verifieds
-             newState = state
-               { stateUnverifiedEmails = newUnverifieds
-               , stateVerifiedEmails = newVerifieds
-               }
```

81

```
-          lift $ writeTVar tvar newState
+      email <- mayEmail `orThrow` D.EmailVerificationErrorInvalidCode
+      let auths = stateAuths state
+          mayUserId = map fst . find ((email ==) . D.authEmail . snd) $ auths
+      uId <- mayUserId `orThrow` D.EmailVerificationErrorInvalidCode
+      let verifieds = stateVerifiedEmails state
+          newVerifieds = insertSet email verifieds
+          newUnverifieds = deleteMap vCode unverifieds
+          newState = state
+            { stateUnverifiedEmails = newUnverifieds
+            , stateVerifiedEmails = newVerifieds
+            }
+      lift $ writeTVar tvar newState
+      return (uId, email)
```

Nothing much changed from the previous implementation. An extra functionality added here was getting the UserId from the given Email. We later return this UserId along with Email. We also introduce a helper function orThrow. What this helper function does, basically, is to throw the given error from the second parameter if the first parameter is Nothing.

The final piece we need to modify is in the Lib module, to glue everything together. The first thing we need to modify is our application's monad, App. Since we want logging functionality from Katip, we need to add KatipContextT and derive an instance for KatipContext and Katip. If you are wondering why our monad stack is ReaderT State (KatipContextT IO) not KatipContextT (ReaderT State IO), my answer would be: it doesn't matter. Both would work. I just arbitrarily chose the former one.

```
  newtype App a = App
-    { unApp :: ReaderT State IO a
-    } deriving (Applicative, Functor, Monad, MonadReader State, MonadIO)
+    { unApp :: ReaderT State (KatipContextT IO) a
+    } deriving ( Applicative, Functor, Monad, MonadReader State, MonadIO
+               , KatipContext, Katip)
```

In addition to that, we need to modify the run function, since our application's monad stack changes. We accept another parameter, LogEnv, which is used by Katip for logging. We then use this LogEnv in runKatipContextT.

```
- run :: State -> App a -> IO a
- run state = flip runReaderT state . unApp
+ run :: LogEnv -> State -> App a -> IO a
+ run le state =
+   = runKatipContextT le () mempty
+   . flip runReaderT state
+   . unApp
```

Finally, we just edit someFunc to initialize LogEnv.

```
+ withKatip :: (LogEnv -> IO a) -> IO a
+ withKatip app =
+   bracket createLogEnv closeScribes app
+   where
+     createLogEnv = do
+       logEnv <- initLogEnv "HAuth" "prod"
+       stdoutScribe <- mkHandleScribe ColorIfTerminal stdout InfoS V2
+       registerScribe "stdout" stdoutScribe defaultScribeSettings logEnv
  someFunc :: IO ()
- someFunc = do
+ someFunc = withKatip $ \le -> do
    state <- newTVarIO M.initialState
-   run state action
+   run le state action
```

We are done with the implementation. If you run someFunc in REPL, you will see the log printed on the terminal. Notice that UserId, which we set as the log context, appears in the log.

Summary

In this chapter, we have added logging capabilities to our application using Katip, a Haskell library for logging. We learned many concepts about Katip, such as Item, LogEnv, KatipContext, etc. We learned how to leverage existing functions in Katip to do our logging effectively.

CHAPTER 5

Databases

For most web-based applications, storing data in memory is usually not practical. The data will be wiped out when the application terminates. It's not a rare case for an application to be terminated, for example, when you want to deploy a newer version of the same application.

Another downside of storing data in-memory is that you may not able to share the data between application instances. We sometimes need multiple application instances for availability and scalability. If one of the instances is down, we still can serve user requests by using the other instances (availability). If there are too many requests to handle, we can add more instances to cope (scalability).

For those reasons, we usually store the data in a database that is outside of the application.

There are many databases to choose from, each having its own characteristic that may suit certain types of use cases. Redis, for example is a key-value store that stores the data in-memory. Since it's in-memory, it means the lookup is very fast but the data could be lost when Redis is down. Knowing this limitation, Redis is better suited for caching. In this book we will be using PostgreSQL and Redis. Both databases are popular and versatile while being more than enough for our use cases.

PostgreSQL

In this section, we will look in detail how we could integrate PostgreSQL to our application. We will start by discussing ways to interact with an SQL database and the available packages from the community. Then we will have a deep-dive on how to use a specific package to interact with PostgreSQL. Finally, we will build a repository implementation for our application using PostgreSQL.

85

© Ecky Putrady 2018
E. Putrady, *Practical Web Development with Haskell*, https://doi.org/10.1007/978-1-4842-3739-7_5

ORM vs. Non-ORM

A common way to interface with PostgreSQL or other relational DB is by using object-relational mapping (ORM). Using ORM has its pros and cons. On the pros side, ORM allows us to easily switch databases. Although they are all relational databases, there are slight differences in SQL among relational databases that make the same SQL statement possibly not run on other relational databases. ORM solves this problem by giving a higher level abstraction for application developers. Another pro is that it's easier to do Create, Read, Update, and Delete (CRUD) operations. ORM handles the SQL generation and mapping between SQL result and types that the programming language understands.

On the cons side, using ORM can be perceived as adding complexity to the problem. Learning ORM doesn't mean you don't have to learn SQL and the actual relational database you will be using. This means, in addition to learn SQL and the database, you also need to learn how ORM works. You might as well drop ORM altogether, since it is simpler overall. Another con is that the generated query might not always be the most optimized. If your application needs a complex query, such as grouping and window functions, ORM is useless. You will need to drop to the SQL level and issue a query.

In my experience, ORM is usually more of a hassle than a help. In addition to the cons described, my biggest issue with it is it's very tempting to mix database concern with domain concern. This is a violation of port and adapter architecture. In an ideal world, database models map exactly to the domain model. In the real world, however, this is less likely the case. The database might be shared with other applications, and those applications need extra data that is not relevant to our domain. There are also the cases where some data get duplicated intentionally for performance reasons. For those reasons, we won't be using ORM in this book.

postgresql-simple

In Haskell, there are well-known packages for interfacing with PostgreSQL. If you are keen on ORM, you might want to use persistent[1] and esqueleto.[2] persistent is designed to work with SQL and NoSQL back end, while esqueleto is built on top of persistent and provides capabilities to do joins on SQL back end.

---

[1] www.stackage.org/lts-10.3/package/persistent-2.7.1
[2] www.stackage.org/lts-10.3/package/esqueleto-2.5.3

For non-ORM packages, we have hasql[3] and postgresql-simple.[4] hasql is known to be faster compared with postgresql-simple, but postgresql-simple is more mature.

In this book we will use the postgresql-simple package.

Connection Management

Before issuing any query to the database, we need to open a new connection. The function to do that is connectPostgreSQL. It accepts a connection string as specified in PostgreSQL docs.[5] It returns a Connection that can later be used to issue queries to the database. Once you are done with the connection you can close it with the close function provided by the package. The function accepts a Connection that we acquire from connectPostgreSQL. The following code snippet shows how to open and close a connection:

```
openAndClose = do
  conn <- connectPostgreSQL "postgresql://localhost/hauth"
  close conn
```

Connection Pool

PostgreSQL has a constraint on the maximum simultaneous open connections. By default, we can only open 100 connections simultaneously. Now, consider if you have a very busy server serving a lot of users. It would be possible for you to open more than 100 connections at the same time. This means you hit the connection limit and you will get an error from PostgreSQL. This is of course not desirable. In addition to the connection limit, opening a new connection is also not a cheap operation. It would be more efficient to keep the connection open and reuse it.

A common solution to the problem is by using a connection pool. The idea of a connection pool is that you have a number of open connections in the pool and your application will take it from the pool before using and then return it to the pool when done. With a connection pool, we can limit the number of actual opened connections to the database and not have to create and close connections every time.

---

[3]www.stackage.org/lts-10.3/package/hasql-1.1.1
[4]www.stackage.org/lts-10.3/package/postgresql-simple-0.5.3.0
[5]www.postgresql.org/docs/current/static/libpq-connect.html#LIBPQ-CONNSTRING

In Haskell, the package for managing a connection pool is `resource-pool`.[6] To be precise, this package actually is not specialized for connection. It is general enough to be used for anything.

`resource-pool` is a fairly simple package with minimal APIs. There are only three essential functions worth knowing about: `createPool`, `destroyAllResources`, and `withResources`. Let's look into each of them.

`createPool` is a function to create the pool. It returns `IO (Pool a)` and receives the following input in order:

1. `IO a`: the action to create the resource

2. `(a -> IO ())`: the action to destroy resource a

3. `Int`: the number of stripes (subpools) to maintain

4. `NominalDiffTime`: amount of time that an unused resource is kept alive

5. `Int`: maximum number of resource to keep alive per stripe

`resource-pool` has a concept of "Stripe." Stripe is a subpool within the pool. The purpose of having multiple stripes is to reduce contention. Acquiring a resource from a stripe requires a locking mechanism. Only one thread can acquire a resource at a given time. Other threads need to wait until the resource acquisition is completed. This might be a bottleneck for a busy application. With multiple subpools, it's possible for multiple concurrent processes to acquire resources from each pool. Figure 5-1 illustrates the relationship between pool, stripes, and resource.

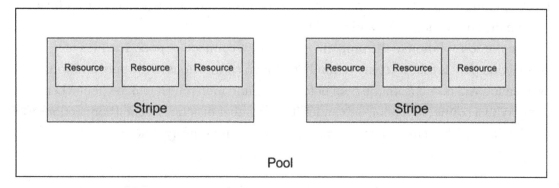

Figure 5-1. `resource-pool`—*pool contains stripes; stripes contain resources*

---

[6]`www.stackage.org/package/resource-pool`

destroyAllResources is a function of type Pool a -> IO (). It basically destroys all resources that are alive in the pool by calling the destroy action defined when we create the pool. It's best to call this function whenever we don't need the pool anymore, for example, during application shutdown.

withResource has the following type signature:

```
withResource :: MonadBaseControl IO m => Pool a -> (a -> m b) -> m b
```

Please just ignore MonadBaseControl IO for now. In practice, we will use IO as the m. This function accepts the pool and an action, given the resource. What will happen is that we will take a resource from the pool temporarily, execute the action in the second parameter, then return the resource back to the pool. If there is an idle resource in the pool, the resource will be used immediately. If there is no idle resource in the pool and the pool still has room for more resources, then a new resource is created and used immediately. If the pool is at full capacity, then this function will be blocked until a resource is available. In the case of the action throwing an exception, the resource will be destroyed.

Database Migration

When we start our application, the very next thing that we want to do is to set up or modify database tables to the latest version so that our application can interact with it. This process is known as database migration. We will use postgresql-simple-migration,[7] a member of the postgresql-simple package ecosystem that focuses on doing database migration.

Among many functions provided, we are just interested with runMigrations. The function has the following type signature:

```
runMigrations :: Bool -- Run in verbose mode?
              -> Connection -- The postgres connection to use
              -> [MigrationCommand] -- The commands to run
              -> IO (MigrationResult String) -- The result of the migration
```

---

[7]www.stackage.org/lts-10.3/package/postgresql-simple-migration-0.1.11.0

We use it like this:

```
migrate :: Connection -> IO ()
migrate conn = do
  result <- withTransaction conn (runMigrations False conn cmds)
  case result of
    MigrationError err -> throwString err
      _ -> return ()
  where
    cmds =    [ MigrationInitialization
              , MigrationDirectory "src/Adapter/PostgreSQL/Migrations"
              ]
```

withTransaction is a function that comes from postgresql-simple that is used to perform an action within a database transaction. withTransaction receives a connection and an action. If the action finishes without error, the transaction will be committed. On the other hand, if the action throws an error, the transaction will be rollbacked before rethrowing the error. We wrap our migration action inside a transaction so that if there is any error during the migration, everything is aborted instead of partially applied.

We pass in two MigrationCommands as the last parameter for runMigrations: MigrationInitialization and MigrationDirectory. MigrationInitialization is a command to initialize required tables in our database to track the migrations. We will cover how this works later. MigrationDirectory is a command to execute SQL files, in alphabetical order, in a given directory. In the preceding example, the directory happens to be src/Adapter/PostgreSQL/Migration.

Finally, we interpret the result of the migration. If the migration fails, we want to purposefully crash the application. In our case, having a working database is a prerequisite of running the application. That's why we crash our application if the migration fails.

Suppose that we have files named 00000_auths.sql and 00001_posts.sql in the migration directory. If you run the migration, we may look into our database and we will find a table named schema_migrations. schema_migrations is a table created by

`MigrationInitialization` command and is used to manage the migrations. If you do a select all for that table, you will get the following output:

```
filename       |        checksum        |       executed_at
---------------+------------------------+--------------------------
00000_auths.sql | PD4DRG/ODR5xk2tDVLmNeg== | 2018-01-20 09:35:16.712525
00001_posts.sql | AAFSVH/ASc68sa9cnISnbG== | 2018-01-20 09:37:02.638962
```

The `schema_migrations` table has three columns: `filename`, `checksum`, and `executed_at`. Whenever we run migrations, each file being executed is checked against this table. The checksum of the file is checked to make sure the one that is going to be executed now is the same one as the one executed last time. If it's not the same, the migration is aborted. So, **once a file is executed in a migration, you should not alter the file anymore**. If a file is executed successfully, it will then be written to this table.

Queries

In `postgresql-simple`, there are only six functions for issuing database queries. They are different in terms of whether the query should return a value and how many parameters the query accepts. Please refer to the following chart for the comparison between functions:

	Return nothing	**Return values**
No parameter	execute_	query_
One parameter	execute	query
Many parameters	executeMany	returning

`execute_` is used for queries that don't return any values and require no parameters, for example, creating a new database, dropping a table, or updating a row to a specific value.

```
> execute_ conn "update auths set is_email_verified = 't'"
```

In the preceding example, we update every row in the `auths` table to have the `is_email_verified` column set to true.

query_ is similar to execute_, but it returns values.

```
> query_ conn "select (2+4)" :: IO [Only Int]
[Only {fromOnly = 6}]

> query_ conn "select (1+2), (3+4)" :: IO [(Int, Int)]
[(3, 7)]

> query_ conn "select (1+2), (3+4)" :: IO [(Int, Int, Int)]
*** Exception: ConversionFailed {errSQLType = "2 values: [\"int4\",\"int4\"]",
errSQLTableOid = Nothing, errSQLField = "", errHaskellType = "at least 3
slots in target type", errMessage = "mismatch between number of columns to
convert and number in target type"}

> query_ conn "select (1+2), (3+4)" :: IO [(Int, Text)]
*** Exception: Incompatible {errSQLType = "int4", errSQLTableOid = Nothing,
errSQLField = "?column?", errHaskellType = "Text", errMessage = "types
incompatible"}
```

As we can see from the preceding examples, we need to specify the return type so that the compiler knows what function to use to parse the result. In the first example, since the number of columns being returned is one, then we need to use Only to wrap the expected value. In the second example, there are two columns being returned, so we use a tuple to parse it. The third and fourth examples are showing what happens if we choose the wrong types. Yes, it will result in runtime errors. Since the error is a runtime one, we need to be very careful when dealing with the postgresql-simple package. It's best if we have full automated test coverage for each query.

Up next, we have execute. It's used for queries that don't return any value but require a parameter.

```
> execute conn "update auths set is_email_verified = ?" (Only True)

> execute conn "update auths set is_email_verified = ? where user_id = ?"
(True, 123)
```

execute accepts two parameters: the query and the query parameter. As you can see, when we write a query, we may put a ? as a placeholder for query parameter. If there is only one query parameter, we need to wrap it with Only, as shown by the first code in the snippet. If we have more than one parameter, we may put our parameters in a tuple, as shown by the second code in the snippet. You might notice that many things can go wrong there: mismatched number of parameters, mismatched query parameter type, etc. If any of those things happen, the function will throw an error.

Next, we have executeMany. It's similar to execute, but you want to accept multiple query parameters instead of one parameter. One good use case for that is when you want to insert multiple rows of data.

```
> executeMany conn "insert into auths (pass, email, email_verification_code,
is_email_verified) values (?, ?, ?, ?)" [("pass1","email1@test.com",
"vcode1", False), ("pass2", "email2@test.com", "vcode2", False)]
```

query is another function for querying. This is the function that you will often use. We use query for issuing a query with parameters and a return value. One example is to fetch some data from the database as follows:

```
> query conn "select id, pass from auths where id < ?" (Only 15) :: IO
[(Integer, Text)]
```

Another example is to get some values from the database after writing, as shown here:

```
> query conn "update auths set is_email_verified = ? returning id, is_
email_verified"
(Only True) :: IO [(Integer, Bool)]
```

The last query-related function that we want to explore is returning. We use that for a query that requires many parameters and returns values, such as:

```
> returning conn "insert into auths (pass, email, email_verification_code,
is_email_verified) values (?, ?, ?, ?) returning id, pass" [("pass1",
"email1@test.com", "vcode1", False), ("pass2", "email2@test.com", "vcode2",
False)] :: IO [(Integer, Text)]
```

Transaction

If you are working with an SQL database in a nontrivial application, sooner or later you will encounter the need to use a transaction. We will not explore in deep how a transaction works in SQL as it's not the focus of this book. We will only look into the function in postgresql-simple that does a transaction.

The function that we are interested in is `withTransaction`. It has the following type signature:

```
withTransaction :: Connection -> IO a -> IO a
```

The function accepts `Connection` as the first argument and an `IO  a` as the second argument. Since the second argument is an `IO`, we can nest as many actions as we want.

`withTransaction` will begin the transaction before executing the second argument. If the second argument finishes without throwing any exception, then the transaction will be committed. On the other hand, if the second argument throws any exception, then the transaction will be rollbacked before the exception is rethrown.

An example usage of `withTransaction` is as follow:

```
multiUpdates = withTransaction conn $ do
  execute conn "update auths set is_email_verified = ?" (Only True)
  execute conn "update posts set is_visible = ?" (Only True)
```

In the preceding example, we do modifications on two tables inside a transaction. If both are run successfully, then the transaction will be committed. Otherwise it will be rollbacked before the exception is rethrown. Some examples of an exception that may happen would be violations of database constraints or a malformed query.

Implementation

We have done quite a walkthrough of the package; now we are ready to integrate PostgreSQL to our project. At the high level, the steps that we are going to take for integrating the package are the following:

1. Import required dependencies

2. Prepare migration file and code

3. Implement repositories

4. Tie everything together

Let's start my importing the required dependencies. Add the following lines to the `package.yaml` file:

```
dependencies:
- resource-pool # NEW!
- postgresql-simple # NEW!
```

Let's move on to the migration file. For our project, we only need one table for storing user authentication. We write it in 00000_auths.sql the src/Adapter/PostgreSQL/ Migrations folder. Yes, we put the migrations folder under a sibling folder of Haskell source codes. The contents of 00000_auths.sql are as follows:

```
create extension citext;
create extension pgcrypto;

create table auths (
  id bigserial primary key not null,
  pass text not null,
  email citext not null unique,
  email_verification_code text not null,
  is_email_verified boolean not null
);
```

We enable the citext extension so that we can compare two texts with case-insensitivity. As you can see, we use citext for the email field. Email is case insensitive, so citext neatly applies to it. pgcrypto is an extension that allows us to do encryption and decryption using an SQL statement. We will use it for storing a user password in an encrypted format.

The filename 00000_auths.sql is purposefully selected due to the behavior of the MigrationDirectory command that applies the SQL files in alphabetical order. If we want to apply a new migration, we just need to increment the number part, for example 00001_new_migration.sql.

Next, we write the code to execute the migration in the Adapter.PostgreSQL.Auth module:

```
module Adapter.PostgreSQL.Auth where

import ClassyPrelude
import Data.Pool
import Database.PostgreSQL.Simple.Migration
import Database.PostgreSQL.Simple

type State = Pool Connection
```

```
migrate :: State -> IO ()
migrate pool = withResource pool $ \conn -> do
  result <- withTransaction conn (runMigrations False conn cmds)
  case result of
    MigrationError err -> throwString err
    _ -> return ()
  where
    cmds = [ MigrationInitialization
           , MigrationDirectory "src/Adapter/PostgreSQL/Migrations"
           ]
```

We begin the previous snippet with imports to various modules that we will be using. Next, we declare a type synonym for `Pool Connection` so that it's easier to type for upcoming functions that we will be implementing.

Next, we write the implementation of the migration function. The function acquires connection from the pool using the `withResource` function. The connection is then used in the `runMigrations` function. The migration is run within a transaction, provided neatly by the `withTransaction` function. Since we run our migration in a transaction, if any error happens during the migration, the whole migration will be aborted.

The migration reads files from the `src/Adapter/PostgreSQL/Migrations` folder and executes it in alphabetical order. One would think that hardcoding the migration folder is not a best practice. However, I'd argue that this is something that you don't want to change. So let's keep it simple and hardcode.

Alright, we have implemented the migration function. But wait, how do we get `State` in the first place? Glad you asked; that's exactly what we are going to do next. Add the following code in the same file as before:

```
import Data.Time

data Config = Config
  { configUrl :: ByteString
  , configStripeCount :: Int
  , configMaxOpenConnPerStripe :: Int
  , configIdleConnTimeout :: NominalDiffTime
  }
```

```
withPool :: Config -> (State -> IO a) -> IO a
withPool cfg action =
  bracket initPool cleanPool action
  where
    initPool = createPool openConn closeConn
                 (configStripeCount cfg)
                 (configIdleConnTimeout cfg)
                 (configMaxOpenConnPerStripe cfg)
    cleanPool = destroyAllResources
    openConn = connectPostgreSQL (configUrl cfg)
    closeConn = close

withState :: Config -> (State -> IO a) -> IO a
withState cfg action =
  withPool cfg $ \state -> do
    migrate state
    action state
```

We want the user of this module to tweak the connection pool configuration and also the PostgreSQL connection string. So, we created a Config type so that the user can easily discover what things can be configured.

withPool internally calls the bracket function. We have seen bracket in a previous chapter. Whenever there is an object with a "lifetime," that is, it needs to be destroyed after use, then it's best to manage the creation and destruction with bracket. Here, we use bracket to create and destroy the pool.

The pool creation is handled by initPool. initPool calls createPool, a function that comes from the Data.Pool module. We pass in some values from Config type into createPool function to set the pool configuration. openConn and closeConn are functions that we use to open and close a PostgreSQL connection, respectively.

withState is a simple function that internally calls withPool and immediately executes database migration before continuing on executing action from the function parameter. We have this because it's common for an application to have database migration executed during startup.

Let's now move on to the repositories implementation. We start by implementing the addAuth function. This function is meant to store a new authentication into PostgreSQL.

```
import qualified Domain.Auth as D
import Data.Has
import Text.StringRandom

type PG r m = (Has State r, MonadReader r m, MonadIO m, MonadThrow m)

withConn :: PG r m => (Connection -> IO a) -> m a
withConn action = do
  pool <- asks getter
  liftIO . withResource pool $ \conn -> action conn

addAuth :: PG r m
        => D.Auth
        -> m (Either D.RegistrationError (D.UserId, D.VerificationCode))
addAuth (D.Auth email pass) = do
  let rawEmail = D.rawEmail email
      rawPassw = D.rawPassword pass
  -- generate vCode
  vCode <- liftIO $ do
    r <- stringRandomIO "[A-Za-z0-9]{16}"
    return $ (tshow rawEmail) <> "_" <> r
  -- issue query
  result <- withConn $ \conn ->
    try $ query conn qry (rawEmail, rawPassw, vCode)
  -- interpret result
  case result of
    Right [Only uId] -> return $ Right (uId, vCode)
    Right _ -> throwString "Should not happen: PG doesn't return userId"
    Left err@SqlError{sqlState = state, sqlErrorMsg = msg} ->
      if state == "23505" && "auths_email_key" `isInfixOf` msg
        then return $ Left D.RegistrationErrorEmailTaken
        else throwString $ "Unhandled PG exception: " <> show err
  where
    qry = "insert into auths \
          \(email, pass, email_verification_code, is_email_verified) \
          \values (?, crypt(?, gen_salt('bf')), ?, 'f') returning id"
```

We define a constraint synonym `PG r m`. This constraint synonym basically says that `m` is a monad where you can perform IO action (via `MonadIO`), throw an exception (via `MonadThrow`), read `r` from environment (via `MonadReader r`), and you can get `State` from `r` (via `Has State r`). This constraint synonym is defined so that it's easier to type, as the functions that we will define later share the same constraints.

`withConn` is a small helper function to execute PostgreSQL-related functions, given you are in `PG r m` context. It first gets the connection pool from the environment, then acquires connection from that connection pool. The acquired connection is later handed over to the `action` from the function parameter.

The type signature of `addAuth` is the same as the one in the `Domain.Auth` module: we receive an `Auth` and we return either `RegistrationError` or a tuple of `UserId` and `VerificationCode`. This function is divided into three chunks of logic: generating `VerificationCode`, issuing a query to PostgreSQL, and interpreting the result.

Generating the `VerificationCode` part is done by concatenating the email with 16 random alphanumeric characters. The `VerificationCode` must be unique system-wide and unguessable. The email part helps to ensure the uniqueness property, while the random alphanumeric characters help to ensure the unguessable property.

The query that we issue basically inserts the auth to the `auths` table, as you can see in the preceding code. The query is quite straightforward, except for the `crypt(?, gen_salt('bf'))` part. That part is for encrypting the user's salted password so that it can be stored securely in our database. Those functions are SQL functions that come from the `pgcrypto` extension.

`try` is a function that we have access to by importing ClassyPrelude. The function has the following type signature:

```
try :: (Exception e, MonadCatch m) => m a -> m (Either e a)
```

`try` executes the first argument (`m a`) and catches a synchronous exception with type e that is thrown. If the exception is indeed thrown, then this function will return `Left e`. If no exception is thrown, the function will return `Right a`.

We use `try` to wrap the `query` action, as it may throw an exception and we are interested in handling the exception that may be thrown.

The last chunk is for interpreting the result. As you can see, we pattern match on the `Right [Only uId]` since we expect the function to return one row and one column that contains `UserId`. If that's the result that we get, we return `Right (uId, vCode)`. The next pattern match, Right _ should not happen. Well, it might happen, but it means that we have introduced a bug to our program. For this case, we just want to throw an error with a meaningful error message.

You might be thinking that a String-based exception is not a good practice and we should use our own exception data type here. The reason that a String-based exception is bad is because it's error prone to catch that specific exception. However, in this case, we don't have the need to handle such an exception. So, unless we have the need to handle it, I wouldn't bother to introduce a new exception data type.

Finally, the last pattern match is to check for SqlError. One case that is possible is when we insert an email that already exists in our system. We put a unique constraint for the email in our table. So, inserting a duplicated email will result in an error. This is a legit use case that we want to handle. So, what we did is to inspect the SqlError and check whether the error state is 23505, which means unique constraint violation,[8] and whether msg contains the auths_email_key string, that is, the constraint name for email column in our table. If the exception did occur, we just return Left RegistrationErrorEmailTaken, otherwise, we want to throw an error, as it's not something that should happen.

Let's move on to implement the setEmailAsVerified function. Write the following code in the same file as previously:

```
setEmailAsVerified :: PG r m
                   => D.VerificationCode
                   -> m (Either D.EmailVerificationError (D.UserId,
                   D.Email))
setEmailAsVerified vCode = do
  result <- withConn $ \conn -> query conn qry (Only vCode)
  case result of
    [(uId, mail)] -> case D.mkEmail mail of
      Right email -> return $ Right (uId, email)
      _ -> throwString $ "Should not happen: email in DB is not valid: " <>
      unpack mail
    _ -> return $ Left D.EmailVerificationErrorInvalidCode
```

---

[8]www.postgresql.org/docs/10/static/errcodes-appendix.html

where
```
  qry = "update auths \
        \set is_email_verified = 't' \
        \where email_verification_code = ? \
        \returning id, cast (email as text)"
```

In this function, we basically want to modify a row in our auths table that has the given verification code and set the is_email_verified column to t. After that, we want to get the UserId and Email of the modified auths. If you see the preceding query, that's basically what we do. One that needs a bit more explanation is the cast (email as text) part. Remember that we define the email column in our table as citext, as it is case-insensitive? Unfortunately, postgresql-simple doesn't know how to parse that to Text. So, we cast it to text in PostgreSQL so that postgresql-simple will be able to parse that.

The result of the query is pattern matched. There are two possible cases of query result. The first one is when the query returns exactly one row. The second one is when the query returns 0 or more than 1 row.

The first case is the happy case. We successfully modified a row. In this case, we get the UserId and Email from the returned row. The email we get from the row is a Text, but we want it to be Email. So, we need to use the mkEmail function to parse the Text. Since mkEmail also does input validation, we pattern-match the resulting validation. If it's a Right, then good, just return it. Otherwise we throw an error. If an error is indeed thrown, then it means that there is a bug in our addAuth function. This should never occur if our program is correct.

The second case is the unhappy case. This happens when we can't find the given verification code in our database. In this case, we just return a Left EmailVerificationErrorInvalidCode.

The next function to implement is findUserByAuth, and the code is as follows:

```
findUserByAuth :: PG r m
                 => D.Auth -> m (Maybe (D.UserId, Bool))
findUserByAuth (D.Auth email pass) = do
  let rawEmail = D.rawEmail email
      rawPassw = D.rawPassword pass
  result <- withConn $ \conn -> query conn qry (rawEmail, rawPassw)
```

```
return $ case result of
  [(uId, isVerified)] -> Just (uId, isVerified)
  _ -> Nothing
where
  qry = "select id, is_email_verified \
        \from auths \
        \where email = ? and pass = crypt(?, pass)"
```

In this function, we basically want to find a `UserId` and information on whether the user has his email verified or not. To do this we do a select by filtering `Email` and `Password`. Since the password is encrypted in the database, we need to use `crypt()`, a function from the `pgcrypto` extension.

The result of that query can be one row or no row. In the case of one row being returned, we just wrap it in `Just` and return it. Otherwise, we return `Nothing`, as it means such a record doesn't exist in our database.

The last function that we want to implement is `findEmailFromUserId` and the code is as follows:

```
findEmailFromUserId :: PG r m
                    => D.UserId -> m (Maybe D.Email)
findEmailFromUserId uId = do
  result <- withConn $ \conn -> query conn qry (Only uId)
  case result of
    [Only mail] -> case D.mkEmail mail of
      Right email -> return $ Just email
      _ -> throwString $ "Should not happen: email in DB is not valid:
      " <> unpack mail
  _ ->
  return Nothing
where
    qry = "select cast(email as text) \
          \from auths \
          \where id = ?"
```

This function is quite straightforward. We get an email in our `auths` table where the id is the same as the input parameter. Again, we parse the input to `Email` and throw an error if the email is not valid.

Phew, we have finished writing the repositories implementation. Now it's time to tie everything together. Let's open the Lib module and write the following code:

```
+import qualified Adapter.PostgreSQL.Auth as PG

-type State = TVar M.State
+type State = (PG.State, TVar M.State)
 newtype App a = App
   { unApp :: ReaderT State (KatipContextT IO) a
   } deriving ( Applicative, Functor, Monad, MonadReader State, MonadIO
-              , KatipContext, Katip)
+              , KatipContext, Katip, MonadThrow)

 instance AuthRepo App where
-  addAuth = M.addAuth
-  setEmailAsVerified = M.setEmailAsVerified
-  findUserByAuth = M.findUserByAuth
-  findEmailFromUserId = M.findEmailFromUserId
+  addAuth = PG.addAuth
+  setEmailAsVerified = PG.setEmailAsVerified
+  findUserByAuth = PG.findUserByAuth
+  findEmailFromUserId = PG.findEmailFromUserId
```

We modify our State definition. Previously, it was equivalent to TVar M.State. Now, since we want to support both in-memory and PostgreSQL implementation, we add PG. State to our State.

We also need to modify the deriving clause of our App definition by adding MonadThrow. MonadThrow is necessary because we define MonadThrow m as one of the constraints for executing PostgreSQL-related functions. There will be a compile error if we don't add MonadThrow here.

In addition to modifying State and App, we also modify our AuthRepo instance implementation. Previously, we used functions from the Adapter.InMemory.Auth module. Now, we want to use our PostgreSQL implementation that we have just defined. So, we just swap out existing functions to functions from the Adapter.PostgreSQL.Auth module.

We are not done yet; further modifications need to be done in the `someFunc` function as follows:

```
 someFunc :: IO ()
 someFunc = withKatip $ \le -> do
-  state <- newTVarIO M.initialState
-  run le state action
+  mState <- newTVarIO M.initialState
+  PG.withState pgCfg $ \pgState -> run le (pgState, mState) action
+  where
+    pgCfg = PG.Config
+            { PG.configUrl = "postgresql://localhost/hauth"
+            , PG.configStripeCount = 2
+            , PG.configMaxOpenConnPerStripe = 5
+            , PG.configIdleConnTimeout = 10
+            }
```

We simply add the `PG.withState` function here to acquire `PG.State`. Then, we use it to build our `State` that will later be passed in to the `run` function. For simplicity, we hardcode our PostgreSQL configuration. We could improve it later by parsing the configuration from the environment.

Now, we may open REPL and run `someFunc`. If you have the PostgreSQL database running and have a database named `hauth`, you should see that the code is still working as expected.

Great! With that, we have finished integrating our application with PostgreSQL.

Redis

Up next, we are going to integrate Redis to our application. Why Redis? What do we use it for? Well, we use it to store `SessionId` to `UserId` mapping. Once a user is logged in, the user gets a `SessionId` that will be used to authenticate with our application for every interaction that requires authentication. For this, we need to look up the `UserId` based on the given `SessionId`. This operation will occur often and we want it to be very fast. The fastest way is to store the mapping in the application's memory. However, this wouldn't work if you have multiple instances of the application running. What if the user's request is going to the instance that has no such mapping? So, we need a dedicated key-value system to store such mapping. Sure, we can store it in PostgreSQL, but since PostgreSQL saves the values to disk, it is not as fast as getting it from memory. So, we want a database of in-memory key-value store. Redis is one such database. It's quite popular and widely used in the industry.

hedis

There is a good package in Haskell for interacting with Redis, called hedis.[9] hedis is complete and low level, as in, it mimics Redis commands.[10] It's the similar level of abstraction as the postgresql-simple package that we have used earlier.

In this section we will explore a bit about how to use the package. Redis actually does so much more than just key-value store. However, for our use case, setting and getting values from a key-value store is enough. For that reason, we will only look into those functions. Moreover, exploring other functions on your own should be straightforward once you understand the basics laid out in this section. I would suggest looking into the documentation and playing around with it in the REPL if you would like to explore.

For opening a connection to Redis using the hedis package, the function we want to use is checkedConnect. It has the following type signature:

```
checkedConnect :: ConnectInfo -> IO Connection
```

This function initiates the connection to Redis and checks whether the connection is established; that's why it has "checked" as part of its name. It returns a Connection, which actually is a connection pool. Unlike postgresql-simple, hedis already managed the connection pool. Internally, it uses the resource-pool package. It's the same package that we used previously for PostgreSQL.

---

[9]http://hackage.haskell.org/package/hedis-0.10.0
[10]https://redis.io/commands

ConnectInfo is a configuration for creating Connection. You can use the defaultConnectInfo function to construct a default configuration. By default, the values for ConnectInfo will be as follows:

```
connectHost           = "localhost"
connectPort           = PortNumber 6379 -- Redis default port
connectAuth           = Nothing          -- No password
connectDatabase       = 0                -- SELECT database 0
connectMaxConnections = 50               -- Up to 50 connections
connectMaxIdleTime    = 30               -- Keep open for 30 seconds
connectTimeout        = Nothing          -- Don't add timeout logic
```

Should you wish to override any of the configurations, you can do the following:

```
let cfg = defaultConnectInfo { connectHost = "127.0.0.1"
                             , connectMaxConnections = 100
                             }
```

Another approach that I actually prefer is to use parseConnectInfo. It accepts a string in the format of redis://uname:pass@host:port/db, for example, redis://user:pass@localhost:6379/0, and converts it to ConnectInfo. The type signature for parseConnectInfo is as follows:

```
parseConnectInfo :: String -> Either String ConnectInfo
```

As you can see, it returns an Either. It may return Left in the case of malformed input.

For setting values to Redis, we use the set function. set has the following type signature:

```
set :: RedisCtx m f => ByteString -> ByteString -> m (f Status)
```

set receives two arguments: the key and the value that both are in ByteString. It returns a seemingly confusing type m (f Status). RedisCtx m f is basically a constraint that applies to all Redis-related operations. It has two concrete types: Redis and RedisTx. The first one is normal Redis action, while the second one is for Redis transaction. For our application, we only need the Redis type. We don't have a need for RedisTx. If we specialize the preceding function to Redis, the type signature becomes:

```
set :: ByteString -> ByteString -> Redis (Either Reply Status)
```

```haskell
data Reply
  = SingleLine ByteString
  | Error ByteString
  | Integer Integer
  | Bulk (Maybe ByteString)
  | MultiBulk (Maybe [Reply])
```

```haskell
data Status
  = Ok
  | Pong
  | Status ByteString
```

We can just ignore all of those Reply and Status constructors. What we are interested in is that set should return Right Ok in a successful scenario.

For getting a value from Redis, the function to use is get:

```
get :: RedisCtx m f => ByteString -> m (f (Maybe ByteString))
```

Again, for simplicity sake, we can just specialize this to Redis so it will be:

```
get :: ByteString -> Redis (Either Reply (Maybe ByteString))
```

The first argument it accepts is the key. It then returns Maybe ByteString, the value. It is wrapped in Maybe because the value might not exist.

The last function we are interested in is runRedis. Basically, this function turns Redis action into IO, as we can infer from the type signature:

```
runRedis :: Connection -> Redis a -> IO a
```

The following example shows how all the functions that we have seen previously work together:

```haskell
main :: IO ()
main = do
  conn <- checkedConnect defaultConnectInfo
  world <- runRedis conn $ do
    set "hello" "world"
    get "hello"
  print world
```

That wraps up our brief introduction to the hedis package. We can now proceed to integrate the package to our application.

Implementation

In this section, we are going to integrate Redis with our application using hedis, the package that we have just explored.

First thing first: import the package. We want to use at least version 0.10.0 of the hedis package. The reason is that the parseConnectInfo function is only available starting with version 0.10.0. At the time of this writing, the version is not yet available in Stackage. So, we need to list it in our extra-deps section in stack.yaml:

```
extra-deps:
- hedis-0.10.0
```

We also need to import that in our package.yaml:

```
dependencies:
- hedis
```

Next, let's create a new module Adapter.Redis.Auth and write the necessary imports:

```
module Adapter.Redis.Auth where

import ClassyPrelude
import qualified Domain.Auth as D
import Text.StringRandom
import Data.Has
import qualified Database.Redis as R
```

Next, we write the necessary function to acquire a connection:

```
type State = R.Connection

-- | Create state from redis url string.
-- format: redis://user:pass@host:port/db
-- sample: redis://abc:def@localhost:6379/0
withState :: String -> (State -> IO a) -> IO a
```

```
withState connUrl action = do
  case R.parseConnectInfo connUrl of
    Left _ ->
      throwString "Invalid Redis conn URL"
    Right connInfo -> do
      conn <- R.checkedConnect connInfo
      action conn
```

Here we define State as a type synonym for R.Connection. This is for consistency with the existing PostgreSQL implementation as well as for future proofing. Should we, in the future, need more than just R.Connection, we can just edit the State type synonym.

withState is quite straightforward. We just parse a String, which is supposed to be the Redis connection URL, make a Redis connection, and then execute the action from the parameter. In the case of an invalid connection string URL, we just throw an error.

Moving on, we implement the newSession function from the SessionRepo typeclass:

```
type Redis r m = (Has State r, MonadReader r m, MonadIO m, MonadThrow m)

withConn :: Redis r m => R.Redis a -> m a
withConn action = do
  conn <- asks getter
  liftIO $ R.runRedis conn action

newSession :: Redis r m => D.UserId -> m D.SessionId
newSession userId = do
  sId <- liftIO $ stringRandomIO "[a-zA-Z0-9]{32}"
  result <- withConn $ R.set (encodeUtf8 sId) (fromString . show $ userId)
  case result of
    Right R.Ok -> return sId
    err -> throwString $ "Unexpected redis error: " <> show err
```

We define the Redis r m constraint synonym. It's pretty similar to PostgreSQL that we have seen previously. Functions with Redis r m constraint basically say that the function can perform IO (via MonadIO), throw an exception (via MonadThrow), read r from environment (via MonadReader r), and we can get State from r (via Has State r).

withConn is a small helper function to execute R.Redis under Redis r m constraint. What we do is basically get the connection from the environment, then execute the R.Redis action using the R.runRedis function.

In newSession, we create a SessionId; it's a random alphanumeric generated by the stringRandomIO function. Then, we store the mapping between the SessionId and UserId from the function parameter to Redis. Since R.set only accepts ByteString, we need to convert both values to ByteString.

The result of setting the key and value to Redis is then inspected. If it's a Right R.Ok, then the operation was successful and we just return the generated SessionId. Otherwise, we just throw an error with a meaningful message.

findUserIdBySessionId is the last function in the SessionRepo typeclass that we want to implement:

```
findUserIdBySessionId :: Redis r m => D.SessionId -> m (Maybe D.UserId)
findUserIdBySessionId sId = do
  result <- withConn $ R.get (encodeUtf8 sId)
  return $ case result of
    Right (Just uIdStr) -> readMay . unpack . decodeUtf8 $ uIdStr
    err -> throwString $ "Unexpected redis error: " <> show err
```

It's quite straightforward; just do an R.get with the given SessionId and inspect the result. In the case of Right (Just uIdStr), we just parse the uIdStr from ByteString to UserId. decodeUtf8 is a function to convert ByteString to Text. unpack is a function to convert Text to String. This functions chain is necessary, since readMay receives a String.

We are done with the repository implementation. Now, we're moving on to the Lib module to finally integrate the functions we have just written.

We start by importing Adapter.Redis.Auth and modifying State type synonym, since we want to introduce Redis:

```
+import qualified Adapter.Redis.Auth as Redis

-type State = (PG.State, TVar M.State)
+type State = (PG.State, Redis.State, TVar M.State)
```

Next, since we want to store user sessions in Redis instead of in-memory, we modify the SessionRepo instance to the following:

instance SessionRepo App where

```
- newSession = M.newSession
- findUserIdBySessionId = M.findUserIdBySessionId
+ newSession = Redis.newSession
+ findUserIdBySessionId = Redis.findUserIdBySessionId
```

As you can see, we just change the functions. Previously, it was from the Adapter. InMemory.Auth module, now it is from the Adapter.Redis.Auth module.

Finally, we modify the someFunc function to include Redis initialization:

```
 someFunc :: IO ()
 someFunc = withKatip $ \le -> do
+  mState <- newTVarIO M.initialState
-  PG.withState pgCfg $ \pgState -> run le (pgState, mState) action
+  PG.withState pgCfg $ \pgState ->
+    Redis.withState redisCfg $ \redisState ->
+      run le (pgState, redisState, mState) action
   where
+    redisCfg = "redis://localhost:6379/0"
     pgCfg = PG.Config
               { PG.configUrl = "postgresql://localhost/hauth"
               , PG.configStripeCount = 2
               , PG.configMaxOpenConnPerStripe = 5
               , PG.configIdleConnTimeout = 10
               }
```

It's basically the same as before but we just added Redis.withState and redisCfg.

Now, if you go to REPL and run someFunc, you'll see the application still works as usual provided you have a running Redis instance.

That's it. Congratulations! We have successfully integrated Redis to our application.

Summary

In this chapter, we have reached quite a milestone: integrating databases to our application. Most web applications use some sort of database for storing data, so it's important for us to know how to do that.

We started by learning about the `postgresql-simple` package. It's a package for integrating with the PostgreSQL database. We learned how to open and close a database connection as well as managing them efficiently using the `resource-pool` package. We explored six important queries-related functions in the library and learned how to write a query, passing parameters and parsing the query result.

We finished our journey by integrating Redis to our application using the `hedis` package. Like PostgreSQL, we also learned how to open and close a connection as well as reading and writing data to Redis.

CHAPTER 6

Queues

In this chapter, we will integrate our application with RabbitMQ.[1] RabbitMQ is a popular queueing system. One common use case of RabbitMQ is for running a background task. A background task is a task that need not be done within a request-response cycle. Having a background task to handle a noncritical process helps make your application more responsive.

But wait, Haskell supports multithreading. Why don't we just spawn a new thread to run the task and call it a day? Well, there are multiple reasons why an external queueing system is more preferable than just spawning a new thread.

The first reason is that spawning a thread blindly may hog your application, especially if the task takes a long time to finish. In this case, an external queueing system acts as a buffer so that the tasks are consumed according to the capacity of the processors.

The second reason is that the tasks will survive application shut down. Suppose that a single node of your application spawns 100 threads, each working on these tasks. Suddenly the application shuts down for any reason. In this case, those tasks will be gone for good. An external queueing system acts as a store for those tasks and we can reprocess it again later.

The third reason is to distribute the tasks evenly across many nodes. You may also spawn background-process-only nodes and connect them to the queueing system.

In our application, we will use RabbitMQ for sending a verification email upon user registration. This doesn't seem like much, and probably you can get away with just doing it without a queueing system. However, this is just for the purpose of showing you how to integrate with an external queueing system.

---

[1] www.rabbitmq.com/

© Ecky Putrady 2018

E. Putrady, *Practical Web Development with Haskell*, https://doi.org/10.1007/978-1-4842-3739-7_6

We will not be covering the basics of RabbitMQ, as it is not the focus of this book. However, the official RabbitMQ website has a great section on the concepts[2] and tutorials.[3]

amqp Package Overview

amqp[4] is a Haskell package for interfacing with RabbitMQ. In this section, we will learn how to use it to interface with RabbitMQ.

Connection and Channel

Since RabbitMQ is an external system to your application, you need to acquire a connection and open a channel in order to communicate with it. Unlike PostgreSQL, the connection is thread-safe. It means that multiple threads can use it concurrently.

The following code shows functions to acquire and close a RabbitMQ connection:

```
openConnection'' :: ConnectionOpts -> IO Connection
closeConnection :: Connection -> IO ()
```

ConnectionOpts is the data structure that describes parameters pertaining to RabbitMQ connection. It has the following fields:

```
data ConnectionOpts = ConnectionOpts {
  coServers :: ![(String, PortNumber)],
  -- ^ A list of host-port pairs.
  coVHost :: !Text,
  -- ^ The VHost to connect to.
  coAuth :: ![SASLMechanism],
  -- ^ The 'SASLMechanism's to use for authenticating with the broker.
  coMaxFrameSize :: !(Maybe Word32),
  -- ^ The maximum frame size to be used. If not specified, no limit is
     assumed.
  coHeartbeatDelay :: !(Maybe Word16),
```

---

[2]www.rabbitmq.com/tutorials/amqp-concepts.html
[3]www.rabbitmq.com/getstarted.html
[4]www.stackage.org/lts-10.3/package/amqp-0.18.1

```
-- ^ The delay in seconds for receiving Heartbeat
coMaxChannel :: !(Maybe Word16),
-- ^ The maximum number of channels the client will use.
coTLSSettings :: Maybe TLSSettings,
-- ^ Whether or not to connect to servers using TLS.
coName :: !(Maybe Text)
-- ^ optional connection name (will be displayed in the RabbitMQ web
   interface)
}
```

To create a `ConnectionOpts`, you may use the `defaultConnectionOpts` function and override each fields as necessary, for example:

```
defaultConnectionOpts { coName = Just "hauth" }
```

Another method to use is the `fromURI` function. It builds a `ConnectionOpts` from a string with the following format: `amqp://<user>:<pass>@<host>:<port>/<vhost>`. If any part is missing, then the value will be the same one as the default. An example would be:

```
fromURI "amqp://guest:guest@localhost:5672/%2F"
```

Now that we know how to open a connection, it's time to learn how to open a channel. The following functions are used to open and close a channel, respectively:

```
openChannel :: Connection -> IO Channel
closeChannel :: Channel -> IO ()
```

Closing a channel manually is usually unnecessary because closing a connection implicitly closes all channels.

A `channel` in this package is thread-safe. Many threads can interact with RabbitMQ using the same channel concurrently without you needing to manually manage the locking mechanism.

After opening a channel, you may want to adjust the prefetch count. Prefetch count is the limit of the amount of data the server delivers to the client before requiring acknowledgements. The function to do it is `qos`:

```
qos :: Channel -> Word32 -> Word16 -> Bool -> IO ()
qos chan prefetchSize prefetchCount global
```

The second parameter, `prefetchSize`, should always be 0, otherwise this function will throw an exception. The reason for such a strange design decision is that this package is designed for AMQP in general instead of just RabbitMQ. RabbitMQ is just one implementation of AMQP. However, RabbitMQ doesn't support `prefetchSize`. That's why it's required to be 0.

The third parameter is the prefetch count.

The fourth parameter is a `Bool` indicating whether this restriction is for a per-consumer or per-channel basis. If the value is `True`, then the prefetch count applies to the whole channel, that is, the number of unacknowledged messages across all consumers that consume from this channel is capped. On the other hand, if the value is `False`, then the number of unacknowledged messages applies to each consumer instead of the whole channel.

I would suggest using the global prefetch count. Think of it as the maximum number of threads that you allow to be running at any given time to handle RabbitMQ messages.

Finally, you may want to add a listener to a channel whenever there is an exception being thrown. It will be helpful to log those exceptions for troubleshooting issues in production. The following functions allow us to do that:

```
addChannelExceptionHandler :: Channel -> (SomeException -> IO ()) -> IO ()
addChannelExceptionHandler chan callback
```

The callback receives `SomeException` and returns an `IO` action. `SomeException` comes from the `GHC.Exception` module. `SomeException` is the base of all exceptions. You may convert this to a human-friendly string using the `displayException` function.

Declaring Exchange, Queue, and Binding

The very next thing that you want to do after establishing a connection and a channel is to declare all exchanges, queues, and bindings. The following function is the one to use for declaring an exchange:

```
declareExchange :: Channel -> ExchangeOpts -> IO ()
```

ExchangeOpts has the following data structure:

```
data ExchangeOpts = ExchangeOpts
  { exchangeName :: Text,
    -- ^ (must be set); the name of the exchange
```

```
exchangeType :: Text,
-- ^ (must be set); the type of the exchange
exchangePassive :: Bool,
-- ^ (default 'False'); If set, the server will not create the exchange.
exchangeDurable :: Bool
-- ^ (default 'True'); Non-durable exchanges are purged if a server
   restarts.
exchangeAutoDelete :: Bool,
-- ^ (default 'False');
-- If set, the exchange is deleted when all queues have finished using it.
exchangeInternal :: Bool,
-- ^ (default 'False');
-- Internal exchanges are used to construct wiring that is not visible
   to applications.
exchangeArguments    :: FieldTable
-- ^ (default empty); A set of arguments for the declaration.
}
```

To create one, we can use newExchange and override the necessary fields, as shown in the following example:

```
newExchange
  { exchangeName = "auth"
  , exchangeType = "topic"
  }
```

For declaring queues, we have a similar function to an exchange. It's called declareQueue:

```
declareQueue :: Channel -> QueueOpts -> IO (Text, Int, Int)
```

It returns a tuple of three values. The first value is the name of the queue. You can create a queue with an empty name, but then RabbitMQ will autogenerate the name. The second value is the number of messages in the queue. If it's a new queue, this value should be 0. The third value is the number of consumers for this queue.

117

QueueOpts has the following fields:

```haskell
data QueueOpts = QueueOpts
  { queueName :: Text,
    -- ^ (default \"\"); the name of the queue;
    -- if left empty, the server will generate a new name
    queuePassive :: Bool,
    -- ^ (default 'False'); If set, the server will not create the queue.
    queueDurable :: Bool,
    -- ^ (default 'True');
    -- Non-durable queues are purged if the server restarts.
    queueExclusive :: Bool,
    -- ^ (default 'False');
    -- Exclusive queues may only be consumed from by the current connection.
    queueAutoDelete :: Bool,
    -- ^ (default 'False');
    -- If set, the queue is deleted when all consumers have finished using it.
    queueHeaders :: FieldTable
    -- ^ (default empty);
    -- Headers to use when creating this queue.
  }
```

Similar to an exchange, to create a new QueueOpts, we can use newQueue and override the fields as necessary:

```haskell
newQueue
  { queueName = "emailVerification"
  , queueDurable = False
  }
```

For binding a queue to an exchange, the function to use is bindQueue:

```haskell
bindQueue :: Channel -> Text -> Text -> Text -> IO ()
```

The first parameter is the channel to use to declare the binding. The second parameter is the queue name. The third parameter is the exchange name. The fourth parameter is the routing key. The routing key is a RabbitMQ concept and is used to route messages augmented with the key to a specific queue. For example, let's say that you bind a queue named "myQueue" to an exchange "myExchange" with routing key "myRoutingKey." When a message with routing key "myRoutingKey" is sent to the "myExchange" exchange, the message will then be routed to "myQueue" queue.

Publishing Messages

For publishing a message to RabbitMQ, the function to use is the following:

```
publishMsg :: Channel -> Text -> Text -> Message -> IO (Maybe Int)
publishMsg channel exchange routingKey msg
```

It returns a Maybe Int, which represents the sequence number of the message. This number is wrapped in a Maybe because this only happens if the channel is in "publisher confirm" mode. If the channel is not in that mode, the return value will be Nothing.

In short, "publisher confirm" mode is a mode where the publisher receives a confirmation back from the server. It's good to be in this mode so that we can make sure the message is indeed received by the server. To enable "publisher confirm" mode in a channel, you can just use the following function:

```
confirmSelect :: Channel -> Bool -> IO ()
confirmSelect channel noblock
```

The second parameter, noblock, is a flag that tells whether this function should block or not. If noblock is True, then this function will not block until the confirmation is received. We can get the confirmation by some other means, like using the waitForConfirms function or addConfirmationListener function.

The last parameter of publishMsg is a Message. Message has the following fields:

```
data Message = Message
  { msgBody :: BL.ByteString,
    -- ^ the content of your message
    msgDeliveryMode :: Maybe DeliveryMode,
    msgTimestamp :: Maybe Timestamp,
    -- ^ use in any way you like; this doesn't affect the way the message
    is handled
    msgID :: Maybe Text,
    -- ^ use in any way you like; this doesn't affect the way the message
    is handled
    msgType :: Maybe Text,
```

```
-- ^ use in any way you like; this doesn't affect the way the message
is handled msgUserID :: Maybe Text,
msgApplicationID :: Maybe Text,
msgClusterID :: Maybe Text,
msgContentType :: Maybe Text,
msgContentEncoding :: Maybe Text,
msgReplyTo :: Maybe Text,
msgPriority :: Maybe Octet,
msgCorrelationID :: Maybe Text,
msgExpiration :: Maybe Text,
msgHeaders :: Maybe FieldTable
}
```

There are two values for `DeliveryMode`: `Persistent` and `NonPersistent`. `Persistent` means that the message will survive after RabbitMQ restarts, provided that the message is sent to the queue that is marked as durable. On the other hand, a `NonPersistent` message will be gone after RabbitMQ restarts.

We can create a new `Message` by using the `newMsg` function and override the fields as necessary. Usually, you just want to override the message body:

```
newMsg { msgBody = "fire the missile!" }
```

Consuming Messages

There are two ways of consuming RabbitMQ messages: poll and push. Push-based consumers are more efficient than the poll-based one. So it's preferable to go for the push-based one if possible.

For polling the message out of a queue, the function to use is `getMsg`. It has the following type signature:

```
getMsg :: Channel -> Ack -> Text -> IO (Maybe (Message, Envelope))
```

The second parameter is of the type `Ack` and it has two possible values: `Ack` and `NoAck`. If `Ack` is passed in as the second parameter, it means we need to acknowledge or reject the message explicitly. Failing to acknowledge or reject the message will result in the same message being sent again in the future. If `NoAck` is passed in as the second parameter, the message will be acknowledged automatically upon being consumed.

It's best to use the Ack mode and acknowledge or reject explicitly after you are done processing the message. That way, if the application crashes during message processing, the message will be sent again in the future.

The third parameter is the queue name to consume the message from.

Finally, it returns a Maybe of (Message, Envelope). The Message structure is the same as we have seen in the previous section. We don't need to care about the Envelope structure, as we won't need to inspect it.

The second approach for consuming a message is to use the push-based consumer:

```
consumeMsgs :: Channel -> Text -> Ack
            -> ((Message, Envelope) -> IO ())
            -> IO ConsumerTag
consumeMsgs chan queue ack callback
```

The parameters are similar to getMsg. The fourth parameter is the callback that will be invoked when we receive a message. The callback is simply an IO action that accepts (Message, Envelope) as its input. The return value of this function is a ConsumerTag, which actually is just a synonym for Text. ConsumerTag is a string that is generated by RabbitMQ that identifies a consumer uniquely.

Please be aware that the callback is executed on the same thread as the channel thread. Every channel spawns its own thread to listen to incoming data. So it's best to immediately spawn a new thread for processing the message.

For acknowledging and rejecting the message, the functions to use are:

```
ackEnv :: Envelope -> IO ()
rejectEnv :: Envelope -> Bool -> IO ()
```

Both receive Envelope as the first parameter. You can get the Envelope when consuming a message.

The second parameter in rejectEnv is a Bool indicating whether the message is requeued or not. If it is a True, then the message will be put into the queue again and the consumer will consume the message again in the future.

Implementation

In this section, we will write the necessary code that integrates RabbitMQ to our application. As we have seen previously, we will use RabbitMQ in our project for offloading the email verification task. Upon user registration, we will send a new message to an exchange named "auth" with a routing key named "userRegistered." We will have a queue named "emailVerification" that is bound to that exchange with "userRegistered" as the routing key. With that network configuration, messages that are published to the "auth" exchange with routing key "userRegistered" will land on the "emailVerification" queue.

The message that we will be sending is a JSON containing email and verification code, something like this:

```
{
  "email": "some.email@test.com",
  "verificationCode": "aisdh934bso908vcAHis90"
}
```

Actually, we can send anything as a message in RabbitMQ, as it accepts `ByteString`. However, let's just stick to JSON as it's a well-supported serialization format.

The messages in the "emailVerification" queue will eventually be received by our application again. Once we receive that, we ideally send the verification email. However, we won't be doing that in this chapter, to keep our focus on RabbitMQ. Instead, we will store the message in an in-memory data structure that we have defined previously in Chapter 3.

Acquiring Connection

It's time to write some actual code. As usual, we start by importing the package in our `package.yaml` file:

```
dependencies:
- amqp
```

Next, we will write code that initializes RabbitMQ integration in our project. Things that need to be done are: acquiring the connection, then creating the network topology (exchanges and queues), and finally initializing the consumers.

We will write such code in the `Adapter.RabbitMQ.Common` module. The code is as follows:

```
import ClassyPrelude
import Network.AMQP

data State = State
  { statePublisherChan :: Channel
  , stateConsumerChan :: Channel
  }

withState :: String -> Integer -> (State -> IO a) -> IO a
withState connUri prefetchCount action = bracket initState destroyState
action'
  where
    initState = do
      publisher <- openConnAndChan
      consumer <- openConnAndChan
      return (publisher, consumer)

    openConnAndChan = do
      conn <- openConnection" . fromURI $ connUri
      chan <- openChannel conn
      confirmSelect chan False
      qos chan 0 (fromInteger prefetchCount) True
      return (conn, chan)

    destroyState ((conn1, _), (conn2, _)) = do
      closeConnection conn1
      closeConnection conn2

    action' ((_, pubChan), (_, conChan)) = action (State pubChan conChan)
```

`withState` is the function to initialize the RabbitMQ state, do the action with the state, then destroy the state. It receives three inputs. The first one is a string that represents the URI, such as `amqp://user:pass@localhost:5678/vhost`. The second parameter is the prefetch count, the maximum number of messages to be received without confirmation. The third parameter is the action to be carried out now that we have constructed the state.

State is composed of two Channels: one for publisher and one for consumer. If you see the implementation in withState, you'll notice that we open two connections to RabbitMQ. This is intentional. It's considered a best practice to separate the connection between publisher and consumer. RabbitMQ may throttle the data being sent per TCP connection. This means that if you are consuming a lot of messages, there is a chance that the publisher will be blocked.

For each connection, we will only open one channel. It's usually recommended to open one channel per thread. However, amqp's Channel is thread-safe. So, we will just open one channel.

For destroying the state, we just need to close the connections. The channels will be closed implicitly.

Creating Network Topology and Initializing Push-Based Consumers

After opening the connection and channel, we will need to declare exchanges, queues, bindings, and consumers. We will start by declaring an exchange:

```
initExchange :: State -> Text -> IO ()
initExchange (State pubChan _) exchangeName = do
  let exchange = newExchange  { exchangeName = exchangeName
                              , exchangeType = "topic" }
  declareExchange pubChan exchange
```

initExchange is a function to create an exchange. Most of the time, you want the exchange type to be "topic." That's why that exchange type is hard-coded here. We use the publisher's channel to create this exchange. Actually, it's just an arbitrary choice. We may as well use the consumer's channel to create the exchange.

```
initQueue :: State -> Text -> Text -> Text -> IO ()
initQueue state@(State pubChan _) queueName exchangeName routingKey = do
  initExchange state exchangeName
  void $ declareQueue pubChan (newQueue { queueName = queueName })
  bindQueue pubChan queueName exchangeName routingKey
```

initQueue is a function to create a queue along with an exchange and the binding. Most of the time, you want to send a message through an exchange with a routing key instead of directly to a queue. This implicitly requires you to set up an exchange, queue, and the binding. This function aims to simplify that process.

Note that declaring an exchange is an idempotent operation. Declaring an exchange with the exact same configuration will do nothing. However, if you declare an exchange with the same name but a different configuration, RabbitMQ will return an error. Declaring a queue also results in this same behavior.

```
initConsumer :: State -> Text -> (Message -> IO Bool) -> IO ()
initConsumer (State _ conChan) queueName handler = do
  void . consumeMsgs conChan queueName Ack $ \(msg, env) -> void . fork $
do
    result <- handler msg
    if result then ackEnv env else rejectEnv env False
```

initConsumer is a function to initialize a consumer. It receives three inputs: RabbitMQ state, queue name to consume from, and an action on the message. The action has a type of (Message -> IO Bool). Basically, we process the RabbitMQ Message and return True if the message is processed successfully and False otherwise. We acknowledge the message using ackEnv when the message processing has finished successfully. We reject the message using rejectEnv if the message processing finished with a failure.

We hard-coded the rejectEnv's last parameter to False. This means that any message being rejected will not be requeued again. In my experience, I rarely requeue the message immediately. If I needed to retry the message processing, I would retry it in the application.

Publishing and Consuming

We will be using JSON as the data format on the wire. In this section, we will create publishing and consuming functions that work with JSON. Let's add the following code into the Adapter.RabbitMQ.Common module.

```
import Data.Has
import Data.Aeson

type Rabbit r m = (Has State r, MonadReader r m, MonadIO m)
```

```
publish :: (ToJSON a, Rabbit r m) => Text -> Text -> a -> m ()
publish exchange routingKey payload = do
  (State chan _) <- asks getter
  let msg = newMsg { msgBody = encode payload }
  liftIO . void $ publishMsg chan exchange routingKey msg
```

We define a `Rabbit r m` constraint synonym. This constraint says that we can get
`State` from m (via `Has State r`, `MonadReader r m`) and are able to do IO (via `MonadIO m`).
The purpose of creating this synonym is purely for minimize typing.

The `publish` function allows us to send any data to RabbitMQ, provided the data
can be serialized to JSON. This can be seen from the `ToJSON a` constraint in the type
signature. What this function does is to get a publisher channel from the environment,
construct the payload, and send it to RabbitMQ.

Up next, we have a function that helps with consuming RabbitMQ messages. We do
expect to receive a JSON, but there is no guarantee that we will receive a JSON all the
time. There might be some error that causes the payload to be malformed. So, we need
to handle that.

import Katip

```
consumeAndProcess :: (KatipContext m, FromJSON a, MonadCatch m)
                  => Message -> (a -> m Bool) -> m Bool
consumeAndProcess msg handler =
  case eitherDecode' (msgBody msg) of
    Left err -> withMsgAndErr msg err $ do
      $(logTM) ErrorS "Malformed payload. Rejecting."
      return False
    Right payload -> do
      result <- tryAny (handler payload)
      case result of
        Left err -> withMsgAndErr msg (displayException err) $ do
          $(logTM) ErrorS "There was an exception when processing the msg.
          Rejecting."
          return False
        Right bool ->
          return bool
```

```
withMsgAndErr :: (KatipContext m, ToJSON e) => Message -> e -> m a -> m a
withMsgAndErr msg err =
 katipAddContext (sl "mqMsg" (show msg) <> sl "error" err)
```

What we do here is decoding the message's body. If the decoding fails, we will then log the error and return False—indicating we want to reject the message. We use the logging functionality from Katip that we learned in Chapter 4.

Upon successful decoding, we will pass the decoded data to the handler function that we receive from the second parameter of the function. We wrap the handler action in a tryAny to catch any synchronous exceptions. tryAny becomes accessible for use once we import ClassyPrelude. tryAny requires us to operate under the MonadCatch typeclass. Since we have generalized our function and have not pinned it to the IO monad, we add MonadCatch as a constraint for m.

If there's a synchronous exception, we will log it and return False. Since we use tryAny, the exception will be of the type SomeException. SomeException is basically a catch-all exception. We want to catch any exception here to prevent our application from crashing. displayException is a function that comes from the Exception typeclass and is used for displaying the exception as a string. If there is no exception, then we are on a happy path. Simply return True and the message will be acknowledged.

Repository Implementation

In the previous section, we've written some functions that are not exactly related to our domain. In this section we will build on top of the code from the previous section to write code that is really related to our domain.

We'll be writing the code in the Adapter.RabbitMQ.Auth module. We'll start with the imports.

```
import ClassyPrelude
import Adapter.RabbitMQ.Common
import qualified Adapter.InMemory.Auth as M
import Network.AMQP
import Katip
import Data.Aeson
import Data.Aeson.TH
import qualified Domain.Auth as D
```

As I have stated before, in this chapter we won't actually be sending the email, to keep our focus on RabbitMQ. Instead, we will store the message in an in-memory database. We are going to reuse `Adapter.InMemory.Auth`. Hence we import it in the preceding import block.

Next, we define the message payload. The payload should contain the email and the verification code:

```
data EmailVerificationPayload = EmailVerificationPayload
  { emailVerificationPayloadEmail :: Text
  , emailVerificationPayloadVerificationCode :: Text
  }
```

In addition to the structure definition, we will also need to make it serializable and deserializable to JSON. The following function is a `TemplateHaskell` to do that.

```
$(let structName = fromMaybe "" . lastMay . splitElem '.' . show
                 $ "EmailVerificationPayload
     lowercaseFirst (x:xs) = toLower [x] <> xs
     lowercaseFirst xs = xs
     options = defaultOptions
                 { fieldLabelModifier = lowercaseFirst . drop (length
                   structName)
                 }
  in deriveJSON options "EmailVerificationPayload)
```

This looks daunting, but this is basically the same code block that we have seen in the JSON section in Chapter 2. This is used to derive the `FromJSON` and `ToJSON` implementation for `EmailVerificationPayload`. Ideally, we will have this as a utility function. However, let's stick with this for now.

The preceding function allows us to convert `EmailVerificationPayload` to a JSON with the following structure:

```
{ "email": "abc@aaa.com", "verificationCode": "bv87sadg9" }
```

Now that we have defined the structure and made it serializable to JSON, it's time to implement the `notifyEmailVerification` function that is defined in the `Domain.Auth` module.

```
notifyEmailVerification :: (Rabbit r m)
                       => D.Email -> D.VerificationCode -> m ()
notifyEmailVerification email vCode =
  let payload = EmailVerificationPayload (D.rawEmail email) vCode
  in  publish "auth" "userRegistered" payload
```

The function is quite straightforward. We just build the message based on the input parameters, and then publish it to the "auth" exchange while using "userRegistered" as the routing key.

Next, we want to implement the consumer of this message. In the previous section, we defined the initConsumer function. The handler that we pass in to that function should be of the type Message -> IO Bool. The following function is the message handler that is supposed to a user registration event.

```
consumeEmailVerification :: (M.InMemory r m, KatipContext m, MonadCatch m)
                       => (m Bool -> IO Bool) -> Message -> IO Bool
consumeEmailVerification runner msg =
  runner $ consumeAndProcess msg handler
  where
    handler payload = do
      case D.mkEmail (emailVerificationPayloadEmail payload) of
        Left err -> withMsgAndErr msg err $ do
          $(logTM) ErrorS "Email format is invalid. Rejecting."
          return False
        Right email -> do
          let vCode = emailVerificationPayloadVerificationCode payload
          M.notifyEmailVerification email vCode
          return True
```

The first parameter is a function that converts m Bool to IO Bool. m is constrained to (M.InMemory r m, KatipContext m, MonadCatch m). KatipContext m and MonadCatch m is there, since we use consumeAndProcess in the function body. M.InMemory r m is there because we will simply store the message in memory for now using a function that we have already defined in Chapter 3.

consumeAndProcess returns m Bool, but we need the function to return IO Bool. This is where the runner function comes into play: to convert m Bool to IO Bool.

In the `handler` inner function, what we do is to parse the email from the payload and check whether it's a valid email or not. If it's not valid, we will just log the error and return `False`. Otherwise, we proceed to call `M.notifyEmailVerification` and return `True`.

Finally, we just need a function to set up the necessary network topology and listener. Let's call this function "init":

```
init  :: (M.InMemory r m, KatipContext m, MonadCatch m)
      => State -> (m Bool -> IO Bool) -> IO ()
init state runner = do
  initQueue state "verifyEmail" "auth" "userRegistered"
  initConsumer state "verifyEmail" (consumeEmailVerification runner)
```

The function is quite simple. We just create a queue, which implicitly creates an exchange as well, and initialize the consumer.

Tying Them All Up

We have finished writing the repository implementation. Now it's time to integrate this implementation to our application. Go to the `Lib` module and write the following import lines:

```
+import qualified Adapter.RabbitMQ.Common as MQ
+import qualified Adapter.RabbitMQ.Auth as MQAuth
```

Next, we need to modify the `State` to include the `MQ.State`:

```
-type State = (PG.State, Redis.State, TVar M.State)
+type State = (PG.State, Redis.State, MQ.State, TVar M.State)
```

Since we need our application monad to be an instance of `MonadCatch`, we will need to modify our monad too. Simply `MonadCatch` as follows:

```
 newtype App a = App
   { unApp :: ReaderT State (KatipContextT IO) a
   } deriving ( Applicative, Functor, Monad, MonadReader State, MonadIO
-             , KatipContext, Katip, MonadThrow)
+             , KatipContext, Katip, MonadThrow, MonadCatch)
```

Next, we will modify the `EmailVerificationNotif` instance implementation of the App. Previously, we put the message in memory using the `M.notifyEmailVerification` function. Now, we want to send it to RabbitMQ before putting it into memory. To do that, we just need to use the `MQAuth.notifyEmailVerification`. So, our implementation will be as follows:

```
 instance EmailVerificationNotif App where
-  notifyEmailVerification = M.notifyEmailVerification
+  notifyEmailVerification = MQAuth.notifyEmailVerification
```

Moving on, we need to modify the `someFunc` function to initialize the RabbitMQ state. The changes required are to call `MQ.withState` and `MQAuth.init`, as follows:

```
someFunc :: IO ()
someFunc = withKatip $ \le -> do
  mState <- newTVarIO M.initialState
  PG.withState pgCfg $ \pgState ->
    Redis.withState redisCfg $ \redisState ->
      MQ.withState mqCfg 16 $ \mqState -> do
        let runner = run le (pgState, redisState, mqState, mState)
        MQAuth.init mqState runner
        runner action
  where
    mqCfg = "amqp://guest:guest@localhost:5672/%2F"
    redisCfg = "redis://localhost:6379/0"
    pgCfg =
      PG.Config
        { PG.configUrl = "postgresql://localhost/hauth"
        , PG.configStripeCount = 2
        , PG.configMaxOpenConnPerStripe = 5
        , PG.configIdleConnTimeout = 10
        }
```

We arbitrarily pick 16 as the prefetch count. Ideally you would experiment with this value to find one that fits the application use case and the hardware it runs on.

The function is getting too complex now. Let's just refactor a bit and extract the "state initialization" piece to its own function named withState:

```haskell
withState :: (LogEnv -> State -> IO ()) -> IO ()
withState action =
  withKatip $ \le -> do
    mState <- newTVarIO M.initialState
    PG.withState pgCfg $ \pgState ->
      Redis.withState redisCfg $ \redisState ->
        MQ.withState mqCfg $ \mqState -> do
          let state = (pgState, redisState, mqState, mState)
          action le state
  where
    mqCfg = "amqp://guest:guest@localhost:5672/%2F"
    redisCfg = "redis://localhost:6379/0"
    pgCfg = PG.Config
      { PG.configUrl = "postgresql://localhost/hauth"
      , PG.configStripeCount = 2
      , PG.configMaxOpenConnPerStripe = 5
      , PG.configIdleConnTimeout = 10
      }

main :: IO ()
main =
  withState $ \le state@(_, _, mqState, _) -> do
    let runner = run le state
    MQAuth.init mqState runner
    runner action
```

While we are at it, we also rename someFunc to main. Due to this change, we will need to make changes in a few places. Try compiling the code and see if you can fix the compile errors. It should be simple.

Finally, we need to modify the `action` function. Previously, we wrote the email verification notification directly to an in-memory database. So, we expected that the notification was stored immediately. Now, since we're using RabbitMQ, the notification is being processed on a separate thread. This means that the notification will take a while before appearing in our in-memory database. To cater for this, we will repeatedly poll the message, blocking until it's available. That functionality exists in the `pollNotif` function, as you can see in the following code:

```
action :: App ()
action = do
  randEmail <- liftIO $ stringRandomIO "[a-z0-9]{5}@test\\.com"
  let email = either undefined id $ mkEmail randEmail
      passw = either undefined id $ mkPassword "1234ABCDefgh"
      auth = Auth email passw
  register auth
  vCode <- pollNotif email
  verifyEmail vCode
  Right session <- login auth
  Just uId <- resolveSessionId session
  Just registeredEmail <- getUser uId
  print (session, uId, registeredEmail)
  where
    pollNotif email = do
      result <- M.getNotificationsForEmail email
      case result of
        Nothing -> pollNotif email
        Just vCode -> return vCode
```

Try going to the REPL and run the `main` function. Assuming you have Redis, PostgreSQL, and RabbitMQ running, you should see the logs as usual. This means that you have correctly implemented the RabbitMQ integration. Congratulations!

Summary

In this chapter, we have learned to integrate RabbitMQ to our application.

RabbitMQ is a popular queueing system. We use it primarily to offload tasks that are not necessary to be processed immediately. By offloading such tasks, our application should be more responsive to the user.

amqp is a Haskell package for interfacing with RabbitMQ. The library is quite low level but is easy to use. We have learned how to open a connection and a channel, declaring network topology, sending messages, and consuming messages. We use this knowledge to implement email verification logic that is backed by RabbitMQ.

CHAPTER 7

RESTful APIs

In this chapter, we are going to explore how to do web programming in Haskell. When building web applications, it's common to use a web framework. Haskell also has such frameworks. The most popular ones are scotty,[1] servant,[2] and yesod.[3] All those frameworks are built on top of wai.[4] wai is a Haskell package that defines the types for HTTP request and response. It has no actual implementation. The only production-ready implementation of wai is warp.[5]

scotty is a minimal web framework for Haskell. "Framework" may be an overstatement. scotty is more like a library that handles routing, parsing HTTP requests, and building HTTP responses.

servant is another minimal web framework. It's newer than scotty. The differentiating feature of servant is that you'll use advanced type-level programming to define routes and handle the request. However, the downside is that compilation errors are usually harder to understand.

yesod, unlike the others, is a fully fledged web framework.

In this book, we will use scotty as our web framework. I find that scotty is very pleasant to work with and easy to grok.

Scotty Basics

scotty is just a thin layer on top of wai. It provides a friendlier way to do routing, parsing HTTP requests, and building HTTP responses. In this section, we will explore each one of them to get a better understanding of how to use them.

---

[1]www.stackage.org/lts-10.3/package/scotty-0.11.0
[2]stackage.org/lts-10.3/package/servant-0.11
[3]www.stackage.org/lts-10.3/package/yesod-1.4.5
[4]www.stackage.org/lts-10.3/package/wai-3.2.1.1
[5]www.stackage.org/lts-10.3/package/warp-3.2.13

© Ecky Putrady 2018
E. Putrady, *Practical Web Development with Haskell*, https://doi.org/10.1007/978-1-4842-3739-7_7

Hello, Scotty

Let's start by writing a simple hello world application with scotty. First, list scotty as our dependency in a package.yaml file:

```
dependencies:
- scotty
```

We will write our hello world code in a module named Adapter.HTTP.Main. The code is as follows:

```
module Adapter.HTTP.Main where

import ClassyPrelude hiding (delete)
import Web.Scotty.Trans

main :: IO ()
main =
  scottyT 3000 id routes

routes :: (MonadIO m) => ScottyT LText m ()
routes =
  get "/hello" $ text "Hello!"
```

In the preceding code, we define a GET route, /hello, that will return a text Hello!. Before explaining in more detail about the code, let's first try running that to make sure it works. Open the REPL and type the following snippet:

```
> :l Adapter.HTTP.Main -- load the file
> main
Setting phasers to stun... (port 3000) (ctrl-c to quit)
```

Open http://localhost:3000/hello in your browser and you should see "Hello!" being printed on the screen.

Now let's dive a bit into the code. First, we look into scottyT. scottyT is the function that "kicks" the scotty application to run. The type signature for that function is:

```
scottyT :: (Monad m, MonadIO n)
        => Port
        -> (m Response -> IO Response)
        -> ScottyT e m ()
        -> n ()
```

The first parameter, Port, is just a synonym for Int. It specifies to which port our application listens. In our case, we set it to 3000.

The second parameter is a function to transform the monad m we are using in our Scotty application into IO. In our case, our monad m is IO. It means we are asked to supply a function IO Response -> IO Response. Since we don't do anything with it, we supply id as the function. Recall that id is the "identity" function. It returns the input as the output.

The third parameter is the Scotty application to be run. We define our Scotty application in the routes function. We will look into that function in more detail in the next section.

Routing

Defining routes in Scotty is straightforward. I'll write some code first, and then explain what they are.

```
routes :: (MonadIO m) => ScottyT LText m ()
routes = do

  get "/" $ text "home"

  get "/hello/:name" $ do
    name <- param ":name"
    text $ "Hello, " <> name

  post "/users" $ text "adding user"

  put "/users/:id" $ text "updating user"

  patch "/users/:id" $ text "partially updating users"

  delete "/users/:id" $ text "deleting user"

  matchAny "/admin" $ text "I don't care about your HTTP verb"

  options (regex ".*") $ text "CORS usually use this"

  notFound $ text "404"
```

In the preceding code, the pieces before $ are the routes definition, while the pieces after $ are "action" that will be carried out when the route is requested.

The routes are processed from top to bottom. The first route that matches the request will have its action executed. Once a route is a match, the rule matching logic will not be carried out for the subsequent routes.

As you can see, Scotty supports common HTTP verbs: GET, POST, PUT, PATCH, DELETE, and OPTIONS.

matchAny will match any verb. In the preceding code, the action in /admin path will be executed regardless of the verb in the request.

notFound actually matches any verb and any path. So, make sure to put it at the very end of your routes definition. You define this route to handle requests that don't match any route.

The first parameter of those functions (get, put, etc.) is path definition. There are multiple ways to define the path.

The first one is with String, like "/users". By using this approach, you are looking for an exact path match.

The second one is also with String, but you supply a path parameter, like "/users/:id". This definition matches /users/ecky or /users/jack. The :id part is a parameter that you can later get in the action. We will see more about this in the next section. You may also define multiple path parameters, like "/users/:userId/books/:bookId".

The third one is using regex, like regex "^/page.*". That regex matches anything that starts with /page. You may also capture the path using standard regex capture syntax, like regex "^/users/(\\d+)/books/(\\d+)$". We will see more about capturing path parameters in the next section.

Request Parameters

There are multiple ways to get a user's input from the HTTP request. The first one is to read parameters from the path. The second one is by parsing the query parameters. The third one is to read from HTTP headers. Finally, we can also parse the HTTP request body.

As we have seen in the previous section, we can define parameters in the path by using String and regex. Let's study the following code:

```
routes :: (MonadIO m) => ScottyT LText m ()
routes = do
  get "/users/:userId/books/:bookId" $ do
    userId <- param "userId"
    bookId <- param "bookId"
    text $ userId <> " - " <> bookId

  get (regex "^/users/(.+)/investments/(.+)$") $ do
    fullPath <- param "0"
    userId <- param "1"
    investmentId <- param "2"
    text $ fullPath <> " : " <> userId <> " - " <> investmentId
```

To get the path parameter, we use the param function with the parameter name. If we define the path using String, we can use the exact parameter name from the path as the parameter in the param function. However, if we use regex, we need to use their position as the name.

For parsing query parameters, the function to use is also param. param reads from multiple places in the request. It first looks at the path and sees if there is any matching parameter. If it's not found, then it looks into the HTTP request body. If the request body is in URL-encoded format and the parameter being searched appears in the body, then it will return it. If the parameter does not exist there, then it will look into the query parameters. Finally, if it's still not found, it will throw a ScottyError. We will see how to handle exceptions in a later section.

param has the following type signature:

```
param :: (Parsable a, ScottyError e, Monad m) => Text -> ActionT e m a
```

ActionT e m a is a monad for a single route. From the preceding type signature, we can infer that param returns any type that is an instance of Parsable a. scotty comes with predefined Parsable instances, such as instances for Bool, Text, or Int. If you need, you can also create a new instance for your type.

If param found the parameter but the type doesn't match, this route is simply skipped. For example, let's say we have the following route:

```
routes =
  get "/add/:p1/:p2" $ do
    p1 <- param "p1"
    p2 <- param "p2"
    let sum = p1 + p2 :: Int
    text "Finish adding!"
```

If the HTTP request is GET /add/not/number, the action defined in the preceding code will not be executed. To get the parameter in the HTTP request header, the functions to use are:

```
header :: (ScottyError e, Monad m) => LText -> ActionT e m (Maybe LText)
headers :: (ScottyError e, Monad m) => ActionT e m [(LText, LText)]
```

The difference between those two functions is that the first one gets the header value with the given parameter, while the second one gets all headers. As you can see, the first one returns a Maybe, indicating that the value might not be found.

To get the raw HTTP request body, the function to use is as follows:

```
body :: (ScottyError e, MonadIO m) => ActionT e m LByteString
```

scotty provides a utility function to parse JSON from the HTTP request body with the following function:

```
jsonData :: (FromJSON a, ScottyError e, MonadIO m) => ActionT e m a
```

The FromJSON a constraint says that this function will decode the raw HTTP request body to a value that is an instance of the FromJSON typeclass. In a case where the HTTP request body can't be converted to the target type, this function will throw an exception. You will see how to handle the exception in the next section.

Handling Exceptions

ScottyError is a typeclass for exceptions that can be thrown from within the route action. Actually, this is not a technically correct term. ScottyError has no relation at all to Haskell's exception. ScottyError is more like a short-circuit mechanism for scotty. However, the way it is designed feels like an exception mechanism, as we will see shortly. For this reason, we will just call this an "exception" although it's not technically correct.

For throwing exceptions, we can use the raise function that has the following type signature:

```
raise :: (ScottyError e, Monad m) => e -> ActionT e m a
```

One instance of ScottyError that by default comes from scotty is LText. It means that we can just pass in LText to the raise function.

If raise is executed in a route, the code following after it will not be executed. For example, let's study the following code:

```
routes :: (MonadIO m) => ScottyT LText m ()
routes =
  get "/users" $ do
    raise "Something failed!"
    text "will never be executed"
```

If you run the code and call GET /users endpoint, you will encounter an internal server error. That is because of the raise function there.

We can recover from ScottyErrors using rescue. rescue has the following type signature:

```
rescue :: (ScottyError e, Monad m)
       => ActionT e m a -> (e -> ActionT e m a) -> ActionT e m a
```

An example usage of rescue would be like the following:

```
routes :: (MonadIO m) => ScottyT LText m ()
routes =
  get "/users" $
    raise "Something failed!" `rescue` \_ -> text "just kidding!"
```

If we run the preceding program, the server will respond with "just kidding!".

One common use case for `rescue` is if you want to have a default value for query parameters. Query parameters, by convention, are optional. However, as we have seen, the `param` function will throw an exception if the parameter can't be found within the request. By using `rescue` after `param`, we can provide a default value for such cases. For example:

```
routes :: (MonadIO m) => ScottyT LText m ()
routes =
  get "/hello" $ do
    name <- param "name" `rescue` \_ -> return "anonymous"
    text $ "Hello, " <> name
```

If we run the preceding program and perform a request to GET `/hello`, the server will respond with `Hello, anonymous`. On the other hand, if we perform a request to GET `/hello?name=John`, the server will respond with `Hello, John`.

All uncaught exceptions are by default converted to a 500 (internal server error) response with an error string. We may override this behavior using the `defaultHandler` function. For example:

```
routes :: (MonadIO m) => ScottyT LText m ()
routes = do
  get "/users" $
    raise "Something failed!"

  defaultHandler $ \_ ->
    text "Something went wrong. We are looking into it!"
```

Building Responses

There are multiple parts of the HTTP response that we can build: status code, headers, and body.

For setting status code, the function to use is `status`:

```
status :: Monad m => Status -> ActionT e m ()
```

The first parameter is of the type `Status`. This type comes from the `http-types`[6] package. If you are going to use this function, then you need to list `http-types` in

---

our package.yaml and import the Network.HTTP.Types.Status module. There are predefined status codes available from that module, for example, ok200, accepted202, and internalServerError500.

The function to add response headers is addHeader:

```
addHeader :: Monad m => LText -> LText -> ActionT e m ()
addHeader key value
```

For writing raw LByteString to the HTTP response body, the function to use is raw:

```
raw :: Monad m => LByteString -> ActionT e m ()
```

In practice, actually, you will rarely use raw. You usually want to use one or more of the following functions:

```
text :: (ScottyError e, Monad m) => LText -> ActionT e m ()
html :: (ScottyError e, Monad m) => LText -> ActionT e m ()
json :: (ToJSON a, ScottyError e, Monad m) => a -> ActionT e m ()
```

In addition to writing the given value to the HTTP response body, the preceding functions also set the correct HTTP header. For example, json adds Content-Type: application/json; charset=utf-8 to the header.

An example of how one would set HTTP response would be:

```
routes :: (MonadIO m) => ScottyT LText m ()
routes =
  get "/hello" $ do
    status unauthorized401
    addHeader "serverName" "gandalfService"
    text "you shall not pass!"
```

Middleware

When you are building a web application, there might be some shared functionalities that you want to run on all HTTP requests—for example, intercepting a request for a static resource, logging, or gzipping response.

Middleware is a way to organize such shared behavior. Middleware runs before the HTTP request enters your application and after the response is produced by your application. Figure 7-1 illustrates this relationship.

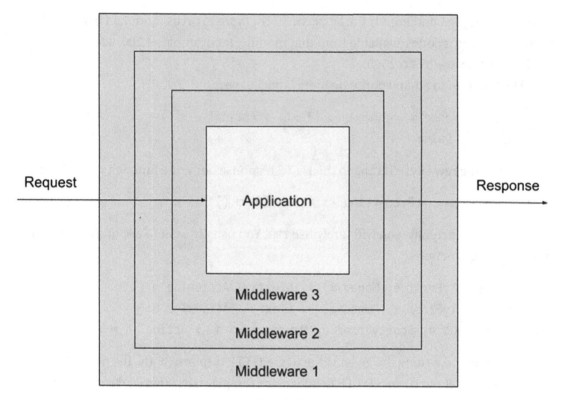

Figure 7-1. *Relationship between middleware and application*

There are several middlewares already available, for example:

- Gzip[7]: allows response to be GZipped depending on client's sent headers

- VHost[8]: routes requests to a configured wai application

- HttpAuth[9]: HTTP Basic Authentication

- Static[10]: serves static files

- RequestLogger[11]: logs HTTP request

---

[7]www.stackage.org/haddock/lts-10.3/wai-extra-3.0.21.0/Network-Wai-Middleware-Gzip.html

[8]www.stackage.org/haddock/lts-10.3/wai-extra-3.0.21.0/Network-Wai-Middleware-Vhost.html

[9]www.stackage.org/haddock/lts-10.3/wai-extra-3.0.21.0/Network-Wai-Middleware-HttpAuth.html

[10]www.stackage.org/package/wai-middleware-static

[11]www.stackage.org/haddock/lts-10.4/wai-extra-3.0.22.0/Network-Wai-Middleware-RequestLogger.html

If you look into the documentation of the preceding, you will notice that each of them has a function that outputs a `Middleware` type. Once we have this `Middleware` type, we can use scotty's `middleware` function to enable the middleware. The following code snippet shows how the function is used:

```
routes :: (MonadIO m) => ScottyT LText m ()
routes = do
  -- gzip
  middleware $ gzip (def { gzipFiles = GzipCompress })
  -- request logging
  middleware logStdout
  -- serve static files
  middleware static

  get "/hello" $
    text "Hello!"
```

The middleware that is first declared is the first one that is executed before entering the application and the last one to be executed after the response is produced by the application. In other words, the first declared middleware is the outermost middleware, as shown in Figure 7-1.

Cookies

A cookie is a piece of data that the server sends to the browser and the browser will resend this data back to the server on subsequent requests. It is a common mechanism for maintaining a user's state.

Let's see an example. Say that a browser sends the following HTTP request:

```
GET /index.html HTTP/1.1
Host: www.test.com
```

The server responds with two `Set-Cookie` headers:

```
HTTP/1.1 200 OK
Set-Cookie: key1=val1
Set-Cookie: sessionId=123abc
```

The browser will store these cookies somehow and will resend them on subsequent requests. For example, let's say that the browser sends another HTTP request to a different path:

```
GET /about.html HTTP/1.1
Host: www.test.com
Cookie: key1=val1; sessionId=123abc
```

Notice that the cookies that the server sent earlier are being resent back in a header with key Cookie.

There's more to Set-Cookie than just key and values. There are other settings such as HttpOnly and Expires that allow you to control the behavior of the cookie. You may look into the documentation provided by Mozilla[12] for the list of available parameters.

Since Set-Cookie and Cookie follow a certain format, there is a Haskell package that allows us to work with the format easily. The package is neatly called cookie.[13]

For creating a Set-Cookie value, we can use the defaultSetCookie function and override some fields as necessary. For example:

```
defaultSetCookie
  { setCookieName = "cookieName"
  , setCookieValue = "cookieValue"
  , setCookiePath = Just "/"
  , setCookieMaxAge = Just 7200
  , setCookieHttpOnly = True
  , setCookieSameSite = Just sameSiteLax
  }
```

defaultSetCookie produces SetCookie type. To convert this type to the actual Set-Cookie format, the function to use is renderSetCookie. renderSetCookie receives SetCookie and produces Builder. Builder comes from the blaze-builder[14] package. We won't dive deep into the details of this library, as we won't use it much. We just need to know that this package has a toLazyByteString function that allows us to convert Builder to LByteString.

---

[12]https://developer.mozilla.org/en-US/docs/Web/HTTP/Headers/Set-Cookie
[13]www.stackage.org/lts-10.3/package/cookie-0.4.3
[14]www.stackage.org/lts-10.3/package/blaze-builder-0.4.0.2

scotty's addHeader function expects an LText. So we need to convert this LByteString to LText. The function to use is decodeUtf8.

All in all, the following code snippet shows how one would send cookies in scotty:

```
setCookie :: (ScottyError e, Monad m) => SetCookie -> ActionT e m ()
setCookie =
  addHeader "Set-Cookie" . decodeUtf8 . toLazyByteString . renderSetCookie
```

Moving on to parsing cookies that are sent by the browser: as you can see in the preceding code, cookies are sent via HTTP headers named Cookie. So, we first need to get the whole value from the header using scotty's header function. header returns an LText. However, the function to parse the cookies, parseCookies, expects a ByteString. So, we need to convert this LText to ByteString. The function to use is encodeUtf8 . toStrict.

parseCookies returns Cookies type, which is a synonym for [(ByteString, ByteString)]. It's a list of key-value pairs.

The following code snippet shows how one would get a cookie value with a specific key:

```
getCookie :: (ScottyError e, Monad m) => Text -> ActionT e m (Maybe Text)
getCookie key = do
  mCookieStr <- header "Cookie"
  return $ do
    cookie <- parseCookies . encodeUtf8 . toStrict <$> mCookieStr
    let bsKey = encodeUtf8 key
    val <- lookup bsKey cookie
    return $ decodeUtf8 val
```

Input Validation

Validating input is always necessary when developing a web application. We can't just trust the user input. The user might send a payload that doesn't conform to the structure that we expect or send a string where it should have been an integer.

For handling input validation, the package to use is digestive-functors.[15] This package makes validating and reporting errors easier. For example, in JSON, you'll get the error message in the same fields as the input.

---

[15]https://www.stackage.org/package/digestive-functors

There are two important types to know in this package: Form v m a and View v. Form is used for doing the validation, while View is used for error reporting.

The v in Form v m a is used to indicate the error type. The m is the monad we are operating with. The a is the result of the validation. For example, Form Text IO Email means this form operates under the IO monad, outputs Email on successful validation, and outputs Text as the error message.

Let's use our own Auth type for an example. Recall that Auth has the following structure:

```
newtype Email = Email { rawEmail :: Text }

newtype Password = Password { rawPassword :: Text }

data Auth = Auth

  { authEmail :: Email
  , authPassword :: Password
  }
```

We also have a special validation function for email and password: mkEmail and mkPassword:

```
mkEmail :: Text -> Either [ErrMsg] Email
mkPassword :: Text -> Either [ErrMsg] Password
```

We can create the Form as follows:

```
import Text.Digestive.Form ((.:))
import qualified Text.Digestive.Form as DF

authForm :: (Monad m) => DF.Form [Text] m Auth
authForm =
  Auth <$> "email" .: emailForm
       <*> "password" .: passwordForm
  where
    emailForm = DF.validate (toResult . mkEmail) (DF.text Nothing)
    passwordForm = DF.validate (toResult . mkPassword) (DF.text Nothing)

toResult :: Either e a -> DF.Result e a
toResult = either DF.Error DF.Success
```

((.:)) is used to label a part of the form. Later, such a label is used for parsing the correct field from the input and error reporting. For example, if the input is a URL-encoded string, the labels correspond to the key value in the string, for example, email=abc@def. com&password=abcDEF123. On the other hand, if your input is JSON, the labels will match:

```
{
  "email": "abc@def.com"
  "password": "abcDEF123"
}
```

DF.Validate has the following type:

```
DF.validate :: (Monad m, Monoid v)
            => (a -> DF.Result v b) -> DF.Form v m a -> DF.Form v m b
DF.Result v a = DF.Error v | DF.Success a
```

The first parameter is a function that is used to validate the input. It returns DF. Result, a type that is similar to Either. Our mkEmail and mkPassword function returns an Either. So, we need to convert that to DF.Result. We created a small function named toResult to do this conversion.

In the preceding example, we use DF.text Nothing as the second parameter of the DF.validate function. That particular part means that we are getting a Text from the input and there is no default value. There are other functions that we can use to read from the input, for example, DF.bool and DF.stringRead. Much more can be found in the official documentation.

Now that we have defined a Form, we need to run it against our input. For JSON input, we would need to include the digestive-functors-aeson[16] package. This package provides two functions:

```
digestJSON :: Monad m
           => Form v m a
           -- ^ The form to evaluate.
           -> Value
           -- ^ The JSON document to use for validation.
           -> m (View v, Maybe a)

jsonErrors :: ToJSON v => View v -> Value
```

---

[16]https://www.stackage.org/package/digestive-functors-aeson

digestJSON returns (View v, Maybe a). If the form evaluation is successful, the Maybe will be a Just. Otherwise, it will be a Nothing. View will always be available regardless of the form evaluation result. View contains the error messages as well as the actual input. Typically, you will handle the result of form evaluation as follows:

```
evaluateFormAndHandle someJSON = do
  result <- digestJSON authForm someJSON
  case result of
    (_, Just val) -> -- handle success
    (v, _) -> -- handle failure
```

jsonErrors is a small function to convert View to Value. It will format the errors so that it corresponds to the input—for example, if you give an input like this:

```
{ "email": "email", "password": "notAPassword" }
```

Then jsonErrors will output the following assuming the error type is a list of Text:

```
{
  "email": ["your defined error message"],
  "password": ["your defined error message"]
}
```

In this section, we only saw briefly how digestive-functors is used to validate JSON input. In the later chapter, we will see how digestive-functor is used to handle HTML forms.

Implementing RESTful API

Our application has four main functionalities: registration, email verification, login, and getting the user details. In this section, we will implement RESTful APIs so that those functionalities can be invoked via HTTP.

Overview

Let's first define the APIs:

```
Registration:
  Request:
    POST /api/auth/register
    {
      "email": "abc@def.com",
      "password": "abcDEF123"
    }

  Response:
    Wrong email or password format:
      400
      {
        "email": "errmsg",
        "password": "errmsg"
      }

    Email taken:
      400
      "EmailTaken"

    Success:
      200

Email verification:
  Request:
    POST /api/auth/verifyEmail
    "verificationCode"

  Response:
    Invalid input:
      400
      "required"
```

```
    Invalid code:
      400
      "InvalidCode"

    Success:
      200

Login:
  Request:
    POST /api/auth/login
    {
      "email": "abc@def.com",
      "password": "abcDEF123"
    }

  Response:
    Invalid input:
      400
      {
        "email": "errmsg",
        "password": "errmsg"
      }

    Invalid auth:
      400
      "InvalidAuth"

    Email not yet verified:
      400
      "EmailNotVerified"

    Success:
      200

Get User:
  Request:
    GET /api/users
```

```
Response:
  Not authenticated:
    401
      "AuthRequired"

  Succes:
    200
    "abc@def"
```

We also want to add a gzip compression on every request to improve performance.
We start by adding the necessary dependencies in `package.yaml`:

```
dependencies:
```

- http-types

- scotty

- cookie

- wai

- wai-extra

- blaze-builder

- digestive-functors

- digestive-functors-aeson

Also, add extra dependencies in `stack.yaml` if necessary. For example:

```
extra-deps:
```

- digestive-functors-0.8.3.0

- digestive-functors-aeson-1.1.22

For implementing the HTTP-related code, we will split the code into three modules:

1. `Adapter.HTTP.API.Auth`: Handle HTTP routings for auth related
   functionalities

2. `Adapter.HTTP.Common`: Common functionalities that may be
   shared throughout other HTTP routes, for example, setting and
   reading cookies

3. `Adapter.HTTP.Main`: Compose the routes and start the HTTP server

Adapter.HTTP.Common Implementation

We will begin our implementation from Adapter.HTTP.Common module with the function to parse and validate JSON input:

```
module Adapter.HTTP.Common where

import ClassyPrelude
import Web.Scotty.Trans
import qualified Text.Digestive.Form as DF
import qualified Text.Digestive.Types as DF
import qualified Text.Digestive.Aeson as DF
import Data.Aeson hiding (json)
import Network.HTTP.Types.Status

parseAndValidateJSON :: (ScottyError e, MonadIO m, ToJSON v)
                        => DF.Form v m a -> ActionT e m a
parseAndValidateJSON form = do
val <- jsonData `rescue` (\_ -> return Null)
validationResult <- lift $ DF.digestJSON form val
case validationResult of
  (v, Nothing) -> do
    status status400
    json $ DF.jsonErrors v
    finish
  (_, Just result) ->
    return result
```

The main use of the parseAndValidate function is to parse JSON from the HTTP request body and run the form. If the validation results in an error, we want to immediately respond with 400, indicating a bad request, and put the error messages in the HTTP response body.

jsonData is a function that comes from scotty. It's the function that parses the HTTP body to JSON. The function may throw an error in the case of malformed JSON. In this case, we want to recover the error and just return a Null JSON value.

DF.digestJSON comes from Text.Digestive.Aeson and is used to run the given form against the parsed JSON value.

Next, we have a small function that is related to form: toResult. It's used to convert Either to DF.Result that is used by digestive-functors for form validation.

```
toResult :: Either e a -> DF.Result e a
toResult = either DF.Error DF.Success
```

We have seen the following functions in the previous section. These functions are used to manage cookies:

```
import Blaze.ByteString.Builder (toLazyByteString)
import Web.Cookie

setCookie :: (ScottyError e, Monad m) => SetCookie -> ActionT e m ()
setCookie =
  setHeader "Set-Cookie" . decodeUtf8 . toLazyByteString . renderSetCookie

getCookie :: (ScottyError e, Monad m) => Text -> ActionT e m (Maybe Text)
getCookie key = do
  mCookieStr <- header "Cookie"
  return $ do
    cookie <- parseCookies . encodeUtf8 . toStrict <$> mCookieStr
    let bsKey = encodeUtf8 key
    val <- lookup bsKey cookie
    return $ decodeUtf8 val
```

In our application, we use the cookies for session management. So, we add the following functions:

```
import Domain.Auth
import Data.Time.Lens

setSessionIdInCookie :: (MonadIO m, ScottyError e) => SessionId ->
ActionT e m ()
setSessionIdInCookie sId = do
  curTime <- liftIO getCurrentTime
  setCookie $ def { setCookieName = "sId"
                  , setCookiePath = Just "/"
                  , setCookieValue = encodeUtf8 sId
                  , setCookieExpires = Just $ modL month (+ 1) curTime
```

```
                , setCookieHttpOnly = True
                , setCookieSecure = False
                , setCookieSameSite = Just sameSiteLax
                }

getCurrentUserId :: (SessionRepo m, ScottyError e) => ActionT e m
(Maybe UserId)
getCurrentUserId = do
  maySessionId <- getCookie "sId"
  case maySessionId of
    Nothing -> return Nothing
    Just sId -> lift $ resolveSessionId sId

reqCurrentUserId :: (SessionRepo m, ScottyError e) => ActionT e m UserId
reqCurrentUserId = do
  mayUserId <- getCurrentUserId
  case mayUserId of
    Nothing -> do
      status status401
      json ("AuthRequired" :: Text)
      finish
    Just userId ->
      return userId
```

setSessionIdInCookie is used to set the cookie that is going to be sent to the client with relevant details. As you can see, we put in the SessionId as the cookie value. We also set the expiry to be one month from now.

getCurrentUserId is used to infer the current UserId from the HTTP request. We first get the relevant cookie that contains SessionId information. Once we have this SessionId, we use the resolveSessionId function from the Domain.Auth module to get the current UserId. Since the request might not contain SessionId, the return value of that function is a Maybe.

reqCurrentUserId is similar to getCurrentUserId. The difference is that we just respond with 401 and finish processing the request. We use this to guard the endpoint that requires the user to be authenticated.

Adapter.HTTP.API.Auth Implementation

We now move to the implementation of `Adapter.HTTP.API.Auth`. This module is responsible for interpreting an HTTP request to our domain logic and vice versa.

```
module Adapter.HTTP.API.Auth where

import ClassyPrelude
import Web.Scotty.Trans
import Domain.Auth
import qualified Text.Digestive.Form as DF
import Text.Digestive.Form ((.:))
import Adapter.HTTP.Common
import Network.HTTP.Types.Status
import Data.Aeson hiding (json, (.:))
import Katip

routes :: ( ScottyError e, MonadIO m, KatipContext m, AuthRepo m
          , EmailVerificationNotif m, SessionRepo m)
       => ScottyT e m ()
routes = do
  -- register
  post "/api/auth/register" undefined

  -- verify email
  post "/api/auth/verifyEmail" undefined

  -- login
  post "/api/auth/login" undefined

  -- get user
  get "/api/users" undefined
```

In the preceding code snippet, we imported the necessary modules and defined the routes in a single function. The long list of type constraints on `routes` is necessary for our implementation later.

Let's implement the "register" route now. Update the "register" route within the routes function to the following:

```
post "/api/auth/register" $ do
  input <- parseAndValidateJSON authForm
  domainResult <- lift $ register input
  case domainResult of
    Left RegistrationErrorEmailTaken -> do
      status status400
      json ("EmailTaken" :: Text)
    Right _ ->
      return ()
```

We use the parseAndValidateJSON function that we have defined in the Adapter. HTTP.Common module. The form that we are using is authForm. We will see the details of that form later. Remember that parseAndValidateJSON will not continue processing if the input does not pass form validation. If the input is valid, we store it in a binding named input. The input is then used as the input for the register function. The register function comes from the Domain.Auth module. The result of that function is an Either. We pattern match on it to see if the process returns any error. If it does, we then just translate it to HTTP response 400 and the error message. If it is a success, then we don't need to do anything, as scotty returns 200 by default.

authForm is defined as follows:

```
authForm :: (Monad m) => DF.Form [Text] m Auth
authForm =
  Auth <$> "email" .: emailForm
       <*> "password" .: passwordForm
  where
    emailForm = DF.validate (toResult . mkEmail) (DF.text Nothing)
    passwordForm = DF.validate (toResult . mkPassword) (DF.text Nothing)
```

This form definition is meant to parse JSON with the following structure:

```
{ "email": "the email", "password": "the password" }
```

Next, we implement the route to handle email verification. Update the corresponding route within the routes function to the following:

```
post "/api/auth/verifyEmail" $ do
  input <- parseAndValidateJSON verifyEmailForm
  domainResult <- lift $ verifyEmail input
  case domainResult of
    Left EmailVerificationErrorInvalidCode -> do
      status status400
      json ("InvalidCode" :: Text)
    Right _ ->
      return ()
```

The preceding logic is not much different from the registration handler.
verifyEmailForm is defined as follows:

```
verifyEmailForm :: (Monad m) => DF.Form [Text] m VerificationCode
verifyEmailForm = DF.text Nothing
```

This form is meant to parse JSON with the following structure:

```
"verification code"
```

Let's move on to the login handler. Update the code to the following:

```
post "/api/auth/login" $ do
  input <- parseAndValidateJSON authForm
  domainResult <- lift $ login input
  case domainResult of
    Left LoginErrorInvalidAuth -> do
      status status400
      json ("InvalidAuth" :: Text)
    Left LoginErrorEmailNotVerified -> do
      status status400
      json ("EmailNotVerified" :: Text)
    Right sId -> do
      setSessionIdInCookie sId
      return ()
```

In the preceding code snippet, we reuse `authForm` because the input structure for registration and login is the same. The logic is more or less the same; however, notice that there is a call to `setSessionIdInCookie`. Since this is a login, we send the `SessionId` in the cookie so that the same client can be authenticated on the subsequent calls.

Finally, we move on to the last route to implement: getting the user details. Like before, please update the code to the following:

```
get "/api/users" $ do
  userId <- reqCurrentUserId
  mayEmail <- lift $ getUser userId
  case mayEmail of
    Nothing ->
      raise $ stringError "Should not happen: SessionId map to invalid UserId"
    Just email ->
      json $ rawEmail email
```

We use `reqCurrentUserId` because the user needs to be authenticated here. If the user is not authenticated, then we will show the HTTP 401 response. The `UserId` that we got from the HTTP request is used in the `getUser` function. The function returns a `Maybe`, which means we need to pattern match it. The `Nothing` case should not happen in practice, since all valid users in our application must have email. So, if it is triggered, there is something wrong with our application code. In that case, we just raise an error. `scotty` will handle this error by responding with HTTP status 500. However, as you will see later, we will override `scotty`'s default behavior so that the error details are not exposed to the client.

Adapter.HTTP.Main Implementation

The `Adapter.HTTP.Main` module is responsible for defining the "higher-level" routes as well as running the actual server. The implementation would be as follows:

```
import Domain.Auth import ClassyPrelude
import Web.Scotty.Trans
import Network.HTTP.Types.Status
import qualified Adapter.HTTP.API.Auth as AuthAPI
import Adapter.HTTP.Common
```

```haskell
import Katip
import Network.Wai
import Network.Wai.Middleware.Gzip

main :: ( MonadIO m, KatipContext m, AuthRepo m
        , EmailVerificationNotif m, SessionRepo m)
     => Int -> (m Response -> IO Response) -> IO ()
main port runner =
  scottyT port runner routes

routes :: ( MonadIO m, KatipContext m, AuthRepo m
          , EmailVerificationNotif m, SessionRepo m)
       => ScottyT LText m ()
routes = do
  middleware $ gzip $ def { gzipFiles = GzipCompress }

  AuthAPI.routes

  defaultHandler $ \e -> do
    lift $ $(logTM) ErrorS $ "Unhandled error: " <> ls (showError e)
    status status500
    json ("InternalServerError" :: Text)
```

In the routes function, we add in gzip middleware. This middleware allows any response that is sent to the client to be compressed with Gzip, provided that the client sends a particular header.

middleware is a function that comes from scotty that accepts Middleware type. The gzip function comes from Network.Wai.Middleware.Gzip. You may refer to the documentation for more details.

After defining middlewares, we put in the AuthAPI.routes that we have just written.

Finally, we define defaultHandler that will catch any uncaught exceptions. In this function, we will just log it with the level set to ErrorS. If this is ever logged, then there's something wrong in our application and we need to look into that. After logging, we just send a 500 with a body of { "error": "InternalServerError" }.

Modification in `Lib` Module

Alright, we're almost finished. The final thing to do is to kick-start our server during application initialization. For this, we need to go to the `Lib` module.

We need to import the module that we have just written in the previous section. Add the following line in the import sections of the `Lib` module:

```
+import qualified Adapter.HTTP.Main as HTTP
```

Then, we need to modify the `withState` function to initialize HTTP port. The code will be as below.

```
-withState :: (LogEnv -> State -> IO ()) -> IO ()
+withState :: (Int -> LogEnv -> State -> IO ()) -> IO ()
 withState action =
   withKatip $ \le -> do
     mState <- newTVarIO M.initialState
     PG.withState pgCfg $ \pgState ->
       Redis.withState redisCfg $ \redisState ->
         MQ.withState mqCfg 16 $ \mqState -> do
           let state = (pgState, redisState, mqState, mState)
-          action le state
+          action port le state
   where
     mqCfg = "amqp://guest:guest@localhost:5672/%2F"
     redisCfg = "redis://localhost:6379/0"
     pgCfg =
       PG.Config
       { PG.configUrl = "postgresql://localhost/hauth"
       , PG.configStripeCount = 2
       , PG.configMaxOpenConnPerStripe = 5
       , PG.configIdleConnTimeout = 10
       }
+    port = 3000
```

`main` function also needs to be modified to be as follows:

```
 main :: IO ()
 main =
-  withState $ \le state@(_, _, mqState, _) -> do
+  withState $ \port le state@(_, _, mqState, _) -> do
     let runner = run le state
     MQAuth.init mqState runner
-    runner action
+    HTTP.main port runner
```

We replace `runner action` with `HTTP.main port runner`. We no longer need the action function. You may remove it if you wish. `HTTP.main` internally calls `scottyT`. `scottyT` blocks forever. It makes sense, since it's running a web server to handle any requests. So, this function will also block.

Running the Application

We have finished writing the necessary code for opening our application to be accessible via RESTful API. It's now time to test drive it. Go to the REPL and run the `main` function in the `Lib` module. You will see that the server runs on port 3000 and it blocks forever. You may use a REST client like Insomnia[17] to send an HTTP request to the server. If you have, you should see that the server behaves as expected.

Congratulations! We have successfully implemented a RESTful API for our application!

Summary

In this chapter, we have built RESTful APIs for our application. We started by exploring the ecosystem of web development in Haskell. Among many web development frameworks and packages, we chose to develop our RESTful APIs using `scotty` due to its simplicity.

We've looked into the basics of `scotty`, such as how to define routes, parsing an HTTP request, building HTTP response, and handling exceptions. `scotty` is pretty minimal regarding functionality.

---

[17]https://insomnia.rest/

It doesn't handle cookies management and input validation. So, we use `cookies` and `digestive-functors`, respectively, to handle them. We also looked into `Middleware`, a way to share common functionalities in a web application. We explored a few ready-to-use middlewares, such as gzip, request-response logger, etc.

The source code for this chapter is available in the attachment of this book with the same name as this chapter's number.

CHAPTER 8

Web Programming

Nowadays, RESTful API consumed by a single page application is a popular way to deliver product functionality over the Internet. This approach is more preferable if the user needs to do many state-changing operations to the application, because it will feel more responsive. However, if the application is meant to be mostly consumed, such as forums and blogs, then having a more traditional, MVC-style web application could be more preferable because it is simpler.

In this chapter, we will learn about building an MVC web application.

Serving Multiple WAI Applications

We can represent our RESTful API web application and our MVC web application as two different WAI applications. We will then use a WAI middleware to route the request to the right application. So, we will structure our HTTP module of the application as follows:

```
API/
    Auth.hs
    Common.hs
    Main.hs
Web/
    static/
        images/
            logo.png
    Auth.hs
    Common.hs
    Main.hs
Common.hs
Main.hs
```

© Ecky Putrady 2018
E. Putrady, *Practical Web Development with Haskell*, https://doi.org/10.1007/978-1-4842-3739-7_8

Anything under the API folder is only related to RESTful API, while anything under the Web folder is only related to the web MVC part.

Both folders contain a Common module. The Common module here is meant to be shared by other modules within the same folder. For example, Common in the API folder might contain a function to build a JSON response, while Common in the Web folder might contain a function to build HTML layouts. There is also a Common module at the top level. This Common module is meant to be shared by both API and Web. It contains functions like setting a cookie.

Main modules are responsible for running the application. In API, the Main module is responsible for creating the RESTful API application. The same thing also happens in the Main module under the Web folder. The Main module at the top level depends on both Main modules and sets up the necessary logic to route the request to the correct application.

Now that we have understood the overall architecture, let's hit our first milestone of properly routing the request to the correct application.

First off, list the required dependencies in `package.yaml`:

dependencies:

- `blaze-html`

- `digestive-functors-blaze`

- `digestive-functors-scotty`

- `wai-middleware-static`

- `warp`

blaze-html[1] is a package to help in building HTMLs. digestive-functors-blaze[2] is a package to bind digestive-functors's View to HTML defined with blaze-html. digestive-functors-scotty[3] is a package to do form validation with scotty. wai-middleware-static[4] is a package to serve static assets. We could use it to serve favicon, CSS, or javascript files. In our case, we will only use it to serve favicon. warp is a package to run a web server that is compatible with wai specification. Internally, scotty uses this. However, since we want to serve Web and API separately, we will need this package.

---

[1]`www.stackage.org/lts-10.3/package/blaze-html-0.9.0.1`
[2]`http://hackage.haskell.org/package/digestive-functors-blaze-0.6.2.0`
[3]`http://hackage.haskell.org/package/digestive-functors-scotty-0.2.0.2`
[4]`www.stackage.org/lts-10.3/package/wai-middleware-static-0.8.1`

Some packages my not be available in stackage, so we need to list them directly under extra-deps in the stack.yaml file:

- digestive-functors-blaze-0.6.2.0

- digestive-functors-scotty-0.2.0.2

Next, we will clean up our code a bit. Let's move some functions that are only related to API from the Adapter.HTTP.Common module to the Adapter.HTTP.API.Common module.

```haskell
module Adapter.HTTP.API.Common where

import ClassyPrelude
import Web.Scotty.Trans
import Domain.Auth
import qualified Text.Digestive.Form as DF
import qualified Text.Digestive.Aeson as DF
import Data.Aeson hiding (json)
import Network.HTTP.Types.Status
import Adapter.HTTP.Common

-- * Forms

parseAndValidateJSON :: (ScottyError e, MonadIO m, ToJSON v)
                     => DF.Form v m a -> ActionT e m a
parseAndValidateJSON form = do
  val <- jsonData `rescue` (\_ -> return Null)
  validationResult <- lift $ DF.digestJSON form val
  case validationResult of
    (v, Nothing) -> do
      status status400
      json $ DF.jsonErrors v
      finish
    (_, Just result) ->
      return result
```

```haskell
-- * Sessions

reqCurrentUserId :: (SessionRepo m, ScottyError e) => ActionT e m UserId
reqCurrentUserId = do
  mayUserId <- getCurrentUserId
  case mayUserId of
    Nothing -> do
      status status401
      json $ errorResponse ("AuthRequired" :: Text)
      finish
    Just userId ->
      return userId

-- * Error response

errorResponse :: (ToJSON a) => a -> Value
errorResponse val = object [ "error" .= val ]
```

Next, we create the Adapter.HTTP.Main module that is responsible for creating a WAI application for RESTful API.

```haskell
module Adapter.HTTP.API.Main where

import Domain.Auth
import ClassyPrelude
import Web.Scotty.Trans
import Network.HTTP.Types.Status
import qualified Adapter.HTTP.API.Auth as Auth
import Adapter.HTTP.API.Common
import Katip
import Network.Wai
import Network.Wai.Middleware.Gzip

main :: ( MonadIO m, KatipContext m, AuthRepo m
        , EmailVerificationNotif m, SessionRepo m)
     => (m Response -> IO Response) -> IO Application
main runner =
  scottyAppT runner routes
```

```
routes :: ( MonadIO m, KatipContext m, AuthRepo m
          , EmailVerificationNotif m, SessionRepo m)
       => ScottyT LText m ()
routes = do
  middleware $ gzip $ def { gzipFiles = GzipCompress }

  Auth.routes

  notFound $ do
    status status404
    json $ errorResponse ("NotFound" :: Text)

  defaultHandler $ \e -> do
    lift $ $(logTM) ErrorS $ "Unhandled error: " <> ls (showError e)
    status status500
    json $ errorResponse ("InternalServerError" :: Text)
```

As you can see, in the main function we use the scottyAppT function instead of
the scottyT function. scottyT internally calls scottyAppT and then runs the resulting
Application using warp. Since we are only interested in creating an Application here,
we use scottyAppT.

We have finished doing necessary changes in the RESTful API part. Let's now move
on to the Web part. For now, we will only create the Adapter.HTTP.Web.Main module
with some dummy routes.

```
module Adapter.HTTP.Web.Main where

import Domain.Auth
import ClassyPrelude
import Web.Scotty.Trans
import Network.HTTP.Types.Status
import Katip
import Network.Wai

main :: ( MonadIO m, KatipContext m, AuthRepo m
        , EmailVerificationNotif m, SessionRepo m)
     => (m Response -> IO Response) -> IO Application
main runner =
  scottyAppT runner routes
```

```
routes :: ( MonadIO m, KatipContext m, AuthRepo m
          , EmailVerificationNotif m, SessionRepo m)
       => ScottyT LText m ()
routes = do
  get "/" $
    text "Hello from web!"

  notFound $ do
    status status404
    text "Not found"

  defaultHandler $ \e -> do
    lift $ $(logTM) ErrorS $ "Unhandled error: " <> ls (showError e)
    status status500
    text "Internal server error!"
```

Finally, let's modify the Adapter.HTTP.Main module to the following:

```
 module Adapter.HTTP.Main where

 import Domain.Auth
 import ClassyPrelude
-import Web.Scotty.Trans
-import Network.HTTP.Types.Status
-import qualified Adapter.HTTP.API.Auth as AuthAPI
-import Adapter.HTTP.Common
+import qualified Adapter.HTTP.API.Main as API
+import qualified Adapter.HTTP.Web.Main as Web
 import Katip
 import Network.Wai
-import Network.Wai.Middleware.Gzip
+import Network.Wai.Handler.Warp
+import Network.Wai.Middleware.Vhost

 main :: ( MonadIO m, KatipContext m, AuthRepo m
         , EmailVerificationNotif m, SessionRepo m)
      => Int -> (m Response -> IO Response) -> IO ()
```

```
-main port runner =
-  scottyT port runner routes
-
-routes :: ( MonadIO m, KatipContext m, AuthRepo m
-          , EmailVerificationNotif m, SessionRepo m)
-          => ScottyT LText m ()
-routes = do
-  middleware $ gzip $ def { gzipFiles = GzipCompress }
-
-  AuthAPI.routes
-
-  defaultHandler $ \e -> do
-    lift $ $(logTM) ErrorS $ "Unhandled error: " <> ls (showError e)
-    status status500
-    json ("InternalServerError" :: Text)
+main port runner = do
+  web <- Web.main runner
+  api <- API.main runner
+  run port $ vhost [(pathBeginsWith "api", api)] web
+  where
+    pathBeginsWith path req = headMay (pathInfo req) == Just path
```

In the main function, we build two Applications, web and api using the Web.main
and API.main functions, respectively. We also use a middleware called vhost. This
function comes from the wai-extra package. It has the following type:

```
vhost :: [(Request -> Bool, Application)] -> Application -> Application
```

The first parameter is a list of tuple. The first part of the tuple is a function that tests
whether to route the request to the application in the second part of the tuple or not.
The second parameter is the default application the request will be routed to, in case the
request does not pass any test function in the list.

In our case, our test function is pathBeginsWith, which basically check whether the
request path begins with "api." The function uses pathInfo function that comes from
Network.Wai. This function receives a Request and outputs a list of string representing
the path. For example, ["api", "auth", "register"] is the output when the path is /
api/auth/register.

Now, we may run the application from the REPL and try to send HTTP request to the application. You'll notice that sending GET http://localhost:3000 will be responded by "Hello from web!" text. On the other hand, if we send a request to POST http://localhost:3000, the response will be a 400 containing a JSON about the error. This indicates that the request is correctly routed to both applications.

Implementing Web Module

In this section, we will fully implement the Web module.

Create an Adapter.HTTP.Web.Common module and write the following code:

```
module Adapter.HTTP.Web.Common where

import ClassyPrelude
import Web.Scotty.Trans
import Domain.Auth
import qualified Text.Digestive.View as DF
import Text.Blaze.Html5 ((!))
import qualified Text.Blaze.Html5 as H
import qualified Text.Blaze.Html5.Attributes as A
import qualified Text.Blaze.Html.Renderer.Text as H
import Adapter.HTTP.Common

-- * Views

renderHtml :: (ScottyError e, Monad m) => H.Html -> ActionT e m ()
renderHtml = html . H.renderHtml

mainLayout :: Text -> H.Html -> H.Html
mainLayout title content =
  H.docTypeHtml $ do
    H.head $ do
      favicon "/images/logo.png"
      H.title $ H.toHtml title
    H.body $ do
      H.div $ H.img ! A.src "/images/logo.png"
      H.div content
```

```
where
  favicon path =
    H.link  ! A.rel    "icon"
            ! A.type_  "image/png"
            ! A.href   path

formLayout :: DF.View a -> Text -> H.Html -> H.Html
formLayout view action =
  H.form  ! A.method  "POST"
          ! A.enctype (H.toValue $ show $ DF.viewEncType view)
          ! A.action  (H.toValue action)

-- * Sessions

reqCurrentUserId :: (SessionRepo m, ScottyError e) => ActionT e m UserId
reqCurrentUserId = do
  mUserId <- getCurrentUserId
  case mUserId of
    Nothing ->
      redirect "/auth/login"
    Just userId ->
      return userId
```

This module implements functions that are meant to be shared by other modules in the Web module.

reqCurrentUserId is a function to get the current UserId from the request. It internally calls getCurrentUserId. However, it will redirect the user to the /auth/login endpoint if the user is not logged in.

mainLayout is a function that builds HTML. As you can see, it uses various functions like H.head, H.body, H.link, etc. Those HTML-related functions come from the blaze-html package.

If you think about it, they are just like normal HTML tags without the angle brackets. Another interesting thing about them is that those are all just functions. It means that we can reuse them in a higher level function to build a more complex view component. This technique can be observed in the favicon and formLayout functions in the preceding code.

The `mainLayout` function will produce the following HTML:

```
<!DOCTYPE HTML>
<html>
  <head>
    <link rel="icon" type="image/png" href="/images/logo.png"/>
    <title>Title form first parameter</title>
  </head>
  <body>
    <div>
      <img src="/images/logo.png"/>
    </div>
    <div>
      Any content from the second parameter
    </div>
  </body>
</html>
```

The type of these HTML functions is H.HTML. However, scotty demands LText to be passed in to the html function. So, we need to convert H.Html to LText. The function to do that is H.renderHtml. To make things easier when we want to render HTML using scotty, we will just define a helper function, renderHtml, as you have seen.

Let's now implement the `Adapter.HTTP.Web.Auth` module. Let's start with the following outline:

```
module Adapter.HTTP.Web.Auth where

import ClassyPrelude
import Web.Scotty.Trans
import Domain.Auth
import Text.Digestive.Scotty
import qualified Text.Digestive.Form as DF
import qualified Text.Digestive.View as DF
import Text.Digestive.Form ((.:))
import Adapter.HTTP.Common
import Adapter.HTTP.Web.Common
import Katip
```

```haskell
import Text.Blaze.Html5 ((!))
import qualified Text.Digestive.Blaze.Html5 as DH
import qualified Text.Blaze.Html5 as H
import qualified Text.Blaze.Html5.Attributes as A

-- * Routes

routes :: ( ScottyError e, MonadIO m, KatipContext m, AuthRepo m
          , EmailVerificationNotif m, SessionRepo m)
       => ScottyT e m ()
routes = do
  -- home
  get "/" $
    redirect "/users"

  -- register
  get "/auth/register" undefined

  post "/auth/register" undefined

  -- verify email
  get "/auth/verifyEmail/:code" undefined

  -- login
  get "/auth/login" undefined

  post "/auth/login" undefined

  -- get user
  get "/users" undefined
```

We imported a lot of modules although they are not used. Rest assured, we will use them later. So ignore any unused warnings for now.

As you can see from the routes function, we defined a few routes:

1. GET /: This redirects to GET /users.

2. GET /auth/register: This shows the registration form.

3. POST /auth/register: This handles the submission of the registration form.

4. `GET /auth/verifyEmail/:code`: This handles email activation.

5. `GET /auth/login`: This shows the login form.

6. `POST /auth/login`: This handles the submission of the login form.

7. `GET /users`: This shows the user email address if the user is logged in.

We'll start implementing from the `GET /users` endpoint:

```
get "/users" $ do
  userId <- reqCurrentUserId
  mayEmail <- lift $ getUser userId
  case mayEmail of
    Nothing ->
      raise $ stringError "Should not happen: email is not found"
    Just email ->
      renderHtml $ usersPage (rawEmail email)
```

In this function, we use the `reqCurrentUserId` that is defined in the `Adapter.HTTP.Web.Common` module. As we have seen before, this function will redirect the user to the login page if the user is not logged in. Once we get the `UserId`, we will then use the `getUser` function from the `Domain.Auth` module to get the user's email. If we get the email successfully, we display it in an HTML page that we build using the `usersPage` function.

The `usersPage` function has the following implementation:

```
usersPage :: Text -> H.Html
usersPage email =
  mainLayout "Users" $ do
    H.div $
      H.h1 "Users"
    H.div $
      H.toHtml email
```

We use the `mainLayout` function defined in the `Adapter.HTTP.Web.Common` module. The content of the page is just a simple title and the email. Figure 8-1 shows how the page will look in the browser.

That was easy; now let's move on to the email verification functionality. Write the following code to handle email verification:

```
get "/auth/verifyEmail/:code" $ do
  code <- param "code" `rescue` const (return "")
  result <- lift $ verifyEmail code
  case result of
    Left EmailVerificationErrorInvalidCode ->
      renderHtml $ verifyEmailPage "The verification code is invalid"
    Right _ ->
      renderHtml $ verifyEmailPage "Your Email has been verified"
```

Users

ecky+1@test.com

Figure 8-1. *Users page*

We first acquire the code from the path. Then the code is passed into the verifyEmail function defined in the Domain.Auth module. The result of that is pattern matched. If it's an invalid code, we return an HTML page stating about the error. Otherwise, we show a success message.

verifyEmailPage is implemented as follows:

```
verifyEmailPage :: Text -> H.Html
verifyEmailPage msg =
  mainLayout "Email Verification" $ do
```

177

```
H.h1 "Email Verification"
H.div $ H.toHtml msg
H.div $ H.a ! A.href "/auth/login" $ "Login"
```

Figure 8-2 shows how the page will look in the browser.

Next, we have registration functionality to work on. The following code implements the handler for user registration:

```
get "/auth/register" $ do
  view <- DF.getForm "auth" authForm
  renderHtml $ registerPage view []

post "/auth/register" $ do
  (view, mayAuth) <- runForm "auth" authForm
  case mayAuth of
    Nothing ->
      renderHtml $ registerPage view []
    Just auth -> do
      result <- lift $ register auth
      case result of
        Left RegistrationErrorEmailTaken ->
          renderHtml $ registerPage view ["Email has been taken"]
        Right _ -> do
          v <- DF.getForm "auth" authForm
          renderHtml $ registerPage v ["Registered successfully"]
```

The GET /auth/register endpoint is just displaying the form. We use DF.getForm to get the empty View of the form. The view is then passed into the registerPage function to build the form. We will see the authForm and registerPage function shortly.

In the POST /auth/register endpoint, we "run" the form using the runForm function from the digestive-functors-scotty package. Basically, this function parses the URL-encoded string from the HTTP request body and runs the form validation against it.

Email Verification

Your Email has been verified
Login

Figure 8-2. *Email verification page*

The result of the runForm is a tuple of View and Maybe Auth. We then pattern match on the mayAuth. If it's a Nothing, then it means that the validation has failed. In this case, view must contain the error messages. So, we just rerender the whole form with the error messages shown.

In the case of successful form validation, we pass in the input into register function from the Domain.Auth module. This function also has a failure scenario. So, we will display the appropriate error message. In a successful registration scenario, we just display an empty registration page with a successful message.

authForm is defined as follows:

```
authForm :: (Monad m) => DF.Form [Text] m Auth
authForm =
  Auth <$> "email" .: emailForm
       <*> "password" .: passwordForm
  where
    emailForm = DF.validate (toResult . mkEmail) (DF.text Nothing)
    passwordForm = DF.validate (toResult . mkPassword) (DF.text Nothing)
```

It's exactly the same as in the API one. However, I think it's better to keep them separated, as the form in API might not be exactly the same as in the Web.

registerPage is implemented as follows:

```
authFormLayout :: DF.View [Text] -> Text -> Text -> [Text] -> H.Html
authFormLayout view formTitle action msgs =
  formLayout view action $ do
    H.h2 $
      H.toHtml formTitle
    H.div $
      errorList msgs
    H.div $ do
      H.label "Email"
      DH.inputText "email" view
      H.div $
        errorList' "email"
    H.div $ do
      H.label "Password"
      DH.inputPassword "password" view
      H.div $
        errorList' "password"
    H.input ! A.type_ "submit" ! A.value "Submit"
  where
    errorList' path =
      errorList . mconcat $ DF.errors path view
    errorList =
      H.ul . concatMap errorItem
    errorItem =
      H.li . H.toHtml

registerPage :: DF.View [Text] -> [Text] -> H.Html
registerPage view msgs =
  mainLayout "Register" $ do
    H.div $
      authFormLayout view "Register" "/auth/register" msgs
    H.div $
      H.a ! A.href "/auth/login" $ "Login"
```

`registerPage` only has two components in it: `authFormLayout` and a link to the login page.

`authFormLayout` is a function that represents a form that captures user registration input. Most of it is just simple `blaze-html` functions; however, there are a few notable pieces there. The first one is the `errorList` function. This function receives a list of `Text` and converts it to an HTML list by combining `H.ul` and `H.li` functions. There is another function called `errorList'` that basically does the same as `errorList` but with the error messages sourced from the form's `View`. As you can see, we use the `DF.errors` function to extract error messages at a specific path.

The second notable piece includes the `DH.inputText` and `DH.inputPassword`. Those functions come from the `digestive-functors-blaze` package. Basically, those functions set up the necessary input field's name and value based on the `view` parameter. If you go back and see our `authForm` function, you should note that we specify some part of the form with some names, such as "email" and "password." Those same names are the input for the first parameter of the `digestive-functors-blaze`'s functions to guide which part of the form to be displayed and captured.

`digestive-functors-blaze` has more functions in addition to `inputText` and `inputPassword`. I strongly suggest checking the documentation[5] to see what the available options are.

Figures 8-3 and 8-4 show how the registration looks in various scenarios.

Let's move on to the login functionality. Write the following code to handle login endpoints:

```
get "/auth/login" $ do
  view <- DF.getForm "auth" authForm
  renderHtml $ loginPage view []

post "/auth/login" $ do
  (view, mayAuth) <- runForm "auth" authForm
  case mayAuth of
    Nothing ->
      renderHtml $ loginPage view []
    Just auth -> do
      result <- lift $ login auth
```

---

[5]https://hackage.haskell.org/package/digestive-functors-blaze-0.6.2.0/docs/
Text-Digestive-Blaze-Html5.html

```
case result of
  Left LoginErrorEmailNotVerified ->
    renderHtml $ loginPage view ["Email has not been verified"]
  Left LoginErrorInvalidAuth ->
    renderHtml $ loginPage view ["Email/password is incorrect"]
  Right sId -> do
    setSessionIdInCookie sId
    redirect "/"
```

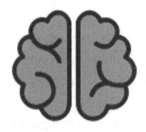

Register

Email

Password

Submit
Login

Figure 8-3. *Empty registration form*

Register

Email wrongEmail

- Not a valid email

Password

- Should be between 5 and 50
- Should contain number
- Should contain uppercase letter
- Should contain lowercase letter

Submit
Login

Figure 8-4. *Registration form with error*

The preceding function is pretty similar with registration ones. Please note that in the successful login scenario, we set the session id in a cookie so that the user could be authenticated in future interactions.

loginPage is also similar to registerPage.

```
loginPage :: DF.View [Text] -> [Text] -> H.Html
loginPage view msgs =
  mainLayout "Login" $ do
```

```
H.div $
  authFormLayout view "Login" "/auth/login" msgs
H.div $
  H.a ! A.href "/auth/register" $ "Register"
```

Since the input that we need is the same as registration, we can just reuse the form. Figures 8-5 and 8-6 show the login page in various scenarios.

We have finished implementing the handler for various authentication functionalities. Now, we need to modify the Adapter.HTTP.Web.Main module to include these new route handlers. Update the routes function to the following:

```
import qualified Adapter.HTTP.Web.Auth as Auth
import Network.Wai.Middleware.Static
import Network.Wai.Middleware.Gzip

routes :: ( MonadIO m, KatipContext m, AuthRepo m
          , EmailVerificationNotif m, SessionRepo m)
       => CacheContainer -> ScottyT LText m ()
routes cachingStrategy = do
  middleware $
    gzip $ def { gzipFiles = GzipCompress }
  middleware $
    staticPolicy' cachingStrategy (addBase "src/Adapter/HTTP/Web")

  Auth.routes

  notFound $ do
    status status404
    text "Not found"

  defaultHandler $ \e -> do
    lift $ $(logTM) ErrorS $ "Unhandled error: " <> ls (showError e)
    status status500
    text "Internal server error!"
```

Login

Email

Password

Submit
Register

Figure 8-5. *Empty login form*

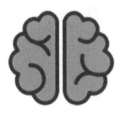

Login

- Email/password is incorrect

Email `wrongEmail@test.com`

Password `•••••••••`

Submit
Register

Figure 8-6. *Login form with errors*

We import the `Adapter.HTTP.Web.Auth` module and use `Auth.routes` in our routes function.

We also add a few middlewares: `gzip` and `staticPolicy'`. We've seen `gzip` in the previous chapter. So we will skip that. `staticPolicy'` is a function from the `middleware-static` package that basically serves static assets.

If you trace back to `mainLayout` function in the `Adapter.HTTP.Web.Common` module, you should see that we use `"/images/logo.png"` as the source path for favicon. However, we store our assets in the `/src/Adapter/HTTP/Web` folder. So, how does `middleware-static` know which path to serve from? The answer is because we define the base path in the second parameter of `staticPolicy'`. What happens here is that on every request, `middleware-static` will first try to serve the static assets. If the asset is not found, then the request is routed to the application.

The first parameter of `staticPolicy'` is a `CacheContainer`. This allows sensible caching headers to be sent along with the asset. We acquire `CacheContainer` from the function parameter.

Now that we have covered the `routes` function, let's move on to the `main` function.

```
main :: ( MonadIO m, KatipContext m, AuthRepo m
        , EmailVerificationNotif m, SessionRepo m)
    => (m Response -> IO Response) -> IO Application
main runner = do
  cacheContainer <- initCaching PublicStaticCaching
  scottyAppT runner $ routes cacheContainer
```

In this function, we initialize the `cacheContainer` and pass it into the `routes` function.

Alright, we have finished all the implementation. Now, you can go to REPL and run the application. You may go to `http://localhost:3000` in your browser and play around with it. Try registering, verifying email, and logging in. You should see that the application works as intended. Note that you should see a favicon as well, indicating that serving static assets functionality works as intended.

Summary

In this chapter, we have exposed our domain functionality via HTML pages. We've seen how to serve multiple WAI applications in a single Haskell executable using `vhost` middleware. We have also seen how easy it is to build composable views using `blaze-html`. For handling form validation and showing error messages, we have `digestive-functors-blaze` and the `digestive-functors-scotty` package that makes achieving those things easy.

CHAPTER 9

HTTP Client

Nowadays, a lot of services expose their functionality over HTTP via RESTful API. Even within the same company, we may use microservices architecture with RESTful API as the primary means of communication. So, it's inevitable that we would need to talk to other services via HTTP.

Haskell's ecosystem fortunately has quite good support for executing an HTTP request. Some of the available packages are:

1. `http-client`[1] and `http-client-tls`[2]

2. `wreq`[3]

3. `req`[4]

4. `http-conduit`[5]

Both `wreq` and `req` are more high level compared with `http-client`. In fact, both depend on `http-client` for doing the actual HTTP request.

`wreq` uses `lens` heavily. `lens` is a well-known library in Haskell for doing data structure manipulation. However, if you are not familiar with it, you might find it a bit daunting.

`req` does not use `lens` but uses rather advanced type level tricks to make sure you are doing the correct stuff according to the HTTP semantics. Depending on your knowledge of Haskell, you may find it complex.

`http-conduit` is another high-level library built on top of `http-client`. It provides extra functionality to process the response in a streaming fashion. It's useful for cases where you have a large response body and you don't want to have it all in memory before processing further. `http-conduit` also provides a simple interface for `http-client`.

---

[1]`www.stackage.org/lts-10.3/package/http-client-0.5.7.1`
[2]`www.stackage.org/lts-10.3/package/http-client-tls-0.3.5.1`
[3]`www.stackage.org/lts-10.3/package/wreq-0.5.2.0`
[4]`www.stackage.org/lts-10.3/package/req-1.0.0`
[5]`www.stackage.org/lts-10.3/package/http-conduit-2.2.4`

© Ecky Putrady 2018
E. Putrady, *Practical Web Development with Haskell*, https://doi.org/10.1007/978-1-4842-3739-7_9

Despite them being high level, I find that http-client is easy enough to use and gets the job done. http-client-tls is used in conjunction with http-client to make secure HTTP requests. Yes, you might not have the one liner to send and read JSON, but I don't find it to be a big turnoff.

http-client package

In this section, we will learn about how to work with the http-client package. There are three main components in this package: Manager, Request, and Response. We will look into them in more detail.

Manager

Manager does connection pooling for our HTTP requests. It keeps the connection to various hosts open for quite some time. So, if there are subsequent requests to the same host, a new connection is not opened but rather the old one is reused. If the connection is idle for some defined amount of time, it is then finally disconnected. Manager is meant to be reused throughout your application.

For creating a manager, the function to use is:

```
newManager :: ManagerSettings -> IO Manager
```

ManagerSettings configures the behavior of the Manager. The following code snippet shows an example of creating and modifying ManagerSettings:

```
let settings = defaultManagerSettings
               { managerConnCount = 20
               , managerIdleConnectionCount = 512
               , managerResponseTimeout = responseTimeoutMicro 30000000
               }
```

Besides the preceding settings, there are a few other settings that you can modify, such as action to modify request or response, action to create connection, etc. However, I find that the common ones to modify are the aforementioned. You may consult the documentation to see the full configuration listing.

In practice, however, we won't use defaultManagerSettings. It's because this setting does not support HTTPS. So, the connection will fail if you try to send a request to an HTTPS endpoint (which should be everywhere nowadays). What you want to do is to use the tlsManagerSettings function from the http-client-tls package.

All in all, here's what we do to create a Manager:

```
manager <- newManager tlsManagerSettings
```

Request

The second component is Request. As the name suggests, this represents the HTTP request to be performed. For creating a Request, we can do the following:

```
initReq <- parseRequest "http://example.com/path/to/resource"
let req = initReq
        { method = "POST"
        , requestHeaders = [ ("x-header-1", "something")
                           , ("x-header-2", "hello")
                           ]
        , requestBody = RequestBodyLBS "{\"hello\":1}"
        , queryString = "param1=hello&param2=world"
        , cookieJar = Nothing
        }
```

As you can see, they are pretty low level. For example, there is no native function to send JSON as the request body. However, I find it not to be an issue. It's very easy to build them without a special function.

The settings you have seen are the ones that are commonly used. There are other configurations like proxy or request timeout as well. Do read up on the docs for those.

Executing a Request

Now that we know how to build a Request, let's learn how to execute it. httpLbs is the function to use:

```
httpLbs :: Request -> Manager -> IO (Response LByteString)
```

This function accepts a `Request` and a `Manager`. This executes the request and reads the HTTP body fully before returning a `Response` `LByteString`. This function may throw a synchronous exception. We will see the exception handling part in a later section.

Response

Once we get the response, we usually want to read various parts of it using the following functions:

```
responseStatus :: Response body -> Status
responseHeaders :: Response body -> ResponseHeaders
responseCookieJar :: Response body -> CookieJar
responseBody :: Response body -> body

-- from http-types package
data Status = Status { statusCode :: Int, statusMessage :: ByteString }
```

`ResponseHeaders` is basically an alias for `[(ByteString, ByteString)]`. For getting a specific header, you may use `responseHeader` with `find`. For example:

```
response <- ... -- get the response somehow
let (Just val) = lookup "Authorization" . responseHeaders $ response
```

`CookieJar` contains the cookies that you get from the server. Usually, we don't do anything with it other than passing it to subsequent requests.

Exceptions

An HTTP request is an IO operation. The nature of IO is that it may throw a synchronous exception. This package is no different. It defines an `HttpException` type for various HTTP-related synchronous exceptions as follows:

```
data HttpException
  = HttpExceptionRequest Request HttpExceptionContent
  | InvalidUrlException String String
```

```
data HttpExceptionContent
  = ResponseTimeout
  | ConnectionTimeout
  | ConnectionClosed
  | TooManyRedirects [Response ByteString]
  | -- and many others
```

I'm not showing the whole list, as it is not a small list. Please check the documentation for the complete listing.

Handling the synchronous exception is no different than normal Haskell's synchronous exception. We use `catch`:

```
let handler e = case e of
  ResponseTimeout -> ...
  ConnectionTimeout -> ...
  _ -> ... -- for other cases
httpLBS request manager `catch` handler
```

RESTful API Client for Our Project

JSON Payload

Since the client and the server are both in Haskell, then it's more beneficial for the client and server to share the Haskell data structures as well as JSON serialization and deserialization. This makes sure that any changes to such structures or logic are correctly propagated to both the client and the server.

So, we start by defining the shared data structures and JSON serde in a dedicated module named `Adapter.HTTP.API.Types.Auth`. However, we also foresee that the JSON serde logic can be reused should a new domain be added to our application. So, we would like to put the common JSON serde logic in a separate module named `Adapter.HTTP.API.Types.AesonHelper`.

Adapter.HTTP.API.Types.AesonHelper Implementation

We start by defining the module and imports.

```
module Adapter.HTTP.API.Types.AesonHelper where

import ClassyPrelude
import Data.Aeson.TH
import Data.Aeson.Types
import Language.Haskell.TH.Syntax
```

Recall that we can generate JSON implementation for any data type using the Template Haskell functions provided by the `aeson` package. In this module, we will use the provided functions with specific options.

For this to compile, we need to include `template-haskell` as our project dependency. Let's do that now by editing our `package.yaml` as follows:

```
dependencies:
- template-haskell
```

The first function that we will create is to parse JSON to types that require a smart constructor. In our project, we have two such types:

```
newtype Email = Email { rawEmail :: Text } deriving (Show, Eq, Ord)
newtype Password = Password { rawPassword :: Text } deriving (Show, Eq)
```

The behavior that we want is that encoding such types should produce the raw values without the enclosing structure. For example, we want these:

```
"eckyputrady@test.com" -- email JSON
"abcDEF123" -- password JSON
```

instead of:

```
{ "rawEmail": "eckyputrady@test.com" }
{ "rawPassword": "abcDEF123" }
```

On the decoding side, we want to parse a value from JSON by leveraging the smart constructor so that it can't be created using an illegal parameter. The following function is a JSON parser that reads a value using the smart constructor provided in the function parameter. This might not make sense for now, but once you see how this is used, it should be obvious.

```
withSmartConstructor :: (a -> Either [Text] b) -> a -> Parser b
withSmartConstructor constructor a =
  case constructor a of
    Left errs -> fail $ intercalate ". " . map unpack $ errs
    Right val -> return val
```

The next function is a helper function to derive JSON for record types. In our application, an example of a record type is Auth.

```
data Auth = Auth
  { authEmail :: Email
  , authPassword :: Password
  } deriving (Show, Eq)
```

For this type, we want the JSON representation to be:

```
{
  "email": "test@test.com",
  "password": "abcDEF123"
}
```

Notice that it doesn't map exactly to our Haskell's record type. Specifically, a few characters at the beginning of the fields are dropped. Our convention for writing a Haskell record is that each field should be prefixed with the record name. So, when serializing to JSON, we want to drop the prefix. The following function does this:

```
deriveJSONRecord :: Name -> Q [Dec]
deriveJSONRecord record =
  let lowerCaseFirst (y:ys) = toLower [y] <> ys
      lowerCaseFirst "" = ""
      structName = nameBase record
      opts = defaultOptions
              { fieldLabelModifier = lowerCaseFirst . drop (length
                structName)
              }
  in deriveJSON opts record
```

As you can see, we override the `fieldLabelModifier` of the default options to omit the prefix and modify the letter casing. We know how many characters to drop based on the record name.

This function receives the `Name` and outputs a `Q [Dec]`. Both come from `template-haskell`. Suffice it to say that the `Name` is the record name and `Q [Dec]` is the generated code.

Next, we want to create a function to derive JSON for sum types. In our application, we use sum types heavily for representing errors. For example, `LoginError`:

```
data LoginError
  = LoginErrorInvalidAuth
  | LoginErrorEmailNotVerified
  deriving (Show, Eq)
```

When we serialize this, we want the output JSON to be a simple string:

```
"InvalidAuth"
"EmailNotVerified"
```

As you can see, we also drop the prefix for each constructor. The following function gets the job done to achieve what we want:

```
deriveJSONSumType :: Name -> Q [Dec]
deriveJSONSumType record =
  let structName = nameBase record
      opts = defaultOptions
              { constructorTagModifier = drop (length structName)
              , tagSingleConstructors = True
              }
  in deriveJSON opts record
```

We modify the default settings. `constructorTagModifier` is used to drop the prefix. `tagSingleConstructor` makes sure that the constructor name is serialized to JSON. If we don't override this value, `"[]"` will be the serialized value instead.

Beside records and sum types, we have one more class of data structure: one that requires a smart constructor. Usually, we use `newtype` to encapsulate the raw value. One example is `Email`:

```
newtype Email = Email { rawEmail :: Text } deriving (Show, Eq, Ord)
```

We want it to be serialized as a simple string without the enclosing structure:

"eckyputrady@test.com"

The following function does the necessary for the previously mentioned behavior. We just override the default settings and set unwrapUnaryRecords to True.

```
deriveToJSONUnwrap :: Name -> Q [Dec]
deriveToJSONUnwrap =
  let opts = defaultOptions { unwrapUnaryRecords = True }
  in deriveToJSON opts
```

Adapter.HTTP.API.Types.Auth Implementation

In this section, we will implement the JSON serialization and deserialization for the domain types. This module should not be complex, as most of the serialization and deserialization logic has been provided by the aeson module.

```
module Adapter.HTTP.API.Types.Auth where

import ClassyPrelude
import Domain.Auth
import Data.Aeson
import Adapter.HTTP.API.Types.AesonHelper

instance FromJSON Email where
  parseJSON =
    withText "Email" $ withSmartConstructor mkEmail

instance FromJSON Password where
  parseJSON =
    withText "Password" $ withSmartConstructor mkPassword

$(map concat . sequence $
    [ deriveJSONRecord "Auth
    , deriveToJSONUnwrap "Email
    , deriveToJSONUnwrap "Password
```

```
, deriveJSONSumType "RegistrationError"
, deriveJSONSumType "EmailVerificationError"
, deriveJSONSumType "LoginError"
])
```

The preceding code snippet is all we have write to make our types JSON convertible.

If you try to compile this module so far, you will get an "orphan instance" warning. An orphan instance warning happens when you define a type A in module A'; define a typeclass B in module B'; but then define the typeclass B instance for type A in module C. This is problematic when, for example, you have defined the same typeclass instances in different modules but then you depend on both modules. The compiler will not compile, because it's not clear which instance implementation you want.

To prevent an orphan instance warning, you may do one of the following:

1. Define the instances where the type is defined.

2. Define the instances where the typeclass is defined.

3. Wrap the type in a newtype and define a typeclass instance for the newtype instead.

In my opinion, if you are building a library that others will depend on, having an orphan instance is a big no-no, as you can't predict how the users will use your library. However, if you are building an application, this is less of an issue. You can fully control the code that you write in your application. So I feel it's justified to ignore this warning.

Based on the preceding reasoning, we can have the compiler ignore an orphan instance in this module by adding the following pragma on the top of the file:

```
{-# OPTIONS_GHC -fno-warn-orphans #-}
```

API Server Refactoring

In the previous section, we have created JSON. Now we can modify our existing API server implementation to use those JSON instances.

Go to the `Adapter.HTTP.API.Auth` module. Then, edit the import sections to add the following line:

```
import Adapter.HTTP.API.Types.Auth ()
```

The preceding line imports the `FromJSON` and `ToJSON` instances definition

After that, edit the routes function to be the following:

```
routes :: ( ScottyError e, MonadIO m, KatipContext m, AuthRepo m
          , EmailVerificationNotif m, SessionRepo m)
          => ScottyT e m ()
routes = do
  -- register
  post "/api/auth/register" $ do
    input <- parseAndValidateJSON authForm
    domainResult <- lift $ register input
    case domainResult of
      Left err -> do
        status status400
        json err
      Right _ ->
        return ()

  -- verify email
  post "/api/auth/verifyEmail" $ do
    input <- parseAndValidateJSON verifyEmailForm
    domainResult <- lift $ verifyEmail input
    case domainResult of
      Left err -> do
        status status400
        json err
      Right _ ->
        return ()

  -- login
  post "/api/auth/login" $ do
    input <- parseAndValidateJSON authForm
    domainResult <- lift $ login input
    case domainResult of
      Left err -> do
        status status400
        json err
```

```
    Right sId -> do
      setSessionIdInCookie sId
      return ()
-- get user
get "/api/users" $ do
  userId <- reqCurrentUserId
  mayEmail <- lift $ getUser userId
  case mayEmail of
    Nothing ->
      raise $ stringError "Should not happen: SessionId map to invalid
      UserId"
    Just email ->
      json email
```

The function is mostly unchanged. The main difference is that we pass in our types directly to the json function provided by scotty. This is now possible because we have defined FromJSON and ToJSON instances in Adapter.HTTP.API.Types.Auth module and import it here.

Module Refactoring

Since we will introduce an HTTP Client for RESTful API, it makes sense to put it somewhere under the Adapter.HTTP.API namespace. Currently, we have the server implementation under this namespace directly. Now, we will move them all to a new namespace: Adapter.HTTP.API.Server. Simply create a folder named Server under API and move Auth.hs, Common.hs, and Main.hs there. As you might have expected, this produces compile errors. However, they are all easy to resolve. Usually, you just need to edit the module name and the import lines. Just follow the compile error messages.

Since this error resolving work is trivial, I will not put the exact changes in this section.

HTTP Client Implementation

We will have two modules for HTTP Client:

1. Adapter.HTTP.API.Client.Common: Defines common types and functions as well as initialization function

2. Adapter.HTTP.API.Client.Auth: Defines functions that are specific to Auth domain, such as registration and login.

Adapter.HTTP.API.Client.Common Module

Let's start by creating the Adapter.HTTP.API.Client.Common module:

```
module Adapter.HTTP.API.Client.Common where

import ClassyPrelude
import Network.HTTP.Client
import Network.HTTP.Client.TLS
import Data.Has
import Data.Aeson
```

As usual, we define the module name and imports.

```
newtype Config = Config
  { configUrl :: String
  }

data State = State
  { stateInitReq :: Request
  , stateManager :: Manager
  }

type HttpClient r m = (MonadReader r m, Has State r, MonadIO m, MonadThrow m)
```

In the preceding snippet, we define the types for configuration. For now, we only have one field for configuration: configUrl. It's meant to configure the URL to hit to when using the HTTP Client.

Next, we define the state. As you can see, we have the initial `Request` and `Manager`. The initial `Request` is meant to be overridden on each HTTP request function. The `Manager` is a requirement for doing an HTTP request.

Finally, we have constraint alias `HttpClient r m`. This alias basically constrains `m` to any type that may throw an exception (via `MonadThrow`), may do IO (via `MonadIO`), and is able to get `State` from the environment (via `MonadReader r m, Has State r`).

```
type Session = CookieJar
```

The preceding snippet defines `Session` as an alias for `CookieJar`. `CookieJar` is a type that comes from `http-client`, as we have seen in an earlier section of this chapter.

```
data UnexpectedResponse a =
  UnexpectedResponse Request (Response a) deriving (Show)
```

```
instance (Typeable a, Show a) => Exception (UnexpectedResponse a)
```

The preceding snippet defines the `UnexpectedResponse` data type. As the name suggest, this is used for representing an error that is caused by an unexpected response from the server.

Since this is an exception, we define the Exception instance of this data type so that we can throw it using `MonadThrow` capability.

```
withState :: Config -> (State -> IO a) -> IO a
withState cfg action = do
  mgr <- newManager tlsManagerSettings
  initReq <- parseRequest $ configUrl cfg
  let initReqWithJson =
        initReq { requestHeaders =
                    [("Content-Type", "application/json; charset=utf-8")]
                }
  action $ State initReqWithJson mgr
```

The preceding function defines how to initialize the `State`. We create a `Manager` and initial `Request`. We then put them in the `State` data structure.

```
parseOrErr :: (MonadThrow m, FromJSON a)
           => Request -> Response LByteString -> m a
parseOrErr req resp =
  case eitherDecode' $ responseBody resp of
    Left _ -> throw $ UnexpectedResponse req resp
    Right a -> return a
```

The preceding function is used to extract JSON from the HTTP response body. We use eitherDecode' from an HTTP response body. If the body is not a parsable JSON, then eitherDecode' will return a Left, otherwise it will be a Right. Using pattern matching, we handle the Left case by throwing UnexpectedResponse.

Adapter.HTTP.API.Client.Auth Module

In this module, we define the actual functions that talk to the HTTP RESTful API endpoint that we have implemented in Chapter 7. The following snippet lists the required imports:

```
module Adapter.HTTP.API.Client.Auth where

import ClassyPrelude
import Network.HTTP.Client
import Data.Has
import qualified Domain.Auth as D
import Network.HTTP.Types
import Adapter.HTTP.API.Types.Auth ()
import Adapter.HTTP.API.Client.Common
import Data.Aeson
```

The first function we define is register, as you can see in the following:

```
register :: HttpClient r m => D.Auth -> m (Either D.RegistrationError ())
register auth = do
  State initReq mgr <- asks getter
  let req = initReq
            { method = "POST"
            , path = "/api/auth/register"
            , requestBody = RequestBodyLBS $ encode auth
            }
```

```
resp <- liftIO $ httpLbs req mgr
case responseStatus resp of
  (Status 200 _) ->
    return $ Right ()
  _ ->
    Left <$> parseOrErr req resp
```

The function signature is similar to the one we see in the Domain.Auth module. We return an Either indicating a success or a failure. However, as this is a network call, it's possible for this function to throw an exception.

This function is quite straightforward. We first get the state from the environment. Then we build an HTTP request. For registration, the endpoint to call is POST /api/auth/register. This aligns with the code that we've previously written. As for the request body, we need to pass in the D.Auth as JSON.

After building the HTTP request, we execute it using the httpLbs function. The response is then interpreted to the domain data types.

The similar pattern is also reused for the verifyEmail function as you can see in the following:

```
verifyEmail :: HttpClient r m
            => D.VerificationCode -> m (Either D.EmailVerificationError ())
verifyEmail code = do
  State initReq mgr <- asks getter
  let req = initReq
            { method = "POST"
            , path = "/api/auth/verifyEmail"
            , requestBody = RequestBodyLBS . encode $ code
            }
  resp <- liftIO $ httpLbs req mgr
  case responseStatus resp of
    (Status 200 _) ->
      return $ Right ()
    _ ->
      Left <$> parseOrErr req resp
```

For the login function, we also reuse the pattern as in the preceding. However, the difference is that we return a Session. Recall that Session is an alias for CookieJar. We can get the CookieJar from the response using the responseCookieJar function.

```
login :: HttpClient r m => D.Auth -> m (Either D.LoginError Session)
login auth = do
  State initReq mgr <- asks getter
  let req = initReq
              { method = "POST"
              , path = "/api/auth/login"
              , requestBody = RequestBodyLBS $ encode auth
              }
  resp <- liftIO $ httpLbs req mgr
  case responseStatus resp of
    (Status 200 _) ->
      return $ Right $ responseCookieJar resp
    _ ->
      Left <$> parseOrErr req resp
```

For getUser, we pass in the Session that we get from login. This Session is set to the request using the cookieJar function. In this function, we assume that the session is always valid. In case it's not valid, the function throws an UnexpectedResponse exception.

```
getUser :: HttpClient r m => Session -> m D.Email
getUser session = do
  State initReq mgr <- asks getter
  let req = initReq
              { method = "GET"
              , path = "/api/users"
              , cookieJar = Just session
              }
  resp <- liftIO $ httpLbs req mgr
  case responseStatus resp of
    (Status 200 _) ->
      parseOrErr req resp
    _ ->
      throw $ UnexpectedResponse req resp
```

Verifying Implementation with REPL

In previous sections, we have implemented the code for the client. In this section, we will verify it using REPL.

We need two REPLs for this. One REPL is used to run the server. The other REPL is used to call the client functions. Type the following commands in the first REPL to start the server:

```
-- load the Lib module
> :l Lib

-- run the server
> main
```

Now that the server has started, let's open the other REPL and type the following commands:

```
> -- load the client module
> :l Adapter.HTTP.API.Client.Auth

> -- Define a helper function to run the client that connects to
localhost:3000
> let cfg = Config "http://localhost:3000"
> let run action = withState cfg $ \state -> flip runReaderT state $ action

> -- Define the `D.Auth` data structure that we use for testing
> let (Right auth) = D.Auth <$> D.mkEmail "hi@hello.com" <*> D.mkPassword
"abcDEF123"

> -- Successful registration test
> run $ register auth
Right ()

> -- Failed registration test due to duplicate email
> run $ register auth
Left RegistrationErrorEmailTaken

> -- Failed login test due to email not yet verified
> run $ login auth
Left LoginErrorEmailNotVerified
```

```
> -- Failed verifyEmail command test due to wrong verification code
> run $ verifyEmail "wrongCode"
Left EmailVerificationErrorInvalidCode

> -- We open the database and get the verification
> -- This verifyEmail command should be successful now
> run $ verifyEmail "\"hi@hello.com\"_sk9v9vXLDt3RuK3V"
Right ()

> -- Try login again, this should now be successful since we have verified
the email
> Right session <- run $ login auth

> -- Get the email of current user using the session we get from previous step
> run $ getUser session
Email {rawEmail = "hi@hello.com"}

> -- Turn off the server

> -- Try to get the user info again now that we have turned off the server
> -- We should get an exception
> run $ getUser session
*** Exception: HttpExceptionRequest Request {
  host               = "localhost"
  port               = 3000
  secure             = False
  requestHeaders     = [("Content-Type","application/json; charset=utf-8")]
  path               = "/api/users"
  queryString        = ""
  method             = "GET"
  proxy              = Nothing
  rawBody            = False
  redirectCount      = 10
  responseTimeout    = ResponseTimeoutDefault
  requestVersion     = HTTP/1.1
}
  (ConnectionFailure Network.Socket.connect: <socket: 15>: does not exist
  (Connection refused))
```

If you run the preceding commands and get a similar result, then our HTTP Client implementation is a success. Congratulations for having reached this far!

Summary

In this chapter, we have learned about working with HTTP Client in Haskell. We have explored some available packages and we settled on `http-client` due to its simplicity.

We learned about the important concepts of the `http-client` package, such as creating a request, executing the request, parsing the response, and handling exceptions.

With the knowledge about the package, we built ourselves a Haskell client library for interacting with our application. Recall that we exposed our application functionalities via RESTful API. Our Haskell client library interacts with this API to invoke the necessary functionalities.

CHAPTER 10

Configuration

When building a web application, there's a good chance you will need to deploy it to multiple environments. For example, besides the production environment, you might have a QA environment for the quality assurance process. The database you connect to in a production environment will have a different host and credential than the one in a QA environment. For this reason, you want your application to read the necessary configuration at runtime.

There are multiple ways to get these configuration values:

1. Environment variables

2. Files

3. Centralized configuration server

If you happen to choose centralized configuration server to manage your configuration, there are many such servers to choose from. One example is Consul.[1] If you use Consul, then you may want to use the `consul-haskell`[2] package.

If you choose files for managing the configuration values, then you can store it as JSON and read it via the `aeson` package. There are Haskell packages that are focused on configuration management, such as `configurator`[3] and `dhall`.[4] Both are quite similar: both provide their own format for putting configuration values. Both also have a feature to read from environment variables. However, one differentiating feature that `configurator` has is that you might get notified when the configuration changes.

---

[1]`www.consul.io/`
[2]`www.stackage.org/package/consul-haskell`
[3]`www.stackage.org/package/configurator`
[4]`www.stackage.org/package/dhall`

209

© Ecky Putrady 2018
E. Putrady, *Practical Web Development with Haskell*, https://doi.org/10.1007/978-1-4842-3739-7_10

I find environment variables to be the simplest among the three. In Haskell, we can interact with environment variables using a System.Environment module provided from the base package.

In this chapter, we will use environment variables to manage the configuration values for our application. I find it to be enough even for bigger applications.

System.Environment Module

An environment variable is basically a key-value pair. So, the operations we are interested in are simply how to set and get values from it. The following code snippet shows such operations:

```
getEnv :: String -> IO String
lookupEnv :: String -> IO (Maybe String)
setEnv :: String -> String -> IO ()
```

The difference between getEnv and lookupEnv is that the former throws an exception if the value is not found, while the latter returns a Nothing if the value is not found.

lookupEnv seems to be more desirable, considering it doesn't throw any exception. However, we usually read configuration values at the start of the program. It's desirable for the program to fail to start if the required configuration value is not found. So, using getEnv would be more fitting for this scenario.

Both functions return a String. However, you may need to read it as a number. So, you might want to use readMay to parse the string to a type that you use in your application.

setEnv is quite straightforward, as is evident by looking at the type. It just receives two inputs: the first one is the key and the second is the value.

Making Our Application Configurable

Now that we have learned about the basics of the System.Environment module, it's time to modify our application so that it reads from environment variables on startup.

First, let's see what values we want to be configurable. Currently, we hardcode our configuration values in the Lib module as follows:

```
withState :: (Int -> LogEnv -> State -> IO ()) -> IO ()
withState action =
  withKatip $ \le -> do
    mState <- newTVarIO M.initialState
    PG.withState pgCfg $ \pgState ->
      Redis.withState redisCfg $ \redisState ->
      MQ.withState mqCfg 16 $ \mqState -> do
        let state = (pgState, redisState, mqState, mState)
        action port le state
  where
    mqCfg = "amqp://guest:guest@localhost:5672/%2F"
    redisCfg = "redis://localhost:6379/0"
    pgCfg = PG.Config
      { PG.configUrl = "postgresql://localhost/hauth"
      , PG.configStripeCount = 2
      , PG.configMaxOpenConnPerStripe = 5
      , PG.configIdleConnTimeout = 10
      }
    port = 3000
```

The values under the where clause are the hardcoded configuration. We want to have some of them read from environment variables. However, you might also notice that for creating a RabbitMQ state, we hardcode a 16 as the second parameter. It would feel cleaner if we have an MQ config data structure that is similar to PostgreSQL. Let's refactor that part now.

Go to Adapter.RabbitMQ.Common and introduce the following type for representing the MQ configuration:

```
data Config = Config
  { configUrl :: String
  , configPrefetchCount :: Integer
  }
```

Then, modify the withState function to receive this Config as the first parameter:

```
withState :: Config -> (State -> IO a) -> IO a
withState config action = bracket initState destroyState action'
  where
    initState = do
      publisher <- openConnAndChan
      consumer <- openConnAndChan
      return (publisher, consumer)

    openConnAndChan = do
      conn <- openConnection" . fromURI . configUrl $ config
      chan <- openChannel conn
      confirmSelect chan False
      qos chan 0 (fromInteger $ configPrefetchCount config) True
      return (conn, chan)

    destroyState ((conn1, _), (conn2, _)) = do
      closeConnection conn1
      closeConnection conn2

    action' ((_, pubChan), (_, conChan)) = action (State pubChan conChan)
```

Now, go back to the Lib module and modify the withState function again:

```
withState :: (Int -> LogEnv -> State -> IO ()) -> IO ()
withState action =
  withKatip $ \le -> do
    mState <- newTVarIO M.initialState
    PG.withState pgCfg $ \pgState ->
      Redis.withState redisCfg $ \redisState ->
        MQ.withState mqCfg $ \mqState -> do
          let state = (pgState, redisState, mqState, mState)
          action port le state
  where
    port = 3000
    redisCfg = "redis://localhost:6379/0"
    mqCfg =
```

```
    MQ.Config
    { MQ.configUrl = "amqp://guest:guest@localhost:5672/%2F"
    , MQ.configPrefetchCount = 16
    }
  pgCfg =
    PG.Config
    { PG.configUrl = "postgresql://localhost/hauth"
    , PG.configStripeCount = 2
    , PG.configMaxOpenConnPerStripe = 5
    , PG.configIdleConnTimeout = 10
    }
```

Next, let's create a `Config` module where we will define the application-wide configuration. We will also define how such a configuration is to be read from the environment variables.

```
module Config where

import ClassyPrelude
import System.Environment
import qualified Adapter.PostgreSQL.Auth as PG
import qualified Adapter.RabbitMQ.Common as MQ
```

Let's first start by defining a `Config` type to represent the application-wide configuration.

```
data Config = Config
  { configPort :: Int
  , configRedis :: String
  , configMQ :: MQ.Config
  , configPG :: PG.Config
  }
```

Next, we define some helper functions to read a value from an environment variable.

```
envFromString :: (IsString a) => String -> IO a
envFromString key = fromString <$> getEnv key
```

The preceding function parses environment variables to anything that is an instance of the IsString typeclass. This can be used, for example, to read environment variable as Text or LByteString. This function throws an exception if the environment variable is not found.

```
envRead :: Read a => String -> IO a
envRead key = do
  rawVal <- getEnv key
  case readMay rawVal of
    Just val -> return val
    Nothing -> throwString $ key <> ": Unable to parse " <> rawVal
```

The preceding function parses the environment variable into any type that is an instance of Read type. This supports a lot of type, for example, Integer or Double. This function throws an exception if the environment variable is not found and if the value of the environment variable is not parsable to the target type.

Now that we have created some helper functions, we can use them to build our Config from environment variables. Add the following code snippet in the same module:

```
fromEnv :: IO Config
fromEnv = Config
  <$> envRead "PORT"
  <*> getEnv "REDIS_URL"
  <*> (MQ.Config
        <$> getEnv "MQ_URL"
        <*> pure 16
     )
  <*> (PG.Config
        <$> envFromString "PG_URL"
        <*> pure 2
        <*> pure 5
        <*> pure 10
     )
```

We use the help of the Applicative typeclass, which IO happens to be an instance of, to create our Config. Notice that we don't read everything from environment variables. The purpose of this is mainly to show you how to hardcode some values, should they have no benefit to be configurable.

In addition to reading from environment variable, we also create a `devConfig` function that creates a `Config` for development purposes.

```
devConfig :: Config
devConfig = Config
  { configPort = 3000
  , configRedis = "redis://localhost:6379/0"
  , configMQ = MQ.Config
    { MQ.configUrl = "amqp://guest:guest@localhost:5672/%2F"
    , MQ.configPrefetchCount = 16
    }
  , configPG = PG.Config
    { PG.configUrl = "postgresql://localhost/hauth"
    , PG.configStripeCount = 2
    , PG.configMaxOpenConnPerStripe = 5
    , PG.configIdleConnTimeout = 10
    }
  }
```

The required changes in the `Config` module are enough. Now, go back to `Lib` module and use the `Config` module during startup.

```
import qualified Config

withState :: Config.Config -> (Int -> LogEnv -> State -> IO ()) -> IO ()
withState config action =
  withKatip $ \le -> do
    mState <- newTVarIO M.initialState
    PG.withState (Config.configPG config) $ \pgState ->
      Redis.withState (Config.configRedis config) $ \redisState ->
        MQ.withState (Config.configMQ config) $ \mqState -> do
          let state = (pgState, redisState, mqState, mState)
          action (Config.configPort config) le state

mainWithConfig :: Config.Config -> IO ()
mainWithConfig config =
  withState config $ \port le state@(_, _, mqState, _) -> do
```

```
  let runner = run le state
  MQAuth.init mqState runner
  HTTP.main port runner

main :: IO ()
main = do
  config <- Config.fromEnv
  mainWithConfig config
```

With the preceding code, running main will read the Config from environment variables. For development purposes, we will also create a function called mainDev. This function uses the devConfig instead of reading from environment variables.

```
mainDev :: IO ()
mainDev = mainWithConfig Config.devConfig
```

Our implementation is done. Let's test drive it. Open REPL and type the following commands:

```
> :l Lib
> main
*** Exception: PORT: getEnv: does not exist (no environment variable)

> mainDev
```

As you can see, running main will crash the application during startup because we have not yet set any environment variables. Running the application using mainDev succeeded, since it uses the hardcoded config for development.

Let's now set the necessary environment variables to make main run successfully. In your terminal, type the following commands to export environment variables:

```
$ export REDIS_URL=redis://localhost:6379/0
$ export MQ_URL=amqp://guest:guest@localhost:5672/%2F
$ export PG_URL=postgresql://localhost/hauth
```

Then, using the same terminal, open REPL again and type the following command:

```
> :l Lib
> main
```

Notice that now the `main` function runs successfully. This is because we have set the necessary environment variables so that the application is able to read them on start, thus not crashing.

Summary

This chapter is short, but we have learned how to make our application configurable by reading configuration values at runtime using environment variables. We use the `System.Environment` module for interfacing with environment variables.

CHAPTER 11

Testing

In real-world software development, automated testing is one of the key practices to ensure our application quality. Automated testing allows us to scale the testing effort once our application gets bigger. Consider this: on every new feature, would you prefer to manually test all existing features to make sure they don't break instead of having an automated process to do that? In addition to catching regression bugs, testing may also act as documentation on how the software should behave.

In this chapter, we will look into how we would test our Haskell application.

Making Our Application More Testable

We want to test each component of our application separately so that we are confident that the component works as intended. For components that are of the adapter type (ones that interact with an external system), we want to test against the real external system if possible. For example, our components that talk to PostgreSQL are better tested against the actual PostgreSQL database. This kind of testing is also known as "integration testing." On the other hand, we also have components that represent the domain. These components talk to the external system by going through port components. For domain components, we want to test against the mocked port components. By mocking these components, we can simulate various scenarios easily without using the actual external system. This makes it possible to have thorough testing and keep the test code fast.

If you look closely at the adapter components, you may notice that they are comprised of two different kinds. One calls the domain, such as HTTP and RabbitMQ consumer, and one that is being called by the domain, such as PostgreSQL and Redis. Let's call the first one a "driving" adapter and the latter one a "driven" adapter.

As I have mentioned earlier, when our domain calls our "driven" adapters, they are called through port components. We can then mock the port components to test our domain. However, in our current implementation, the "driving" adapters call our

© Ecky Putrady 2018
E. Putrady, *Practical Web Development with Haskell*, https://doi.org/10.1007/978-1-4842-3739-7_11

domain directly. This means that we can't test our "driving" adapters separately from our domain. This makes them harder to test. So, before writing any test code, let's refactor our codebase a bit to make it more testable. The main change is that we introduce a new port component that our "driving" adapters use to invoke functionalities in the domain.

The first thing that we will do for refactoring is to split the Domain.Auth module into two modules. One is for types and ports declaration; let's call this Domain.Auth.Types. The second one is where we implement the actual domain logic. Let's call that Domain.Auth.Service.

Domain.Auth.Types has the following content:

```haskell
module Domain.Auth.Types (
  -- * Types
  Auth(..),
  Email(rawEmail),
  mkEmail,
  Password(rawPassword),
  mkPassword,
  UserId,
  VerificationCode,
  SessionId,
  RegistrationError(..),
  EmailVerificationError(..),
  LoginError(..),

  -- * Services
  AuthService(..)
) where

import ClassyPrelude
import Domain.Validation
import Text.Regex.PCRE.Heavy

newtype Email = Email { rawEmail :: Text } deriving (Show, Eq, Ord)

mkEmail :: Text -> Either [ErrMsg] Email
mkEmail =
  validate Email
    [ regexMatches
```

```
      [re|^[A-Z0-9a-z._%+-]+@[A-Za-z0-9.-]+\.[A-Za-z]{2,64}$|]
      "Not a valid email"
    ]
```

```
newtype Password = Password { rawPassword :: Text } deriving (Show, Eq)
```

```
mkPassword :: Text -> Either [ErrMsg] Password
mkPassword =
  validate Password
    [ lengthBetween 5 50 "Should between 5 and 50"
    , regexMatches [re|\d|] "Should contain number"
    , regexMatches [re|[A-Z]|] "Should contain uppercase letter"
    , regexMatches [re|[a-z]|] "Should contain lowercase letter"
    ]
```

```
data Auth = Auth
  { authEmail :: Email
  , authPassword :: Password
  } deriving (Show, Eq)
```

```
type UserId = Int
```

```
type VerificationCode = Text
```

```
type SessionId = Text
```

```
data RegistrationError
  = RegistrationErrorEmailTaken
  deriving (Show, Eq)
```

```
data EmailVerificationError
  = EmailVerificationErrorInvalidCode
  deriving (Show, Eq)
```

```
data LoginError
  = LoginErrorInvalidAuth
  | LoginErrorEmailNotVerified
  deriving (Show, Eq)
```

```
class (Monad m) => AuthService m where
  register :: Auth -> m (Either RegistrationError ())
  verifyEmail :: VerificationCode -> m (Either EmailVerificationError ())
  login :: Auth -> m (Either LoginError SessionId)
  resolveSessionId :: SessionId -> m (Maybe UserId)
  getUser :: UserId -> m (Maybe Email)
```

We have seen most of the preceding code. One notable addition is the AuthService typeclass. This typeclass is the port for "driving" adapters to invoke the domain's functionalities.

The Domain.Auth.Service module contains the remaining code from Domain.Auth that doesn't make it to Domain.Auth.Types:

```
module Domain.Auth.Service where

import ClassyPrelude
import Domain.Auth.Types
import Control.Monad.Except
import Katip

class (Monad m) => AuthRepo m where
  addAuth :: Auth -> m (Either RegistrationError (UserId, VerificationCode))
  setEmailAsVerified :: VerificationCode
                     -> m (Either EmailVerificationError (UserId, Email))
  findUserByAuth :: Auth -> m (Maybe (UserId, Bool))
  findEmailFromUserId :: UserId -> m (Maybe Email)

class (Monad m) => EmailVerificationNotif m where
  notifyEmailVerification :: Email -> VerificationCode -> m ()

class (Monad m) => SessionRepo m where
  newSession :: UserId -> m SessionId
  findUserIdBySessionId :: SessionId -> m (Maybe UserId)

withUserIdContext :: (KatipContext m) => UserId -> m a -> m a
withUserIdContext uId = katipAddContext (sl "userId" uId)

register :: (KatipContext m, AuthRepo m, EmailVerificationNotif m)
         => Auth -> m (Either RegistrationError ())
```

```
register auth = runExceptT $ do
  (uId, vCode) <- ExceptT $ addAuth auth
  let email = authEmail auth
  lift $ notifyEmailVerification email vCode
  withUserIdContext uId $
    $(logTM) InfoS $ ls (rawEmail email) <> " is registered successfully"

verifyEmail :: (KatipContext m, AuthRepo m)
          => VerificationCode -> m (Either EmailVerificationError ())
          verifyEmail vCode = runExceptT $ do
  (uId, email) <- ExceptT $ setEmailAsVerified vCode
  withUserIdContext uId $
    $(logTM) InfoS $ ls (rawEmail email) <> " is verified successfully"
  return ()

login :: (KatipContext m, AuthRepo m, SessionRepo m)
    => Auth -> m (Either LoginError SessionId)
login auth = runExceptT $ do
  result <- lift $ findUserByAuth auth
  case result of
    Nothing -> throwError LoginErrorInvalidAuth
    Just (_, False) -> throwError LoginErrorEmailNotVerified
    Just (uId, _) -> withUserIdContext uId . lift $ do
      sId <- newSession uId
      $(logTM) InfoS $ ls (rawEmail $ authEmail auth) <> " logged in
      successfully"
      return sId

resolveSessionId :: (SessionRepo m) => SessionId -> m (Maybe UserId)
resolveSessionId = findUserIdBySessionId

getUser :: (AuthRepo m) => UserId -> m (Maybe Email)
getUser = findEmailFromUserId
```

The removal of Domain.Auth should trigger compile errors. Just follow those errors and replace Domain.Auth with Domain.Auth.Types. In the HTTP adapter modules, you will notice that there will be complaints about AuthRepo m, EmailVerificationNotif m, and `SessionRepo` m not being found. Remove those constraints and replace them with `AuthService` m and you will be good to go. As the changes for this are quite easy to follow using the compiler errors, I'm not laying out all the changes.

Now we move on to `Adapter.RabbitMQ.Auth`. As you can see, this module talks to `Adapter.InMemory.Auth` directly. We should introduce a port so that it can be mocked or swapped out with something else. We will name the port `EmailVerificationSender`. The content of the `Adapter.RabbitMQ.Auth` module is now as follows:

```
module Adapter.RabbitMQ.Auth where

import ClassyPrelude
import Adapter.RabbitMQ.Common
import Network.AMQP
import Katip
import Data.Aeson
import Data.Aeson.TH
import qualified Domain.Auth.Types as D

data EmailVerificationPayload = EmailVerificationPayload
  { emailVerificationPayloadEmail :: Text
  , emailVerificationPayloadVerificationCode :: Text
  }

class (Monad m) => EmailVerificationSender m where
  sendEmailVerification :: D.Email -> D.VerificationCode -> m ()

init :: (EmailVerificationSender m, KatipContext m, MonadCatch m)
    => State -> (m Bool -> IO Bool) -> IO ()
init state runner = do
  initQueue state "verifyEmail" "auth" "userRegistered"
  initConsumer state "verifyEmail" (consumeEmailVerification runner)

consumeEmailVerification :: (EmailVerificationSender m, KatipContext m,
                            MonadCatch m)
                    => (m Bool -> IO Bool) -> Message -> IO Bool
consumeEmailVerification runner msg =
  runner $ consumeAndProcess msg handler
```

```
where
  handler payload =
    case D.mkEmail (emailVerificationPayloadEmail payload) of
      Left err -> withMsgAndErr msg err $ do
        $(logTM) ErrorS "Email format is invalid. Rejecting."
        return False
      Right email -> do
        let vCode = emailVerificationPayloadVerificationCode payload
        sendEmailVerification email vCode
        return True

notifyEmailVerification :: (Rabbit r m) => D.Email -> D.VerificationCode -> m ()
notifyEmailVerification email vCode =
  let payload = EmailVerificationPayload (D.rawEmail email) vCode
  in  publish "auth" "userRegistered" payload

-- JSON serde

$(let structName = fromMaybe "" . lastMay . splitElem '.' . show $
''EmailVerificationPayload
      lowercaseFirst (x:xs) = toLower [x] <> xs
      lowercaseFirst xs = xs
      options = defaultOptions
                  { fieldLabelModifier = lowercaseFirst . drop (length
                    structName)
                  }
  in  deriveJSON options ''EmailVerificationPayload)
```

Finally, we move on to Lib module to wire these new ports that we have just created. Add the following code:

```
import Domain.Auth.Types
import qualified Domain.Auth.Service as D

instance AuthService App where
  register = D.register
  verifyEmail = D.verifyEmail
```

```
login = D.login
resolveSessionId = D.resolveSessionId
getUser = D.getUser

instance MQAuth.EmailVerificationSender App where
  sendEmailVerification = M.notifyEmailVerification
```

Our refactoring effort has now been completed. It's time to move on to the actual testing.

Test Implementation

In this section, we will implement the actual testing code. We first start by setting up the test framework. After that, we will write a test for the each of the following modules:

1. Domain.Validation

2. Domain.Auth.Service

3. Adapter.PostgreSQL.Auth

4. Adapter.Redis.Auth

5. Adapter.RabbitMQ.Auth

6. Adapter.HTTP.API.Server.Auth

7. Config

Test Framework Setup

There are many test frameworks to choose from for Haskell. A few popular ones are tasty,[1] HTF,[2] HUnit,[3] and hspec.[4] In this book, we will be using hspec. I find hspec to be very intuitive to use; it produces the human-friendliest output; and it has a rich ecosystem around it.

---

[1]www.stackage.org/package/tasty
[2]www.stackage.org/package/HTF
[3]www.stackage.org/package/HUnit
[4]www.stackage.org/package/hspec

Add the hspec package to our package.yaml under the tests.hauth-test.dependencies section:

```
dependencies:
- hspec
```

We will also do one more tweak to the hspec configuration so that hspec will only run tests that were previously failed before running the whole test. This makes the test development cycle much quicker. Execute the following command on the terminal:

```
$ echo --failure-report .hspec-failures >> ~/.hspec
$ echo --rerun >> ~/.hspec
$ echo --rerun-all-on-success >> ~/.hspec
```

To run the test, we can use the following stack command:

```
$ stack test
```

The preceding command will run the test once. However, during development, it's better to automatically rerun the test when any file is changed. To do this, just add --file-watch to the preceding command like so:

```
$ stack test --file-watch
```

Combined with the hspec's "only re-run previously failing tests" functionality, this makes a very productive test development workflow.

The main entry point for test code is the test/Spec.hs file. You may organize your test any way you like, as long as it's being invoked directly or indirectly from this file. For hspec, however, there's a suggested test organization convention. The organization is simple: just create the same module with Spec added to its name. For example, if we have a Domain.Validation module, then the test should be put in the Domain. ValidationSpec module. Effectively, this means that we put the code inside the test/ Domain/ValidationSpec.hs file. In that file, there must be one function named spec. That function will be called to execute the test in the module. Simple, right?

If we organize the tests like that, then we can leverage a neat feature from hspec: automatic test discovery. With this feature, the tests following the organization approach described previously will be automatically included during the test run. This reduces the amount of boilerplate code that we need to write. To enable that feature, change the content of test/Spec.hs to just this line:

```
{-# OPTIONS_GHC -F -pgmF hspec-discover #-}
```

In this book, we will use the aforementioned organization approach and use the automatic test discovery feature for writing our tests.

Testing **Domain.Validation**

Let's start testing the Domain.Validation module. As stated previously, create a file named test/Domain/ValidationSpec.hs and write the following code:

```
module Domain.ValidationSpec where

import ClassyPrelude
import Test.Hspec
import Domain.Validation
import Text.Regex.PCRE.Heavy

spec :: Spec
spec = do
  describe "rangeBetween" $ do
  let validator = rangeBetween 1 10 "fail"
  it "val < min should fail" $
    validator 0 `shouldBe` Just "fail"
  it "val == min should pass" $
    validator 1 `shouldBe` Nothing
  it "min < val < max should pass" $
    validator 5 `shouldBe` Nothing
  it "val == max should pass" $
    validator 10 `shouldBe` Nothing
  it "val > max should fail" $
    validator 11 `shouldBe` Just "fail"

describe "lengthBetween" $ do
  let validator = lengthBetween 1 10 "fail"
  it "val < min should fail" $
    validator [] `shouldBe` Just "fail"
  it "val == min should pass" $
    validator [1] `shouldBe` Nothing
  it "min < val < max should pass" $
```

```
      validator [1..5] `shouldBe` Nothing
    it "val == max should pass" $
      validator [1..10] `shouldBe` Nothing
    it "val > max should fail" $
      validator [1..11] `shouldBe` Just "fail"

describe "regexMatches" $ do
  let validator = regexMatches [re|^hello|] "fail"
  it "if matches found then it should pass" $
    validator "hello world" `shouldBe` Nothing
  it "if no match found then it should fail" $
    validator "world hello" `shouldBe` Just "fail"
```

If we run the test, we should see the following output:

```
Domain.Validation
  rangeBetween
    val < min should fail
    val == min should pass
    min < val < max should pass
    val == max should pass
    val > max should fail
  lengthBetween
    val < min should fail
    val == min should pass
    min < val < max should pass
    val == max should pass
    val > max should fail
  regexMatches
    if matches found then it should pass
    if no match found then it should fail
```

It might not be visible in this book, but there are colors for the preceding output. Lines with green color indicate that the test passed. On the other hand, a red color indicates test failure.

As you can see, the output structure mimics the code that we had written previously. In the preceding code, we observed a few hspec constructs: describe, it, and shouldBe. describe is basically just a grouping of tests. You can nest multiple describe. As you might have expected, every nested call to describe will indent the output within it. it is a function to do the actual test. it can't be nested, unlike describe. shouldBe is an assertion that the two input parameters are equal. If the assertion fails, it will show an informative error message showing the expected and the actual values. There are more hspec constructs; we will discover more of them as we progress in this chapter.

Testing Domain.Auth.Types

In the Domain.Auth.Types module, the functionalities that we want to test are the smart constructors. We write the test in the test/Domain/Auth/TypesSpec.hs file:

```haskell
module Domain.Auth.TypesSpec where

import ClassyPrelude
import Test.Hspec
import Domain.Auth.Types

spec :: Spec
spec = do
  describe "mkEmail" $ do
    describe "should pass" $
      mkEmailSpec "ecky@test.com" True
    describe "should fail" $ do
      mkEmailSpec "invalid email@test.com" False
      mkEmailSpec "email@test." False
      mkEmailSpec "test.com" False

  describe "mkPassword" $ do
    describe "should pass" $
      mkPasswordSpec "abcDEF123" []
    describe "should fail" $ do
      mkPasswordSpec "aA1" ["Should between 5 and 50"]
      mkPasswordSpec (fromString . take 51 . join $ repeat "aA1")
      ["Should between 5 and 50"]
```

```
      mkPasswordSpec "abcDEF" ["Should contain number"]
      mkPasswordSpec "abc123" ["Should contain uppercase letter"]
      mkPasswordSpec "ABC123" ["Should contain lowercase letter"]
mkEmailSpec :: Text -> Bool -> Spec
mkEmailSpec email isValid =
  it (unpack email) $
    case (isValid, mkEmail email) of
      (True, result) ->
        result `shouldSatisfy` either (const False) ((email ==) . rawEmail)
      (False, result) ->
        result `shouldSatisfy` either (["Not a valid email"] ==)
        (const False)

mkPasswordSpec :: Text -> [Text] -> Spec
mkPasswordSpec password errMsgs =
  it (unpack password) $
    case (errMsgs, mkPassword password) of
      ([], result) ->
        result `shouldSatisfy` either (const False) ((password ==) .
        rawPassword)
      (msgs, result) ->
        result `shouldSatisfy` either (msgs ==) (const False)
```

If run, it will output the following:

```
Domain.Auth.Types
  mkEmail
    should pass
      ecky@test.com
    should fail
      invalid email@test.com
      email@test.
      test.com
  mkPassword
    should pass
      abcDEF123
```

```
should fail
  aA1
  aA1aA1aA1aA1aA1aA1aA1aA1aA1aA1aA1aA1aA1aA1aA1
  abcDEF
  abc123
  ABC123
```

One notable thing to take away from the preceding code is that we define two helper functions to build a test scenario: mkEmailSpec and mkPasswordSpec. Bear in mind that hspec functions are by no means anything special. They are just regular functions and we can treat them as such, including calling them in a different function.

Testing Domain.Auth.Service

In the previous sections, we've seen how to test a simple module that doesn't need to call any external dependencies. In this section, we will test a module that requires interaction with external dependencies. We will learn how to mock those external dependencies so that we can test various scenarios easily. Following the test organization approach so far, the test code should be put in the test/Domain/Auth/ServiceSpec.hs file.

As we've discussed earlier, we want to mock the port components. In this case, the port components are AuthRepo, SessionRepo, and EmailVerificationNotif. The functionality that we want to have regarding mocking is that we are able to define what each function of the port components return upon calling on each test case. To achieve this, we first need to define a record containing the functions from each repo as its field:

```
import Domain.Auth.Types

data Fixture m = Fixture
  { _addAuth
      :: Auth -> m (Either RegistrationError (UserId, VerificationCode))
  , _setEmailAsVerified
      :: VerificationCode -> m (Either EmailVerificationError (UserId, Email))
  , _findUserByAuth
      :: Auth -> m (Maybe (UserId, Bool))
  , _findEmailFromUserId
      :: UserId -> m (Maybe Email)
  , _notifyEmailVerification
```

```
      :: Email -> VerificationCode -> m ()
  , _newSession
      :: UserId -> m SessionId
  , _findUserIdBySessionId
      :: SessionId -> m (Maybe UserId)
  }
```

As you can see, the name that we use for each field in the fixture is basically the same as the function name in the port components, except that we add a leading underscore. This underscore is used to prevent name clash.

We also define an empty fixture, which will throw an error if any of the functions are called:

```
unimplemented :: a
unimplemented = error "unimplemented"

emptyFixture :: Fixture m
emptyFixture = Fixture
  { _addAuth = const unimplemented
  , _setEmailAsVerified = const unimplemented
  , _findUserByAuth = const unimplemented
  , _findEmailFromUserId = const unimplemented
  , _notifyEmailVerification = \_ _ -> unimplemented
  , _newSession = const unimplemented
  , _findUserIdBySessionId = const unimplemented
  }
```

Next, we define a monad transformer stack for our application:

```
import Katip

newtype App a = App
  { unApp :: ReaderT (Fixture IO) (KatipContextT IO) a
  } deriving ( Applicative, Functor, Monad, MonadReader (Fixture IO), MonadIO
             , KatipContext, Katip
             )
```

The Katip-related function is there because the functions that we are testing require it. Since we are not interested in testing and mocking the logging functionalities, we will use the real logging from Katip and make it silent.

By defining a specialized monad transformer stack, we can define an instance of AuthRepo, SessionRepo, and EmailVerificationNotif that uses the function defined in the fixture. The code looks as follows:

```
dispatch :: (MonadIO m, MonadReader r m)
         => (r -> a -> IO b)
         -> (a -> m b)
dispatch getter param = do
  func <- asks getter
  liftIO $ func param

dispatch2 :: (MonadIO m, MonadReader r m)
          => (r -> a -> b -> IO c)
          -> (a -> b -> m c)
dispatch2 getter param1 param2 = do
  func <- asks getter
  liftIO $ func param1 param2

instance AuthRepo App where
  addAuth = dispatch _addAuth
  setEmailAsVerified = dispatch _setEmailAsVerified
  findUserByAuth = dispatch _findUserByAuth
  findEmailFromUserId = dispatch _findEmailFromUserId

instance EmailVerificationNotif App where
  notifyEmailVerification = dispatch2 _notifyEmailVerification

instance SessionRepo App where
  newSession = dispatch _newSession
  findUserIdBySessionId = dispatch _findUserIdBySessionId
```

What the preceding dispatch function does is to basically get a function from the fixture using the given getter and then apply the same function with the given param. dispatch2 does the same, but it works for functions with two parameters instead of one parameter.

We also define a function to unwind or run the monad transformer:

```
runApp :: Fixture IO -> App a -> IO a
runApp fixture action = do
  le <- initLogEnv "HAuth" "test"
  runKatipContextT le () mempty . flip runReaderT fixture . unApp $ action
```

We defined Katip's logging environment but we don't define any Scribe. This means the log will not be sent anywhere. This is OK, since we are not interested in the logging.

With the preceding boilerplate, we are ready to mock the external dependencies. Let's see an example of how it is used:

```
it "should fail if the auth is incorrect" $ do
  let fixture = emptyFixture
        { _findUserByAuth =
          \_ -> return Nothing
        }
  runApp fixture (login auth)
    `shouldReturn` Left LoginErrorInvalidAuth
```

In the preceding example, we define our fixture to be the same as emptyFixture but with the _findUserByAuth function overridden to always return Nothing. This setup allows us to test a scenario where the user logs in but we are unable to find the supplied credential in our repository. The fixture is then used in the runApp function as the first parameter, while the function under test, login, is supplied as the second parameter. We use shouldReturn, a function from hspec, to check whether the return value of that action is as expected.

shouldReturn works similarly to shouldBe that we have seen before. The difference is that shouldReturn works on a monad. The following code snippet should give a clearer understanding of the two functions:

```
-- with `shouldReturn`:
runApp fixture (login auth)
  `shouldReturn` Left LoginErrorInvalidAuth

-- with `shouldBe`:
result <- runApp fixture (login auth)
result `shouldBe` Left LoginErrorInvalidAuth
```

Let's see another example of the usage of a fixture:

```
it "should return a session if the login is successful" $ do
  let fixture = emptyFixture
        { _findUserByAuth =
          \_ -> return $ Just (1, True)
        , _newSession =
          \uId -> if uId == 1 then return "sId" else unimplemented
        }
  runApp fixture (login auth)
    `shouldReturn` Right "sId"
```

In the preceding example, we override two functions of the fixture. Remember, since they are just normal functions, you can define anything you like. For example, in _newSession, we check the input parameter and throw an error if it's not as expected.

In general, you have seen how mocking is done in Haskell. We will not go through each test scenario in detail for that reason.

Let's step back to some helper functions that we defined earlier for building our fixture. We are definitely going to need those again if we are to define a fixture in other test modules. So, it's better for them to be moved into their own module for reusability. We'll name the module Fixture and define it in the test/Fixture.hs file. The content of that file would be as follows:

```
module Fixture where

import ClassyPrelude

unimplemented :: a
unimplemented = error "unimplemented"

dispatch :: (MonadIO m, MonadReader r m)
         => (r -> a -> IO b)
         -> (a -> m b)
dispatch getter param = do
  func <- asks getter
  liftIO $ func param

dispatch2 :: (MonadIO m, MonadReader r m)
          => (r -> a -> b -> IO c)
```

```
         -> (a -> b -> m c)
dispatch2 getter param1 param2 = do
  func <- asks getter
  liftIO $ func param1 param2
```

Now that we've refactored those helper functions, the content of the Domain.Auth. ServiceSpec function would be as follows:

```
module Domain.Auth.ServiceSpec where

import ClassyPrelude
import Domain.Auth.Types hiding (AuthService(..))
import Domain.Auth.Service
import Test.Hspec
import Fixture
import Katip

data Fixture m = Fixture
  { _addAuth
      :: Auth -> m (Either RegistrationError (UserId, VerificationCode))
  , _setEmailAsVerified
      :: VerificationCode -> m (Either EmailVerificationError (UserId, Email))
  , _findUserByAuth
      :: Auth -> m (Maybe (UserId, Bool))
  , _findEmailFromUserId
      :: UserId -> m (Maybe Email)
  , _notifyEmailVerification
      :: Email -> VerificationCode -> m ()
  , _newSession
      :: UserId -> m SessionId
  , _findUserIdBySessionId
      :: SessionId -> m (Maybe UserId)
  }

emptyFixture :: Fixture m
emptyFixture = Fixture
  { _addAuth = const unimplemented
  , _setEmailAsVerified = const unimplemented
```

```
  , _findUserByAuth = const unimplemented
  , _findEmailFromUserId = const unimplemented
  , _notifyEmailVerification = \_ _ -> unimplemented
  , _newSession = const unimplemented
  , _findUserIdBySessionId = const unimplemented
  }

newtype App a = App
  { unApp :: ReaderT (Fixture IO) (KatipContextT IO) a
  } deriving ( Applicative, Functor, Monad, MonadReader (Fixture IO), MonadIO
             , KatipContext, Katip
             )

runApp :: Fixture IO -> App a -> IO a
runApp fixture action = do
  le <- initLogEnv "HAuth" "test"
  runKatipContextT le () mempty . flip runReaderT fixture . unApp $ action

instance AuthRepo App where
  addAuth = dispatch _addAuth
  setEmailAsVerified = dispatch _setEmailAsVerified
  findUserByAuth = dispatch _findUserByAuth
  findEmailFromUserId = dispatch _findEmailFromUserId

instance EmailVerificationNotif App where
  notifyEmailVerification = dispatch2 _notifyEmailVerification

instance SessionRepo App where
  newSession = dispatch _newSession
  findUserIdBySessionId = dispatch _findUserIdBySessionId

spec :: Spec
spec = do

  let auth = either (error . show) id
          $ Auth <$> mkEmail "abc@123.com" <*> mkPassword "abcDEF123"

  describe "register" $ do
    it "should notify email verification upon successful registration" $ do
```

```
    tvar <- newTVarIO Nothing
    let fixture = emptyFixture
          { _addAuth =
            \_ -> return $ Right (1, "vcode")
          , _notifyEmailVerification =
            \email vCode -> atomically . writeTVar tvar $ Just
            (email, vCode)
          }
    runApp fixture (register auth) `shouldReturn` Right ()
    readTVarIO tvar `shouldReturn` Just (authEmail auth, "vcode")

  it "should return failure and not notify any email verification" $ do
    let fixture = emptyFixture
          { _addAuth = \_ -> return $ Left RegistrationErrorEmailTaken
          }
    runApp fixture (register auth)
      `shouldReturn` Left RegistrationErrorEmailTaken
    -- the fact that no exception thrown means no email verification is
      triggered

describe "verifyEmail" $ do
  it "should call the correct repo function" $ do
    let fixture = emptyFixture
          { _setEmailAsVerified = \vcode -> case vcode of
              "vCode" -> return $ Right (1, authEmail auth)
              _ -> unimplemented
          }
    runApp fixture (verifyEmail "vCode")
      `shouldReturn` Right ()

  it "should return the failure if writing to repo fail" $ do
    let fixture = emptyFixture
          { _setEmailAsVerified =
            \_ -> return $ Left EmailVerificationErrorInvalidCode
          }
    runApp fixture (verifyEmail "vCode")
      `shouldReturn` Left EmailVerificationErrorInvalidCode
```

```
describe "login" $ do
  it "should fail if the auth is incorrect" $ do
    let fixture = emptyFixture
          { _findUserByAuth =
              \_ -> return Nothing
          }
    runApp fixture (login auth)
      `shouldReturn` Left LoginErrorInvalidAuth
  it "should fail if the email has not been verified" $ do
    let fixture = emptyFixture
          { _findUserByAuth =
              \_ -> return $ Just (1, False)
          }
    runApp fixture (login auth)
      `shouldReturn` Left LoginErrorEmailNotVerified
  it "should return a session if the login is successful" $ do
    let fixture = emptyFixture
          { _findUserByAuth =
              \_ -> return $ Just (1, True)
          , _newSession =
              \uId -> if uId == 1 then return "sId" else unimplemented
          }
    runApp fixture (login auth)
      `shouldReturn` Right "sId"

describe "resolveSessionId" $ do
  it "should return Nothing if the session is not found" $ do
    let fixture = emptyFixture
          { _findUserIdBySessionId =
              \_ -> return Nothing
          }
    runApp fixture (resolveSessionId "sId")
      `shouldReturn` Nothing
  it "should return UserId if the session is found" $ do
    let fixture = emptyFixture
          { _findUserIdBySessionId =
```

240

```
                \sId -> if sId == "sId" then return (Just 1) else unimplemented
            }
      runApp fixture (resolveSessionId "sId")
        `shouldReturn` Just 1

  describe "getUser" $ do
    it "should return Nothing if the user is not found" $ do
      let fixture = emptyFixture
            { _findEmailFromUserId =
              \_ -> return Nothing
            }
      runApp fixture (getUser 1)
        `shouldReturn` Nothing
    it "should return Email if the user is found" $ do
      let expected = Just (authEmail auth)
      let fixture = emptyFixture
            { _findEmailFromUserId =
              \uId -> if uId == 1
                then return expected
                else unimplemented
            }
      runApp fixture (getUser 1)
        `shouldReturn` expected
```

Testing `Adapter.PostgreSQL.Auth`

We will write our test implementation in the test/Adapter/PostgreSQL/AuthSpec.hs
file. Let's start by writing the necessary imports:

```
module Adapter.PostgreSQL.AuthSpec where

import ClassyPrelude
import Test.Hspec
import qualified Domain.Auth.Types as D
import Database.PostgreSQL.Simple
import Adapter.PostgreSQL.Auth
import Text.StringRandom
```

Since we test against the real database, we will need to set up the database first before executing any test. To execute any action at the beginning of the test group once, we can use the beforeAll function from hspec like so:

```
spec :: Spec
spec = beforeAll initDB $ do
  describe "addAuth" $
    it "should return email taken if the email already exists" pending

  describe "setEmailAsVerified" $
    it "should return invalid code if the code is invalid" pending

  describe "findUserByAuth" $ do
    it "should return Nothing if matching auth not found" pending
    it "should find the user (email has been verified) if matching auth
    found" pending
    it "should find the user (email not yet verified) if matching auth
    found" pending

  describe "findEmailFromUserId" $ do
    it "should return Nothing if user id is not found" pending
    it "should return correct email if user id is found" pending
```

In the preceding snippet, we also see a new function from hspec: pending. This basically indicates that the test has not yet been written. When running, a pending test will be marked with yellow color. In addition to passes and failures count, hspec output also shows the pending count.

Next, we define the initDB function:

```
initDB :: IO ()
initDB = do
  conn <- connectPostgreSQL "postgresql://localhost"
  void $ execute_ conn "drop database if exists hauth_test_auth"
  void $ execute_ conn "create database hauth_test_auth"
  close conn
  withState testConf (const $ return ())

testConf :: Config
testConf =
```

```
Config    { configUrl = "postgresql://localhost/hauth_test_auth"
          , configStripeCount = 2
          , configMaxOpenConnPerStripe = 5
          , configIdleConnTimeout = 10
          }
```

In the preceding function, we connect to our PostgreSQL instance as root. Then, we drop the test database and recreate it to make sure that the database is in a pristine state. Finally, we use a `withState` function to connect to the test database. This serves two purposes: to make sure the database is reachable and to perform any database migrations.

Let's see an example of a test:

```
it "should return email taken if the email already exists" $ do
  auth <- randomAuth
  runTestApp (addAuth auth >> addAuth auth)
    `shouldReturn` Left D.RegistrationErrorEmailTaken
```

The preceding test says that we are testing duplicate email behavior. We first generate a random Auth, then we insert the same Auth twice. Finally, we check whether it returns `D.RegistrationErrorEmailTaken`. In the preceding code snippet, we use two helper functions, `randomAuth` and `runTestApp`, which are defined as follows:

```
runTestApp :: ReaderT State IO a -> IO a
runTestApp action =
  withPool testConf $ runReaderT action

randomAuth :: IO D.Auth
randomAuth = do
  email <- stringRandomIO "[A-Za-z0-9]{16}@test\\.com"
  return
    $ either (error . show) id
    $ D.Auth <$> D.mkEmail email <*> D.mkPassword "abcDEF123"
```

`runTestApp` is necessary, considering the definition of the `addAuth` function in our `Adapter.PostgreSQL.Auth` module:

```
type PG r m = (Has State r, MonadReader r m, MonadIO m)

addAuth :: PG r m
        => D.Auth
        -> m (Either D.RegistrationError (D.UserId, D.VerificationCode))
```

243

This function works for any m that fulfills the preceding constraint. ReaderT State IO is one concrete monad transformer stack that fulfills the constraint.

Here's a complete content of the test module:

```haskell
module Adapter.PostgreSQL.AuthSpec where

import ClassyPrelude
import Test.Hspec
import qualified Domain.Auth.Types as D
import Database.PostgreSQL.Simple
import Adapter.PostgreSQL.Auth
import Text.StringRandom

spec :: Spec
spec = beforeAll initDB $ do
  describe "addAuth" $
    it "should return email taken if the email already exists" $ do
      auth <- randomAuth
      runTestApp (addAuth auth >> addAuth auth)
        `shouldReturn` Left D.RegistrationErrorEmailTaken

  describe "setEmailAsVerified" $
    it "should return invalid code if the code is invalid" $
      runTestApp (setEmailAsVerified "invalidCode")
        `shouldReturn` Left D.EmailVerificationErrorInvalidCode

  describe "findUserByAuth" $ do
    it "should return Nothing if matching auth not found" $ do
      auth <- randomAuth
      runTestApp (findUserByAuth auth)
        `shouldReturn` Nothing
    it "should find the user (email has been verified) if matching auth
    found" $ do
      auth <- randomAuth
      runTestApp $ do
        Right (uId, vCode) <- addAuth auth
        void $ setEmailAsVerified vCode
        val <- findUserByAuth auth
        liftIO $ val `shouldBe` Just (uId, True)
```

```
    it "should find the user (email not yet verified) if matching auth
    found" $ do
      auth <- randomAuth
      runTestApp $ do
        Right (uId, _) <- addAuth auth
        val <- findUserByAuth auth
        liftIO $ val `shouldBe` Just (uId, False)

  describe "findEmailFromUserId" $ do
    it "should return Nothing if user id is not found" $
      runTestApp (findEmailFromUserId 0)
        `shouldReturn` Nothing
    it "should return correct email if user id is found" $ do
      auth <- randomAuth
      runTestApp $ do
        Right (uId, _) <- addAuth auth
        mayEmail <- findEmailFromUserId uId
        liftIO $ mayEmail `shouldBe` Just (D.authEmail auth)

initDB :: IO ()
initDB = do
  conn <- connectPostgreSQL "postgresql://localhost"
  void $ execute_ conn "drop database if exists hauth_test_auth"
  void $ execute_ conn "create database hauth_test_auth"
  close conn
  withState testConf (const $ return ())

testConf :: Config
testConf =
  Config  { configUrl = "postgresql://localhost/hauth_test_auth"
          , configStripeCount = 2
          , configMaxOpenConnPerStripe = 5
          , configIdleConnTimeout = 10
          }
```

```
runTestApp :: ReaderT State IO a -> IO a
runTestApp action =
  withPool testConf $ runReaderT action

randomAuth :: IO D.Auth
randomAuth = do
  email <- stringRandomIO "[A-Za-z0-9]{16}@test\\.com" return
    $ either (error . show) id
    $ D.Auth <$> D.mkEmail email <*> D.mkPassword "abcDEF123"
```

Testing **Adapter.Redis.Auth**

We will write our test code in the test/Adapter/Redis/AuthSpec.hs file. Similar to Adapter.PostgreSQL.Auth, this module also needs to be tested against the real database. There's actually not much to be tested in this module, since this module only provides two functions. The whole content of the test file is as follows:

```
module Adapter.Redis.AuthSpec where

import ClassyPrelude
import Test.Hspec
import qualified Database.Redis as R
import Adapter.Redis.Auth

spec :: Spec
spec = beforeAll initDB $
  describe "findUserIdBySessionId" $ do
    it "should return Nothing if session is invalid" $
      runTestApp (findUserIdBySessionId "invalidSession")
        `shouldReturn` Nothing
    it "should return valid user id if session is valid" $ do
      let uId = 1
      runTestApp (newSession uId >>= findUserIdBySessionId)
        `shouldReturn` Just uId

initDB :: IO ()
initDB = do
```

```
  let connInfo = either (error "Invalid Redis conn URL") id
                $ R.parseConnectInfo testConf
  conn <- R.checkedConnect connInfo
  void $ R.runRedis conn R.flushdb

testConf :: String
testConf = "redis://localhost:6379/8"

runTestApp :: ReaderT State IO a -> IO a
runTestApp action =
  withState testConf $ runReaderT action
```

You should see a striking similarity with the test implementation of PostgreSQL. Remember that redis provides multiple databases that we can refer to by index number? For testing, we use database index 8. This use of an index is to avoid clashing with the development database, which is in index 0. In the initDB function, we connect to the test DB and clean it up using the flushdb function from the Database.Redis module. This makes sure that the database is in a pristine state.

Testing `Adapter.RabbitMQ.Auth`

The whole test code for this module is as follows:

```
module Adapter.RabbitMQ.AuthSpec where

import ClassyPrelude
import Test.Hspec
import qualified Domain.Auth.Types as D
import qualified Adapter.RabbitMQ.Common as MQ
import qualified Adapter.RabbitMQ.Auth as MQ
import Katip
import Fixture
import System.Process

newtype Fixture m = Fixture
  { _sendEmailVerification :: D.Email -> D.VerificationCode -> m ()
  }
```

```
newtype App a = App
  { unApp :: ReaderT (Fixture IO) (KatipContextT IO) a
  } deriving ( Applicative, Functor, Monad, MonadIO, MonadReader (Fixture IO)
             , Katip, KatipContext, MonadThrow, MonadCatch
             )

instance MQ.EmailVerificationSender App where
  sendEmailVerification = dispatch2 _sendEmailVerification

runConsumerTestApp :: Fixture IO -> App a -> IO a
runConsumerTestApp fixture action = do
  le <- initLogEnv "HAuth" "test"
  runKatipContextT le () mempty . flip runReaderT fixture . unApp $ action

type PublisherStateApp a = ReaderT MQ.State IO a

runPublisherTestApp :: MQ.State -> ReaderT MQ.State m a -> m a
runPublisherTestApp = flip runReaderT

spec :: Spec
spec = beforeAll initMQ $
  it "send and consume email verification notification should work" $
    MQ.withState testConf $ \mqState -> do
      mvar <- newEmptyMVar
      -- run consumer
      let fixture = Fixture
            { _sendEmailVerification =
                \mail code -> liftIO $ putMVar mvar (mail, code)
            }
      MQ.init mqState (runConsumerTestApp fixture)
      -- publish msg
      let email = either (error . show) id $ D.mkEmail "ecky@test.com"
          vCode = "vCode"
      runPublisherTestApp mqState $ MQ.notifyEmailVerification email vCode
      -- wait till the msg come
      takeMVar mvar `shouldReturn` (email, vCode)

initMQ :: IO ()
initMQ = do
```

```
void  $ readProcessWithExitCode "rabbitmqctl"
        [ "delete_vhost", "hauth_test_auth"
        ] ""
  void  $ readProcessWithExitCode "rabbitmqctl"
        [ "add_vhost", "hauth_test_auth"
        ] ""
  void  $ readProcessWithExitCode "rabbitmqctl"
        [ "set_permissions", "-p", "hauth_test_auth", "guest"
        , ".*", ".*", ".*"
        ] ""
testConf :: MQ.Config
testConf =
  MQ.Config { MQ.configUrl = "amqp://guest:guest@localhost:5672/
  hauth_test_auth"
            , MQ.configPrefetchCount = 8
            }
```

There are two parts of RabbitMQ: The consumer and the publisher part. The main thing that we want to test is whether the message from the publisher is consumed successfully by the consumer. The mechanics of how this is done is by using a mocked `EmailVerificationSender`. When building the fixture, we define it so that we put the parameters into an `MVar`. We can think of an `MVar` as a variable that can be shared by multiple threads. We need this because the consumer runs on separate thread. We use `takeMVar` to get the value back from the `MVar`. This function blocks until the value is available in an `MVar`. Once we get the value, we then assert it against our expectations.

Like other modules with an integration test, we also want to test it in a special test environment and set it up in a pristine state. For RabbitMQ, the environment can be isolated using a virtual host. In development, our virtual host is "/". For testing, we will use "hauth_test_auth".

Before using, we first need to create the virtual host and assign some permissions to our credential. The easiest way to do that is by using `rabbitmqctl`, a command-line utility that comes packaged when we install RabbitMQ in our system. To invoke this command-line utility programmatically from our Haskell program, we can use the `process` package. We won't go into the details of this package, as this is not closely related to web development. Suffice it to say that we just use one function, `readProcessWithExitCode`, in which we invoke a process then wait for it to finish.

The preceding code won't compile, because we have not added the `process` package yet to our test dependencies. To add that, just list it in our `package.yaml` file like so:

```
tests:
  hauth-test:
    dependencies:
    - process
```

Testing `Adapter.HTTP.API.Server.Auth`

The `Adapter.HTTP.API.Server.Auth` module's main functionality is to parse an HTTP request, call the right function in `AuthService` with the correct parameters, and finally convert the result into an HTTP response. So, the testing approach that we want to do is to mock `AuthService`, then send an HTTP request and finally verify whether the resulting HTTP response is correct.

`hspec-wai` Crash Course

For testing a WAI application, it's best to use the `hspec-wai`[5] package. This package provides us with a convenient function to send an HTTP request to our WAI application, as well as HTTP response matchers. In addition to that, we also want to use the `hspec-wai-json`[6] package that allows us to test JSON response easier. This functionality is very helpful for testing a RESTful application that uses JSON. Let's add both packages to our dependencies:

```
tests:
  hauth-test:
    dependencies:
    - hspec-wai
    - hspec-wai-json
```

---

[5]`www.stackage.org/package/hspec-wai`
[6]`www.stackage.org/package/hspec-wai-json`

To make an HTTP request to a WAI application, we can use the following functions:

```
type Path = ByteString
type Body = ByteString

get, options, delete :: Path -> WaiSession SResponse
post, put, patch :: Path -> Body -> WaiSession SResponse
```

SResponse contains any data that you may find in an HTTP response. For completeness, here's how SResponse is defined:

```
SResponse = SResponse
  { simpleStatus :: Status
  , simpleHeaders :: ResponseHeaders
  , simpleBody :: ByteString
  }

data Status = Status
  { statusCode :: Int
  , statusMessage :: ByteString
  }

type ResponseHeaders = [Header]
type Header = (CI ByteString, ByteString)
```

CI ByteString is a case-insensitive ByteString. Basically it allows us to check for equality without caring about the letter casing.

HTTP response from the application can be asserted using the following function:

```
shouldRespondWith :: WaiSession SResponse -> ResponseMatcher ->
WaiExpectation

data ResponseMatcher = ResponseMatcher
  { matchStatus :: Int
  , matchHeaders :: [MatchHeader]
  , matchBody :: MatchBody
  }

data MatchHeader = MatchHeader ([Header] -> Body -> Maybe String)
data MatchBody = MatchBody ([Header] -> Body -> Maybe String)
```

251

`MatchHeader` and `MatchBody` are basically functions that check the header and body of the HTTP request and are meant to return a `Nothing` if the input matches according to our expectation. We may return `Just` with the error message and it will treat the assertion as a failure.

`ResponseMatcher` is an instance of the `Num` typeclass. This means that `ResponseMatcher` can be created from a number. If we create it from a number, then the `ResponseMatcher` will match the HTTP response status code according to the number. Let's see an example:

```
get "/health" `shouldRespondWith` 200
```

In the preceding example, we see that we passed in 200 as the second parameter of the `shouldRespondWith` function. This number will then be converted to a `ResponseMatcher` that matches status code 200.

In addition to `Num`, `ResponseMatcher` is also an instance of the `IsString` typeclass. This means that we can also create `ResponseMatcher` from `String`. If we create a `ResponseMatcher` this way, the `ResponseMatcher` will do an exact match on the HTTP response body. Let's see an example:

```
get "/health" `shouldRespondWith` "healthy"
```

In the preceding example, we passed in `"healthy"` as the second parameter to the `shouldRespondWith` function. This `String` will then be converted to a `ResponseMatcher` that asserts that the HTTP response body has to be `healthy`.

Usually, we want to have multiple assertions of the HTTP response. For example, we want to ensure that the body and status code are of some certain values.

To do that, we can just override the created `ResponseMatcher`. An example of that would be:

```
get "/health" `shouldRespondWith` "healthy" { matchStatus = 200 }
```

The preceding code asserts that the HTTP response should have a status code of 200 and `healthy` as the body.

When testing JSON RESTful API, we can use a quasiquoter that allows us to build JSON easily. This quasiquoter comes from the `hspec-wai-json` package. We use it as follows:

```
post "/login" [json|{"username":"uname", "password":"passw"|]
  `shouldRespondWith` [json|"OK"|] { matchStatus = 200 }
```

This quasiquoter can be used to create both a `ResponseMatcher` as well as a `ByteString`, as we can see from the preceding code snippet. The first instance of a `json` quasiquoter is converted to a `ByteString`, while the second one is converted to a `ResponseMatcher`.

Finally, we will look into one more function: `with`. This function basically expects an `IO Application`. `Application` is a WAI application that we want to test against. All in all, here's what the test with `hspec-wai` and `hspec-wai-json` looks like:

```
app :: IO Application
app = -- some WAI application

spec :: Spec
spec = with app $ do
  describe "GET /health" $ do
    it "responds with 200 and healthy" $ do
      get "/" `shouldRespondWith` "healthy" { matchStatus = 200 }

  describe "POST /auth" $ do
    it "responds with some JSON" $ do
      post "/login" [json|{"username":"uname", "password":"passw"|]
        `shouldRespondWith` [json|"OK"|] { matchStatus = 200 }
```

Refactoring HTTP Module

As we've seen in the `hspec-wai` section, it expects us to provide an `IO Application`. However, when we look into our `HTTP.Main` module, we don't have a function that exposes an `IO Application`. We only have one function, `main`, that runs the WAI application. So, we need to refactor this module a bit so that there is a function that returns an `IO Application`. This is quite an easy change; the updated code looks as follows:

```
module Adapter.HTTP.Main where

import ClassyPrelude
import qualified Adapter.HTTP.API.Server.Main as API
import qualified Adapter.HTTP.Web.Main as Web
import Domain.Auth.Types
import Katip
```

```haskell
import Network.Wai
import Network.Wai.Handler.Warp
import Network.Wai.Middleware.Vhost

app :: (MonadIO m, KatipContext m, AuthService m)
    => (m Response -> IO Response) -> IO Application
app runner = do
  web <- Web.main runner
  api <- API.main runner
  return $ vhost [(pathBeginsWith "api", api)] web
  where
    pathBeginsWith path req = headMay (pathInfo req) == Just path

main :: (MonadIO m, KatipContext m, AuthService m)
    => Int -> (m Response -> IO Response) -> IO ()
main port runner =
  app runner >>= run port
```

Fixture Setup

Let's continue by creating the necessary boilerplate to allow AuthService to be mocked. We will create it in the test/Adapter/HTTP/Fixture.hs file. This is because the fixture can be reused for a Web module test, in addition to an API module test. The fixture code looks as follows:

```haskell
module Adapter.HTTP.Fixture where

import ClassyPrelude
import Domain.Auth.Types
import Katip
import Network.Wai
import qualified Adapter.HTTP.Main as HTTP
import Fixture

data Fixture m = Fixture
  { _register :: Auth -> m (Either RegistrationError ())
  , _verifyEmail :: VerificationCode -> m (Either EmailVerificationError ())
  , _login :: Auth -> m (Either LoginError SessionId)
```

```
  , _resolveSessionId :: SessionId -> m (Maybe UserId)
  , _getUser :: UserId -> m (Maybe Email)
  }

emptyFixture :: Fixture IO
emptyFixture = Fixture
  { _register = const unimplemented
  , _verifyEmail = const unimplemented
  , _login = const unimplemented
  , _resolveSessionId = const unimplemented
  , _getUser = const unimplemented
  }

newtype App a = App
  { unApp :: ReaderT (Fixture IO) (KatipContextT IO) a
  } deriving ( Applicative, Functor, Monad, MonadReader (Fixture IO),
               MonadIO
             , KatipContext, Katip
             )

app :: Fixture IO -> IO Application
app fixture = do
  le <- initLogEnv "HAuth" "test"
  let runner = runKatipContextT le () mempty . flip runReaderT fixture . unApp
  HTTP.app runner

instance AuthService App where
  register = dispatch _register
  verifyEmail = dispatch _verifyEmail
  login = dispatch _login
  resolveSessionId = dispatch _resolveSessionId
  getUser = dispatch _getUser
```

Test Implementation

Let's see one example of a test for this module:

```
spec :: Spec
spec = do
  describe "POST /api/auth/register" $ do
    let emailTakenFixture = emptyFixture
          { _register = \_ -> return $ Left RegistrationErrorEmailTaken }
    with (app emailTakenFixture) $
      it "should reject account creation" $
        post "/api/auth/register"
            [json|{"email": "abc@test.com", "password":"abcDEF123"}|]
              `shouldRespondWith` [json|"EmailTaken"|]
              { matchStatus = 400 }
```

In the preceding code snippet, we created a fixture where calling a `register`
would return a `RegistrationErrorEmailTaken` error. The fixture is then passed as the
parameter for app. Recall that we define app in the `test/Fixture.hs` file. The result of
the app function is an `Application`, a WAI application.

The resulting `Application` is then passed in to the `with` function. After that, we
use the post function to send an HTTP POST request to our application. The endpoint
we are sending the request to requires a JSON body. For this, we use the `[json|...|]`
quasiquoter to build our JSON payload. We verify the response as having the correct
status and JSON body using the `shouldRespondWith` function.

The other tests in this module follow this same pattern, so we will not write all of
them here. You could look into the attached source code for this chapter to see the
complete code for this module.

Testing `Config`

For the `Config` module, the main functionality that we want to test is whether we could
read the configuration values from environment variable or not. We will write the code in
the `test/ConfigSpec.hs` file. Let's see how the code looks:

```
module ConfigSpec environment variables

import ClassyPrelude
```

```haskell
import Test.Hspec
import System.Environment
import Config
import qualified Adapter.PostgreSQL.Auth as PG
import qualified Adapter.RabbitMQ.Common as MQ

spec :: Spec
spec = before initEnv $ do
  it "should fail if PORT is missing" $ do
    unsetEnv "PORT"
    void fromEnv `shouldThrow` anyException
  it "should fail if PORT is not a number" $ do
    setEnv "PORT" "NOT A NUMBER"
    void fromEnv `shouldThrow` anyException
  it "should fail if REDIS_URL is missing" $ do
    unsetEnv "REDIS_URL"
    void fromEnv `shouldThrow` anyException
  it "should fail if MQ_URL is missing" $ do
    unsetEnv "MQ_URL"
    void fromEnv `shouldThrow` anyException
  it "should fail if PG_URL is missing" $ do
    unsetEnv "PG_URL"
    void fromEnv `shouldThrow` anyException
  it "should parse config correctly" $
    fromEnv `shouldReturn` Config
      { configPort = 1234
      , configRedis = "REDIS_URL"
      , configMQ = MQ.Config "MQ_URL" 16
      , configPG = PG.Config "PG_URL" 2 5 10
      }

initEnv :: IO ()
initEnv = do
  setEnv "PORT" "1234"
  setEnv "REDIS_URL" "REDIS_URL"
  setEnv "MQ_URL" "MQ_URL"
  setEnv "PG_URL" "PG_URL"
```

In the preceding code snippet, we have an `initEnv` function to initiate the environment variables. We use the `setEnv` function from the `System.Environment` module to set the environment variables.

`initEnv` is used as the first parameter in the `before` function. The `before` function comes from `hspec`. The main difference between `before` and `beforeAll` is that `before` is executed for every test case (the `it`), while `beforeAll` is only executed once in the test group.

Let's look into some test cases of the preceding code. The first five of the test cases check whether the `fromEnv` will throw an exception if the required environment variable is not set. To check whether the function throws an exception, we use the `shouldThrow` function provided by `hspec`. Since we are fine with any exception, as long as something is thrown, then we use `anyException`. The second parameter of `shouldThrow` is actually a predicate. So, if you have a specific concrete exception you would like to verify, then you can do so as follows:

```
someAction `shouldThrow` (== ExitFailure 1)
```

In the final test case, we check for the happy case: we check whether the environment is parsed successfully. This would require us to make `Config` an instance of the `Eq` typeclass, so make the change as required.

Code Coverage

Code coverage is one of many code quality metrics. It basically tells you how much of your code has been tested. The higher it is, the more confident you are that your application works as intended.

We can generate such metrics using the following command:

```
$ stack test --coverage
```

The preceding command should produce an output that shows where the generated coverage report is located. Figure 11-1 shows what the coverage report looks like. In our case, we managed to reach around 50% of coverage. We can also click into each module to see which part of the code has not been covered. Figure 11-2 shows an example of this.

module	Top Level Definitions		Alternatives		Expressions	
	%	covered / total	%	covered / total	%	covered / total
module hauth-0.1.0.0-9ARw4KOpKXC1NGemd5ootg/Adapter.HTTP.API.Server.Auth	100%	3/3	100%	8/8	92%	93/101
module hauth-0.1.0.0-9ARw4KOpKXC1NGemd5ootg/Adapter.HTTP.API.Server.Common	100%	2/2	100%	4/4	100%	35/35
module hauth-0.1.0.0-9ARw4KOpKXC1NGemd5ootg/Adapter.HTTP.API.Server.Main	100%	2/2	-	0/0	27%	13/48
module hauth-0.1.0.0-9ARw4KOpKXC1NGemd5ootg/Adapter.HTTP.API.Types.AesonHelper	0%	0/4	0%	0/4	0%	0/66
module hauth-0.1.0.0-9ARw4KOpKXC1NGemd5ootg/Adapter.HTTP.API.Types.Auth	22%	4/18	12%	2/16	13%	26/193
module hauth-0.1.0.0-9ARw4KOpKXC1NGemd5ootg/Adapter.HTTP.Common	100%	5/5	100%	2/2	67%	47/70
module hauth-0.1.0.0-9ARw4KOpKXC1NGemd5ootg/Adapter.HTTP.Main	50%	1/2	-	0/0	72%	18/25
module hauth-0.1.0.0-9ARw4KOpKXC1NGemd5ootg/Adapter.HTTP.Web.Auth	0%	0/7	0%	0/13	0%	0/296
module hauth-0.1.0.0-9ARw4KOpKXC1NGemd5ootg/Adapter.HTTP.Web.Common	0%	0/4	0%	0/2	0%	0/60
module hauth-0.1.0.0-9ARw4KOpKXC1NGemd5ootg/Adapter.HTTP.Web.Main	50%	1/2	-	0/0	6%	4/59
module hauth-0.1.0.0-9ARw4KOpKXC1NGemd5ootg/Adapter.PostgreSQL.Auth	81%	13/16	60%	9/15	87%	167/190
module hauth-0.1.0.0-9ARw4KOpKXC1NGemd5ootg/Adapter.RabbitMQ.Auth	87%	7/8	50%	2/4	61%	74/120
module hauth-0.1.0.0-9ARw4KOpKXC1NGemd5ootg/Adapter.RabbitMQ.Common	60%	9/15	50%	3/6	68%	124/182
module hauth-0.1.0.0-9ARw4KOpKXC1NGemd5ootg/Adapter.Redis.Auth	100%	4/4	60%	3/5	79%	55/69
module hauth-0.1.0.0-9ARw4KOpKXC1NGemd5ootg/Config	33%	4/12	100%	2/2	71%	45/63
module hauth-0.1.0.0-9ARw4KOpKXC1NGemd5ootg/Domain.Auth.Service	100%	6/6	100%	3/3	47%	56/117
module hauth-0.1.0.0-9ARw4KOpKXC1NGemd5ootg/Domain.Auth.Types	24%	9/37	-	0/0	97%	45/46
module hauth-0.1.0.0-9ARw4KOpKXC1NGemd5ootg/Domain.Validation	100%	4/4	100%	6/6	100%	38/38
Program Coverage Total	49%	74/151	48%	44/90	47%	840/1778

Figure 11-1. *Coverage report summary*

`never executed` `always true` `always false`

```
1   module Domain.Auth.Service where
2
3   import ClassyPrelude
4   import Domain.Auth.Types
5   import Control.Monad.Except
6   import Katip
7
8   class (Monad m) => AuthRepo m where
9     addAuth :: Auth -> m (Either RegistrationError (UserId, VerificationCode))
10    setEmailAsVerified :: VerificationCode
11                      -> m (Either EmailVerificationError (UserId, Email))
12    findUserByAuth :: Auth -> m (Maybe (UserId, Bool))
13    findEmailFromUserId :: UserId -> m (Maybe Email)
14
15  class (Monad m) => EmailVerificationNotif m where
16    notifyEmailVerification :: Email -> VerificationCode -> m ()
17
18  class (Monad m) => SessionRepo m where
19    newSession :: UserId -> m SessionId
20    findUserIdBySessionId :: SessionId -> m (Maybe UserId)
21
22
23  withUserIdContext :: (KatipContext m) => UserId -> m a -> m a
24  withUserIdContext uId = katipAddContext (sl "userId" uId)
25
26  register :: (KatipContext m, AuthRepo m, EmailVerificationNotif m)
27           => Auth -> m (Either RegistrationError ())
28  register auth = runExceptT $ do
29    (uId, vCode) <- ExceptT $ addAuth auth
30    let email = authEmail auth
31    lift $ notifyEmailVerification email vCode
32    withUserIdContext uId $
33      $(logTM) InfoS $ ls (rawEmail email) <> " is registered successfully"
34
35  verifyEmail :: (KatipContext m, AuthRepo m)
36              => VerificationCode -> m (Either EmailVerificationError ())
37  verifyEmail vCode = runExceptT $ do
38    (uId, email) <- ExceptT $ setEmailAsVerified vCode
39    withUserIdContext uId $
40      $(logTM) InfoS $ ls (rawEmail email) <> " is verified successfully"
41    return ()
42
43  login :: (KatipContext m, AuthRepo m, SessionRepo m)
44        => Auth -> m (Either LoginError SessionId)
45  login auth = runExceptT $ do
46    result <- lift $ findUserByAuth auth
47    case result of
48      Nothing -> throwError LoginErrorInvalidAuth
49      Just (_, False) -> throwError LoginErrorEmailNotVerified
50      Just (uId, _) -> withUserIdContext uId . lift $ do
```

Figure 11-2. *Coverage report detail for a module*

259

Summary

In this chapter, we learned about automated testing of a Haskell application. Doing automated testing requires our application architecture to be testable. The strategy that we took to make our application testable is by using typeclass to separate between the protocol (port) and the actual implementation (adapter). In the test, we mock the protocol so that we can test various scenarios.

The testing framework that we chose was hspec. hspec provides a nice, human-readable API that we can use to build our test cases. For testing a WAI application, we use a package called hspec-wai or hspec-wai-json. Both packages provide a nice, high-level syntax for executing an HTTP request to a WAI application as well as asserting the HTTP response.

In terms of writing the test, we use a mix of unit testing and integration testing. We write integration tests for adapter components. For example, we test the PostgreSQL adapter component against the actual PostgreSQL database. For domain components, we use a unit testing approach with the help of mocks. We've seen how we could easily create test fixtures without resorting to external packages.

Last but not least, we also looked into code coverage report. It's simply just one command line parameter to enable it. We've walked through the report and understood which part of our code has not been covered in test.

The resulting code for this chapter can be found in the files that shipped along with this book.

CHAPTER 12

Deployment

In previous chapters, our main focus was on the development part of the application. We've seen the result: we have a slick web application that we can run locally. However, eventually we will need to deploy it to a server so that more people are able to access it. In this chapter, we will turn our focus into the deployment part of the application. We will first learn to build the application for production and then finally deploy it with Docker.

Building Application for Production

Our application requires some external resources to be able to run correctly, for example, images and SQL migration files. This needs to be taken into consideration when building an application that is easily shippable. In addition to that, we also want to use many tools that statically analyze our code for common Haskell pitfalls. This helps to prevent trivial issues from appearing in production. In this section we will look into code quality tools and how to package our external resources, along with application binary.

GHC Compiler Flags

The first tool that we will look at for ensuring our code quality is not exactly a tool, but rather some flags in our compiler. GHC comes with functionalities that would warn of common mistakes in Haskell source code. We just need to enable that by specifying the correct flags. Add the following lines at the root of your `package.yaml` file for enabling them:

```
ghc-options:
- -Wall
- -Werror
- -Wincomplete-record-updates
- -Wincomplete-uni-patterns
- -Wredundant-constraints
```

© Ecky Putrady 2018
E. Putrady, *Practical Web Development with Haskell*, https://doi.org/10.1007/978-1-4842-3739-7_12

The -Wall flag enables GHC to warn for basic, common mistakes. Some examples of warning produced with this flag are unused imports, usage of tabs, and unused variables.

The -Wincomplete-record-updates flag checks for a record update that might fail at runtime. Let's see an example code:

```
data A
  = B { x :: Int }
  | C

f :: A -> A
f a = a { x = 10 }
```

In the preceding example, the code will compile just fine. However, if f is called with C, then the program will crash at runtime. With -Wincomplete-record-updates enabled, this code will produce a warning.

-Wincomplete-uni-patterns checks for incomplete pattern matching in lambda expressions. For example, the following code will produce a warning if this flag is enabled:

```
a = \[] -> 2
```

-Wredundant-constraints checks for constraints that are unnecessary. For example:

```
f :: (Monad m, MonadIO m) => m ()
```

In the preceding example, Monad constraint is unnecessary because MonadIO already implies Monad constraint

Unfortunately, this flag does not detect redundant constraints in type if we use ConstraintKinds language pragma. For example, the following code does not produce any warning:

```
type Repo m = (Monad m, MonadIO m)
f :: Repo m => m ()
```

-Werror turns any warning into a fatal error during compilation. This effectively causes the build to fail if there is any warning in our code. Without enabling this flag, the warnings will all just be printed and not fail the build. Since our purpose is to build a production-ready application, it's better to turn this flag on to make sure we address any warnings that might cause production issues.

Once we have enabled those flags, we can then run our build command as per normal:

```
$ stack build
```

If you run it in our current codebase, you might notice that we have triggered a lot of warnings. As an exercise, I would suggest cleaning all the warnings by yourself. See how and why they are a warning.

HLint

HLint[1] is a tool that analyzes Haskell code and provides code improvement suggestions. The suggestion could range from style, unnecessary parenthesis, or alternative function to use that leads to a more performant and shorter code.

Install HLint using stack as follows:

```
$ stack install hlint
```

Then, we can use it by:

```
$ hlint .
```

If you run the preceding command in our project, you will notice that there are some warnings being triggered, for example, unnecessary usage of do keywords. Try fixing all those warnings.

It's possible to tell HLint to ignore certain warnings by writing some configurations. HLint reads a configuration file named .hlint.yaml in the same directory where HLint is run. The easiest way to write this file is by fixing all warnings that we think it's necessary to fix, while leaving ones that we think are unnecessary. Then, we run the following command:

```
$ hlint . --default > .hlint.yaml
```

The preceding command will generate a settings file that ignores all outstanding warnings.

---

[1]www.stackage.org/package/hlint

Weeder

Weeder[2] detects, among other things, unused Haskell exports and unused dependencies packages. We accumulate code over time. The stuff that we used previously might not be used anymore due to the code change that we made. Weeder frees us from doing these checks manually.

Install Weeder using `stack` as follows:

```
$ stack install weeder
```

Then, we can run it as follows:

```
$ weeder .
```

If you run the preceding command in our project, you will get a lot of warnings about unused packages. This is because we put all our package dependencies at the top level of our `package.yaml` file. This means our application, library, and test code depend on that module. We did that for simplicity. However, it's better to keep things minimal and clean. So, let's fix those warnings by moving appropriate dependencies to an appropriate compilation group.

Like HLint, we may also choose to ignore certain warnings. Weeder reads a configuration named `.weeder.yaml` in the same directory where the tool is run. We can generate this configuration by issuing the following command:

```
$ weeder . --yaml > .weeder.yaml
```

This puts outstanding warnings in the configuration file and marks them as ignored.

hpc-threshold

hpc-threshold[3] is a tool to ensure that code coverage is above some configurable thresholds. This is useful to keep new code being sufficiently tested over time.

Install this package by issuing the following command:

```
$ stack install hpc-threshold
```

---

[2]`www.stackage.org/package/weeder`
[3]`https://hackage.haskell.org/package/hpc-threshold`

If you get an error saying this package is not found, it means that the package is not available in Stackage yet. We can add the package in our stack.yaml file to fix this:

```
extra-deps:
- hpc-threshold-0.1.0.3
```

Next, we proceed to create a configuration file. This program reads a configuration from a file named .hpc-threshold that presents in the same directory where the program is run. The contents of the configuration file are as follows:

```
[ Threshold
    { thresholdName = "Expressions used"
    , thresholdRegex = "(\\d+)% expressions used"
    , thresholdValue = 45.0
    }
, Threshold
    { thresholdName = "Boolean coverage"
    , thresholdRegex = "(\\d+)% boolean coverage"
    , thresholdValue = 15.0
    }
, Threshold
    { thresholdName = "Alternatives used"
    , thresholdRegex = "(\\d+)% alternatives used"
    , thresholdValue = 45.0
    }
, Threshold
    { thresholdName = "Local declarations used"
    , thresholdRegex = "(\\d+)% local declarations used"
    , thresholdValue = 65.0
    }
, Threshold
    { thresholdName = "Top-level declarations used"
    , thresholdRegex = "(\\d+)% top-level declarations used"
    , thresholdValue = 45.0
    }
]
```

As you might have noticed, the file format is actually a default Show instance of a Haskell record. Each Threshold configuration represents the thing that we need to check. Most of the time, you only want to configure the thresholdValue. This is the threshold that the code coverage needs to reach before it is considered to be passing.

Run this program by using this command:

```
$ stack build --test --coverage
$ (stack hpc report --all 2>&1) | hpc-threshold
```

The first command is used to build the coverage report. In the second command, we use stack hpc report to print those reports to stdout. Please note that 2>&1 is necessary because the stack hpc report command prints the result in stderr. The 2>&1 is there to pipe stderr to stdout. The stdout stream is then piped to hpc-threshold to be processed.

An example output of this program is as follows:

```
$ (stack hpc report --all 2&>1) | hpc-threshold
Code coverage threshold check: FAIL
   Expressions used: 67.0% (< 45.0%)
   Boolean coverage: 14.0% (< 15.0%)
   Alternatives used: 42.0% (< 45.0%)
   Local declarations used: 88.0% (≥ 65.0%)
   Top-level declarations used: 80.0% (≥ 45.0%)
```

Build Script

In the previous sections, we have explored various compiler flags and tools that help improve our Haskell code quality. Ideally, we just want a single command to run all of the above. Hence we need to write a script whose purpose is to build and apply the code quality tools. We want the build to fail if there are any warnings from the tools that we used. The build process also includes packaging external resources, like SQL migration files, images, and other files that are necessary to make our application run correctly.

The simplest way to achieve this is by simply using bash script. Let's name it build.
sh and put it at the root of our project. Here's the content of the script:

```bash
#!/bin/bash
set -e # makes the script fail if any one of the below operation fails

### prepare for distribution

rm -rf dist
mkdir dist

### build & test

echo "Build & test"
stack build --test --coverage
echo "Build & test finished with exit code $?"
cp -r $(stack path --local-install-root)/bin dist/bin

### copy non-hs resources

cp -r app dist/app
cp -r src dist/src
cd dist
find . -name "*.hs" -type f -delete
find . -type d -empty -delete
cd ..

### code quality tools

echo "Installing code quality tools"
stack install hlint weeder hpc-threshold

echo "Running HLint ..."
hlint .
echo "HLint finished with exit code $?"

echo "Running Weeder ..."
weeder .
echo "Weeder finished with exit code $?"
```

```
echo "Running hpc-threshold ..."
(stack hpc report --all 2>&1) | hpc-threshold
echo "hpc-threshold finished with exit code $?"
```

report

```
echo "Build finished. see /dist."
```

At high-level, the script does the following:

1. Prepare `./dist` as the folder for build artifacts distribution.

2. Build and test the application and put the result in the `./dist` folder.

3. Copy extra files that are necessary for running the application.

4. Run code quality tools: HLint, Weeder, hpc-threshold.

By having this script, our build process is simplified from running multiple commands to just one command: `./build.sh`.

Our build result should be available in the `./dist` folder. For running the resulting application, we may do the following:

```
$ cd dist
$ ./bin/hauth-exe
```

It's essential to run the application from `dist` instead of from the `dist/bin` folder. This is so the external resources like SQL migrations and images are picked up correctly when the application is run.

Building and Deploying with Docker

With our existing build process, the compiled Haskell application is unfortunately not portable. For example, if we build the application on a MacBook Air and then try to run it on an Ubuntu machine, then we'll get an error saying that the system can't run the executable. This is because there are missing libraries that are not included in the resulting application. This situation is not ideal, because this forces our build machine to be the same as our target machine—which is not always the case. Fixing the build process is unfortunately quite complicated. Instead of doing that, we will use another approach to make our application easily runnable on any machine.

Nowadays, Docker[4] is one of the most popular choices for shipping an application. There is a big and growing ecosystem around it. Major cloud providers built toolings to support it. For example, Google developed Kubernetes[5] to do container orchestration. Amazon provided ECS[6] that allows us to easily deploy Docker-based applications.

In a nutshell, we can think of a Docker container as a lightweight virtual machine. We can leverage Docker to solve our portability problem. The idea is that we build our application in a Docker container. The result is then packaged into another Docker container. This container is then shipped to the target machine. As long as the target machine has Docker in it, we can run any Docker container, including our application.

We need to separate the container to build the application and the container to run the application. When running the application, we don't need GHC and many other tools that are used to build the application. GHC is heavy in size. Having this in your container considerably increases the size of your container. It's always better to reduce your container to the absolute minimum to run the application.

We will use the following script, `scripts/docker-build.sh`, to build our application in a Docker container:

```
#!/bin/bash
docker run \
    -v ~/.stack:/root/.stack \
    -v .:/root/work \
    eckyputrady/haskell-build-web:lts-10.3

cd scripts
cp -r ../dist ./dist
docker build -t eckyputrady/hauth:latest .
rm -rf ./dist
```

The `docker run ...` command is the one that builds the application inside a docker container. This uses a Docker image—a template to build a docker container—eckyputrady/haskell-build-web. This image contains everything that is necessary to build the application, including GHC, PostgreSQL, RabbitMQ, and Redis. The results of the build are then available in the dist folder of our project.

---

[4]www.docker.com/

[5]https://kubernetes.io/

[6]https://aws.amazon.com/ecs/

The second Docker command, `docker build -t ...`, instructs Docker to package our application into a Docker image named eckyputrady/hauth:latest. The Docker image is created from the `Dockerfile` file in the same folder with the following content:

```
FROM eckyputrady/haskell-run:lts-10.3

COPY ["./dist", "/dist"]
ENTRYPOINT respawn ./bin/hauth-exe
```

Suffice it to say that the preceding script tells Docker to base off the image from another Docker image named eckyputrady/haskell-run:lts-10.3, copy the `dist` folder from our computer into the image, and run `respawn ./bin/hauth-exe` when the container is run.

Now that we have a Docker image for our application, we can ship it to any machine that has Docker in it. A common workflow is to push this image into a Docker Registry—a repository of Docker images—and have your target machine pull the image from this registry and then run it.

Since our machine has Docker in it, then it means we can run the Docker image that we've just build. Since we need PostgreSQL, RabbitMQ, and Redis to be able to run the application, we will use Docker Compose[7] to start it. In a nutshell, Docker Compose is a tool that allows us to orchestrate multiple docker containers. We use the following Docker Compose script that we put in `scripts/docker-compose.yaml`:

```
version: "3.3"
services:
  hauth:
    image: eckyputrady/hauth:latest
    environment:
      - PORT=3000
      - PG_URL=postgresql://hauth:hauthpass@postgres:5432/hauth
      - MQ_URL=amqp://hauth:hauthpass@rabbitmq:5672/%2F
      - REDIS_URL=redis://redis:6379/0
    depends_on:
      - postgres
      - redis
      - rabbitmq
```

---

[7]https://docs.docker.com/compose/

270

```
  ports:
    - "80:3000"

postgres:
  image: postgres:9.6
  environment:
    - POSTGRES_PASSWORD=hauthpass
    - POSTGRES_USER=hauth
    - POSTGRES_DB=hauth
  ports:
    - "5432:5432"

redis:
  image: redis:4
  ports:
    - "6379:6379"

rabbitmq:
  image: rabbitmq:3-management
  hostname: rabbitmq
  ports:
    - "15672:15672"
  environment:
    - RABBITMQ_DEFAULT_USER=hauth
    - RABBITMQ_DEFAULT_PASS=hauthpass
```

We won't dive into the details of Docker Compose in this book. Suffice it to say that the preceding script sets up PostgreSQL, Redis, and RabbitMQ, then finally links them to our application.

We may run this script by going to the scripts folder and typing the following command in our terminal:

```
$ docker-compose up
```

Once everything has been up and running, we may open our browser and go to http://localhost to see that our application is running correctly.

Summary

In this chapter, we've learned about deployment of a Haskell application. We started by ensuring that our application contains a good quality code by running various static analysis tools. Our static analysis tools consist of GHC compiler flags, HLint, Weeder, and `hpc-threshold`. Those tools have done a great job to point out multiple issues in our code.

The build and deployment strategy that we chose is Docker. Docker fixes the portability problem of a Haskell application by allowing it to run on any machine that has Docker in it. We deliberately chose to separate the container to build and to run the application for efficiency purposes.

The modified code and various scripts that we have worked on in this chapter are available in the zip file with the same name as this chapter that comes along with the book.

Index

A

amqp package
   channels, 115–116
   connection, 114–115
   consuming messages, 120–121
   declaring exchange, 116–117
   publishing message, 119–120
   queue, binding, 118
   queues, declaring, 117–118
Application-wide
         configuration, 213
Auth data structure
   create safer domain types, 44
   dependent kind, 39
   Domain.Validation module, 41
   independent kind, 39
   length checking validation, 42
   mkEmail, 40
   RegistrationError, 39
   types, 38
   validate function, 41
Automatic test discovery, 227

B

Build process
   bash script, 267–268
   Docker deployment, 269–271
ByteString array, 11

C

Cabal file, 5–7
CacheContainer, 187
ClassyPrelude
   bracket function, 78
   data structures, 13–15
   enable, 10
   stack build, 10–11
Code coverage report, 258–259
Configurable application
   application-wide configuration, 213
   Config module, 215–216
   devConfig function, 215
   Lib module, 211
   preceding function, 214
   REPL, 216
   withState function, 212
Connection pool, 87–88
Consuming messages, 120–121
Contextual logging, 73–74
Cookie, 145–147

D

Digestive-functors package, 147–150
Docker deployment
   container, 269
   Docker Compose, 270–271
   image, 270

273

E. Putrady, *Practical Web Development with Haskell*, https://doi.org/10.1007/978-1-4842-3739-7

Printed in the United States
By Bookmasters